THE LOST
CONTINENT

GAVIN HEWITT

THE LOST CONTINENT

THE BBC'S EUROPE EDITOR ON EUROPE'S DARKEST HOUR SINCE WORLD WAR TWO

HODDER &
STOUGHTON

First published in Great Britain in 2013 by Hodder & Stoughton
An Hachette UK company

1

Copyright © Gavin Hewitt 2013

A CIP catalogue record for this title is available from the British Library

Hardback ISBN 978 1 444 76479 6
Trade Paperback ISBN 978 1 444 76480 2
Ebook ISBN 978 1 444 76481 9

Typeset by Hewer Text UK Ltd, Edinburgh

Printed and bound by Clays Ltd, St Ives plc

Hodder & Stoughton policy is to use papers that are natural, renewable
and recyclable products and made from wood grown in sustainable forests.
The logging and manufacturing processes are expected to conform
to the environmental regulations of the country of origin.

Hodder & Stoughton Ltd
338 Euston Road
London NW1 3BH

www.hodder.co.uk

For Ava and Maya

Contents

Prologue

1. The Dream
2. Boom Time
3. ...
4. The Night they Ad...
5. Great Race and ...
6. ...
7. Behind Half has ... 113
8. The Shadow of ...
9. ...
10. The Making of ...
11. The Downfall of ...
12. The Madman ...
13. ...
14. A Great Depression
15. The Return of the ... 272
16. ...
17. ...Dolce Vita 338
18. The Long Goodbye

Epilogue
Acknowledgements
Notes
Index

CONTENTS

Prologue 1

1. The Dream 23
2. Boom Time 35
3. 'We ate the money together' 53
4. The Night they Almost Lost the Euro 64
5. Greek Rage and German Resentment 83
6. Opposite Twins 98
7. Ireland: Hell was at the Gates 112
8. The Shadow of Silvio 130
9. Disobedience 148
10. The Turning of Frau Nein 165
11. The Downfall of *Il Cavaliere* 177
12. The 'Madman' from Athens 198
13. The British Outsiders 215
14. A Great Depression 235
15. The Rebellion of Mr Normal 258
16. Spain: Resisting the Men in Black 277
17. Ciao! Dolce Vita 296
18. The Lost Continent 307

Timeline 319
Acknowledgements 323
Sources 325
Index 347

'An era can be said to end when
its basic illusions are exhausted.'

Arthur Miller

Prologue
Delirium

It was the futile act of an angry man. A shaking fist. A moment of rage against greed and ruin.

Thomas O'Malley was a kiosk cop, a police officer who controlled the gates to the Irish Parliament. When the weather blew cold and damp he would retreat into his booth from where he would control those going in and out of Leinster House.

On that afternoon in September 2010, it began with sound. The gunning of an engine. The grating of a missed gear change. It drew O'Malley's eye to the corner of Kildare and Molesworth. There it was, in all its garish rebellion. A cement mixer with the bright red slogan, 'Toxic bank' stamped on its drum. O'Malley stayed watching this truck with its yellow cab as it headed towards him and, at the last moment, veered towards the gates of the Parliament.

The driver, stopped, climbed onto the roof of his cab and locked the doors behind him. O'Malley stared at the man – lean, middle-aged, with sleek, black hair – convinced he was about to pour concrete and seal up the entrance to Parliament. He shouted at him to step down. The man glanced at him and announced the brakes of the truck had been cut and could not be moved.

Joe McNamara was a builder brimming with resentment and debt. On the back of his mixer he had written, 'The people have had enough.' Now, surrounded by police, he stood there waving a hurley stick. It was a solitary gesture of defiance: one man's protest against a government that had rescued reckless banks and left the tax-payers to pick up the bill. He, like others, believed his country was on the verge of insolvency.

Weeks later, the moment came. Sunday, 21 November 2010 was the reckoning. It had been long anticipated but it stung nonetheless. On one raw, unsettled day in late autumn, Ireland was forced to accept a bail-out from the EU and the IMF. Until the final hours, the rumour of a rescue had been denied. The government in Dublin had set up a war room to resist. It had insisted time and again that the country's sovereignty had been 'hard won' and would not be given away to anyone. It proved an empty promise.

Ireland believed it had escaped the poverty of its past and had been reborn as the Celtic Tiger. Now it faced humiliation. The country had revelled in its new-found reputation as a nimble, economic powerhouse. In a short period of time, it had become the second richest nation in the world; it owned more Mercedes per head of population than the Germans. Dublin had grown into one of Europe's weekend party cities. The road south from the capital led to steep hillsides over-looking azure bays: the hideaways for Ireland's expanding community of the rich and famous. Bono, Enya, Neil Jordan, Van Morrison and Maeve Binchy all hunkered down there. It was a small island bursting with pride.

Now the future of the country had passed into other's hands. Unknown people. European Commissioners. Officials from the European Central Bank. A team from the International Monetary Fund, the IMF, had arrived in town. Their reputation went before them: unsentimental administrators who forced broken states into adopting tough regimes of austerity. Photographers managed to catch the fund's top European official, Ajai Chopra, walking past a beggar, a symbol of what Ireland had become.

The Celtic Tiger had been built on a property bubble, fuelled by cheap money. The Irish had had a swagger about them. It had been dazzling while it lasted, but there had been fears that old Ireland had not gone away, that the country would be drawn back into its past. On that November day, Dublin's 'pram women' were selling grapes and bunches of fruit from battered baby carriages. They had hard-lined, outdoor faces. They were women who would out-lip you. And they took you back to another time. On Grafton Street, there was a man in charcoal-grey, statue-still, his long coat, his kepi hat and his face all charcoaled. Even the live pigeon that inexplicably rested on his shoulder had a grey dusting. He was a human statue playing General de Gaulle. No one had the time or the money for the street artist. The party was over. Nearby was an old man, sunk back into the wall, his flat cap half obscuring his face. In his hands were two string puppets of young Irish girls, which he jigged to some fiddle music. That, too, took you back to an older, half-forgotten Ireland.

With the bail-out came a national shudder, serious enough for the *Irish Times*, in its editorial, to borrow its headline from W.B. Yeats and his poem about the Great War, 'September 1913'.

'Was it for this the wild geese spread
The grey wing upon every tide;
For this that all that blood was shed
. . . all that delirium of the brave?'

In posing the question, 'Was it for this?' the paper asked its readers to confront what the financial crisis had done to the country. 'Having obtained our political independence from Britain to be masters of our own affairs, we have surrendered our sovereignty to the European Commission, the European Central Bank and the International Monetary Fund. Their representatives ride into Merrion Street today.' There were many who shared the paper's lament: 'The shame of it all.'

It hurt because the Irish had embraced being European. In their struggle to be independent, they had defined themselves by what they were not. And that was British, that big – some-time occupying, sometime bullying – neighbour. The Irish would gently mock the British as stubborn, wary and insular; some of whose people had even feared the Channel Tunnel would finish Britain as an island nation. The Irish had shed their doubts; they had found their place in the world. They were Europeans. It sounded modern, even enlightened. Some of their best and brightest had headed to Brussels.

The roots of the crisis lay exposed along the country's high-ways. From the capital, it is a short undulating drive to the Irish Midlands and the rolling hills of the Republic. In autumn, the late afternoon light is often soft with the mist hanging low to the ground. And then emerging from the haze, like intrud-ers, are clusters of recently built town houses. Row after row of them. Mostly empty. These became the ghost towns, the thousands of houses left unsold when the bubble burst. Concrete and speculation lay behind the Irish miracle.

In 2002 Ireland – enthusiastically – had exchanged its currency, the punt, for the euro. The single currency was the symbol of European integration. It lay at the heart of the dream of the European Union's founding fathers. At its launch, it had been celebrated as 'far more than a medium of exchange. It is part of the identity of a people.' But this new currency ended up seducing countries like Ireland.

Even before it adopted the euro, Ireland was fast-charging with growth of 9.6 per cent a year. Within the euro-zone, there was one interest rate for all. It suited some but not others. Low rates, which were right for the conservative German economy, were potentially dangerous elsewhere. Despite its already strong growth, Irish interest rates halved. Money became even cheaper. Capital flowed in from countries like Germany and stoked the boom. In just ten years, property prices quadrupled and Ireland gorged itself.

In 2008, the financial crash struck. It started in America and engulfed all western countries. Financial institutions like Lehman Brothers collapsed and credit dried up. Over the next two years, house prices in Ireland plunged 30 per cent. The banks were left nursing huge losses and the Irish government decided to take extraordinary measures to save them. It guaranteed the loans of the banks and placed their debts on the government's books. It had no realistic means of repaying these sums, and the country reeled towards bankruptcy.

On the road to Kilkenny is a ruin and beside it a graveyard. The dates on the gravestones do not go back much beyond a century, for before that – in the 1840s – there had been famine, and waves of Irish emigrants had joined the huddled masses heading west to the New World and Ellis Island. The Irish thought they had seen the end to emigration. In the years of the economic miracle, in fact, thousands of East Europeans had come to the island to work, but they had left on the economic low tide. Once again, emigration fairs returned to Irish towns, pulling in the crowds and calling young people away. In time, 1,700 young people a week would be leaving. Town after town saw the rituals of departure: the farewell gathering in the pub, the embraces, the tears and the unspoken fears that the promises of return would not be honoured.

A taxi ride in Dublin is rarely silent. The drivers like to talk, to savour the *craic*. A grey-haired driver with pale blue eyes spoke about his fifteen-year-old daughter, Lily. He feared that in a few years he would lose her. She would emigrate and join the Irish diaspora. The thought gnawed away at him to the point he confided in a stranger. Lily would go to Australia or Canada, far-away places, and he hated those who had broken his country. 'Mass emigration,' said the writer, Fintan O'Toole, 'had always been the index of Ireland's failure.'

Another driver spoke of the craziness, the delirium of the boom. His grown children had been offered thousands on their credit cards without anyone checking their income. Everyone knew people were printing out false P60 forms to inflate their take-home pay, but neither the banks nor the finance houses cared; they just doled out the mortgages. All lies and greed, the driver said bitterly.

The road south out of the Spanish capital is flanked by hundreds of stores with flashing signs announcing *muebles*, *tienda de azulejos*, *materiales de construccion*, *cemento*. A casual glance would leave the impression that there was really only one business in town: construction. And, in a way, that had been true and the reason for Spain's economic downfall.

At the edge of Madrid the billboards are more faded. They still advertise chalets *en venta*, 'for sale'. Even though the prices are slashed, almost no one is buying. Property is yesterday's dream. Beyond the clutter of the city's edge are cement silos and then the dry lands of La Mancha. It is desolate, flat, sun-baked and inhospitable in summer; the terrain where Cervantes's Don Quixote tilted at windmills.

After a forty-minute drive from the capital, a dark, muscular block rises from the parched plateau. From a distance it could be a penitentiary, but these are the solid, Soviet-style apartment blocks of Seseña; a brown-bricked housing complex made up of twelve towers intended to house 30,000 people in 13,000 apartments.

It is eerily quiet as almost no one lives there now. A metal fence surrounds the project to keep out squatters and the thieves who come to strip out the piping and radiators. The project was aimed at those who could not afford the prices of Madrid, but it stands alone, set apart from the nearest town, on a dry, waterless piece of scrubland with few trees. The roads between the blocks are deserted, apart from the occasional patrol by the security guards. There is still an *oficina de ventas*, offering three-bedroom apartments at 89,000 euros, but more often than not the shutters are down. Seseña has become a destination for the curious rather than the buyer. In time, the prices would be slashed further and the banks would settle for rock-bottom offers just to get the project off its books.

The developer, Francisco Hernando, had long gone. Locals referred to him as *El Pocero* – the pitman. He had once sold coal from the back of a cart, having left school scarcely able to read and write. In time he would own a 235-foot yacht with a helipad. *Cemento* made millionaires, dozens of them. But the craze for construction ruined Spain.

Nearby to Seseña are chalets that appear like sugar cubes with shuttered windows. They can be bought for 153,000 euros, but they look out onto a wasteland, where hundreds of red power cables peek out of the scrub. These are the abandoned foundations of buildings that will never be completed. Beside them are piles of scaffolding, roof tiles and concrete drains discarded by the construction workers as they drove away, their wages no longer paid by bankrupt developers.

Seseña and other Spanish ghost towns are monuments to the delirium that, as in Ireland, gripped the country. Spain, too, had gone on a building binge; at times it was consuming more concrete than France, Belgium, Germany and Italy put together. A second home almost became an accessory. It did not matter where. It might be a flat on a sun-baked plot beside a rutted track or an apartment in the towers that choked and disfigured the coastline. It did not matter. A belief had set in that you would never lose money with property. In the space of a decade, land prices rose by over 500 per cent. For a time, Spain had the largest number of mortgages per capita in the world.

When the bubble burst, the banks were stuffed full of bad debts: 200 billion euros. Perhaps more. No one was really sure. The construction sites were mothballed. The numbers of unemployed soared to the highest levels in Europe. There were more than 5 million out of work, with over half of all young people without a job.

Early on a Monday, a queue begins forming in Calle de Evaristo San Miguel in Madrid. The first people have secured their place in the line by seven-thirty in the morning, even though the doors of the drab *oficina de empleo* do not open until nine. Soon there are 200 people. There is little conversation between them. Many sit on the pavement reading. A casual glance would judge it a queue for a lecture theatre: a young man flips through a book on architecture, another is engrossed in business studies; a woman is learning German, another is studying for a part in a play. They are all waiting to claim unemployment benefit. Spain describes them as *ni-ni*s: *ni estudia, ni tranaja,* 'not in education, not in work'. They are also called a lost generation, highly educated, the best and brightest. Eduardo Paniagua is twenty-eight. He has filled in nearly 1,000 application forms and had only a handful of replies, all of them rejections. The years without work have spawned a social revolution: most Spanish people in their early thirties can only afford to stay living with their parents.

The Spanish, like the Irish, were eager Europeans. They had only recently shed the dictatorship of General Franco. They yearned to be normal, to enjoy the freedoms of others. Weary of fluctuating exchange rates and devaluations, they had fought hard to join the euro but, most of all, they wanted to be modern Europeans.

Golden years followed. They had joined a club with low interest rates. The banks offered easy money to developers and homeowners. Spain was creating more jobs than anywhere else in Europe. With the euro had come streams of foreign investment and cheap credit. The single currency was transforming a society. The country spoke of a Spanish fiesta, but it changed the national character. Where once the Spanish had been conservative and frugal, they now gambled their future on property and condemned future generations to sorting out their debts.

Europe took time to realise an immense storm was building. Its officials had been lulled by the currency's early success. The euro had defied the critics who said countries with such different economies could not share the same coins and notes. In a matter of years, the euro had become the world's reserve currency.

In October 2009 everything changed. Greece had held an election and elected a new prime minister, George Papandreou. He was trim, a jogger; a middle-aged politician who had lost most of his hair while what remained was grey, including his moustache. Politics ran in his family. His father and grandfather had been prime ministers. Some called him 'Little George'. Others, however, saw him as a stranger in his own country. He had been born in St Paul, Minnesota, America, and had been educated at Amherst. He was a guitar strummer, a boomer from the counter-culture. His English was better than his Greek. Some derisively called him 'Geoff' rather than 'Giorgios'.

During the election, he and his socialist party had promised real wage rises and extra spending on welfare. Within days of taking power, his new finance minister insisted on a meeting. He came to Maximos Mansion, a former ship-owner's house, which was now the prime minister's office. He told George Papandreou that they had been going through the national accounts. The previous government, he said, had been publishing false statistics; the figures were as good as fakes. The deficit was not 6.7 per cent but closer to 13 per cent. 'We were shocked at the discrepancies,' the prime minister said. He also knew that he had been lied to by the previous administration. In a moment, he understood that all his election promises now counted for little. There would be no funds to increase benefits. More importantly, he realised that without a dramatic plan, the country would be unable to borrow money to pay its debts.

The news seeped out almost immediately and the new government decided not to disguise the scale of the problem. The finance minister described the situation as a 'national emergency'. The prime minister George Papandreou said, 'This is without doubt the worst economic crisis since the restoration of democracy in Greece.'

Cheating was nothing new. Wall Street titans had helped massage the figures so that Greece could meet the criteria for joining the euro. Those who had expressed doubts over whether the Greek economy qualified for sharing the new currency were ignored. 'You could not say "No" to the country of Plato,' was the view at the time. Athens, however, squandered its new membership. Like Ireland and Spain, it found it could borrow at the same rates as Germany. It could not resist the lure of easy money to expand its already bloated public sector.

The announcement that the country was in crisis baffled many Greeks. They had come to believe that membership of the euro immunised them from financial shocks. Some assumed that EU tax-payers would ride to their help if they were in trouble. Others thought the prime minister was exaggerating, summoning up a ruse to renege on election promises made.

Other countries before had run up huge debts, but the problem for Greece was that it was locked into a monetary union: there were limits to what it could do. It could not devalue or print money as in the past. The only way the deficit and the debts could be reduced was to cut spending: taking the axe to benefits, wages and pensions.

In the European quarter in Brussels, officials appeared stunned by the revelations. Countries in the euro-zone were supposed to limit their deficits to 3 per cent of gross domestic product (GDP), although the rules had regularly been broken. Suddenly, officials were facing a dilemma they had never planned for: how to manage a country inside the euro-zone that might not be able to settle its debts. There were early flashes of Greek pride. The finance minister, George Papaconstantinou, snapped, 'We are not Iceland; we are not Dubai,' – two countries that had recently gone broke. 'There will be no bail-out,' he insisted.

In late 2009, Europe's leaders were initially uncertain how to judge the news from Athens. After all, Greece's economy was relatively small; it made up just 2 per cent of Europe's GDP. The Swedish prime minister, Fredrik Reinfeldt, said the Greek deficit was a domestic problem that had to be addressed with domestic solutions.

Papandreou told the Greek people, 'We must change or sink.' The country, he said, was in intensive care. He tried to set a personal example, shedding the official Mercedes for an electric car and encouraging his ministers to do the same. What Greece had done was to focus attention on the debts run up by European governments. A senior MP in Angela Merkel's party in Germany warned that Greece was 'just the tip of the iceberg', but as European officials headed off for their long Christmas break in 2009, there was no appreciation of the magnitude of the crisis. It was assumed that spending cuts and tax increases would bring Greece back into line. They did not. Lean times provoked opposition and resistance.

In 2010 a sterner tone emerged from Europe's political class. 'No one can live beyond their means for ever – not even governments,' said one official. It soon became apparent, however, that Greece was struggling to reduce its deficit and that it was running out of money. The Germans in particular were against rescuing Greece. One of the rules they had insisted on when they gave up their beloved Deutsche Mark was that countries would not have to take on the debts of others.

By May 2010, Europe's leaders feared the euro-zone might break up. Plan after plan to save Greece had failed. The politicians were scrambling to find solutions but the agenda was being set elsewhere. The financial markets were kings. They cast an unblinking, unsentimental eye on the debts that had been racked up across the continent. They judged Europe to be a risky investment and forced up the costs of borrowing. These vigilantes, as officials liked to call them, were bitterly resented in Brussels. Later, and after another long crisis meeting, the president of the European Commission, José Manuel Barroso, would snap: 'There is no sovereignty any more. Only the markets are sovereign.'

An epic struggle was to follow, pitting Europe's leaders against the markets. There were financial rescues and bail-outs, but Europe's leaders could not extinguish the fire. The crisis enveloped not just Ireland, Spain and Greece but Italy and Portugal too. Eventually, it would bring down governments and force leaders from office. The fear was that if countries like Italy could no longer service its debts, then it was too big an economy to be rescued and that would trigger a collapse in the European banking system.

What at first had seemed like a little local difficulty would, over time, shake the European Union to its core and threaten the global economy. It would lead in Chancellor Merkel's view to 'Europe's toughest hour since World War Two'. The governor of the Bank of England, Sir Mervyn King, described it 'as the most serious crisis we have had since the thirties, if not ever'. The American president was frequently on the phone to Europe's leaders demanding action. The French president Nicolas Sarkozy argued that the crisis threatened peace. 'Those who destroy the euro,' he said, 'will take responsibility for the resurgence of conflict on our continent.' The French and German leaders said that the end of the euro would be the end of Europe. A continent lost. 'For us,' said Sarkozy 'it is not simply an economic issue; it has to do with our identity as Europeans.'

The crisis managers were the French and Germans. They had always dominated the European Union. One of its founding fathers, Robert Schuman, had said that, 'The gathering of the nations of Europe demanded the elimination of the age-old antagonism between France and Germany.' The Union had been largely a French and German dream, designed to ensure that war never again returned to the continent. Now the two countries believed they were fighting to save the project that had helped rebuild Europe after World War Two.

The German and French leaders could not have been more different. German Chancellor Angela Merkel was cautious, analytical; a former scientist who trusted facts more than her emotions. The Americans judged her to be 'risk averse and rarely creative'. Her closest advisers referred to her as *Mutti*, 'Mother'.

The French President, Nicolas Sarkozy, on the other hand, was hyperactive; a leader who would come up with a hundred ideas before breakfast. He was mercurial, impulsive, short-fused. His close friend, Alain Minc, said: 'Sarkozy is a man who creates stress.' One US cable stated 'Just being in the same room with Sarkozy is enough to make anyone's stress levels increase.' His predecessor, Jacques Chirac, described him as, 'Nervous, impetuous, bubbling over with ambition, doubting nothing, least of all himself.'

Chancellor Merkel was mindful of German history and the lessons from the Weimar Republic; that inflation left unchecked could destroy democracy. She praised the wisdom of the Swabian housewife, a model Southern German citizen, famed for her frugality and thrift. Her instinctive attitude to the Greeks and others was that they had to be taught a lesson; that they needed to live within their means. Her medicine of choice was austerity.

President Sarkozy disliked the very word 'austerity' or '*la rigueur*' – he banned it from conversation in the Elysée Palace. He wanted the Germans to show solidarity, to use their economic power to help save the euro. Initially, Merkel disliked and mistrusted his Gallic style. When they met he kissed her hand and was always touching her, which she loathed. There were frequent rows and arguments. Privately, he called her 'La Boche', the French equivalent of 'Kraut'. She made fun of his gestures and the way he walked. There was an exchange between them at a European summit when the French president told her, 'We are made to get on,' and that, 'We are the head and legs (of the EU).'

'No, Nicolas,' she replied. 'You are the head and legs. I am the bank.'

Over time, these two very different personalities would realise that the survival of the European project depended on them working closely together. They would phone each other regularly and meet almost every ten days. The blending of their views led the French press to write of a single personality called 'Merkozy'. President Sarkozy joked, 'I've been spending more time with Angela than I have with my wife.' They had the confidence to tease each other. Sarkozy would say to her, 'Don't take butter with your cheese because of your weight.' After he left office, he said it was one fight he never won.

It was a period, however, marked by tension. A financial crisis evolved into a political crisis. The leaders felt impotent in the face of market forces they did not understand and could not control. They would attend summits and judge them a success, only for financial markets to dismiss their agreements within days. On occasions, the animosity could barely be disguised. Although the French president had dined in

Downing Street with his wife Carla Bruni, it did not stop him rounding on David Cameron, the British prime minister. 'Why don't you take the opportunity to shut up,' he shouted at Cameron at a particularly difficult moment. 'I am sick and tired of hearing every day David Cameron criticising us,' he went on.

Italy was one country that had the potential to bring down the currency. 'The future of the euro will be decided at the gates of Rome,' said David Riley of the ratings agency, Fitch. It had debts of 1.9 trillion euros. It was simply too big an economy to bail-out or rescue. Yet for much of the crisis it was led by Silvio Berlusconi, who seemed less like a modern prime minister and more like an emperor in a late Roman imperial drama. The Italian leader had interrupted one summit to say, 'Why don't we talk about football and girls?' Italian police intercepted a phone call from the prime minister to an escort girl, in which he joked that 'in my spare time I am prime minister.' One exchange made it into the official record when he suggested to Angela Merkel that she did as he did and take a lover and still, he told her, his popularity ratings were above 60 per cent. Not surprisingly, she despised him.

Behind the disagreements lay a fundamental dilemma: a monetary union on its own was inherently unstable; it also needed a fiscal union where budgets and tax and spending were co-ordinated and controlled. But if decisions on tax and spending were being decided at a European level, then that made the case for a full political union. That was way beyond what the people of Europe wanted. The voters had expressed no interest in swapping their nation states for a United States of Europe. Yet as the crisis deepened, many believed that Europe faced a stark choice: a political union or the break up of the currency.

Germany, once again, held the key to Europe's future. One German paper said that the 'Germans had become the indispensable nation'. For the first time in Europe's post-war history, Germany emerged as the unquestioned leader. 'France was having to adjust to a subordinate role,' said one long-time observer of the European scene. The Germans did not seek this role but their economic strength delivered them influence and power. Their economy minister, Rainer Brüderle, was not boasting when he said that 'quite simply, we are the motor for the entire European economy'.

It was a great irony of history that the EU, set up to keep German power in check, should end up with Germany holding the future of Europe in its grasp. One German paper said that Germans had spent decades pretending to be smaller than they really were: 'Now they're suddenly realising that the world is relying on them to save the euro and avert a disaster for the global economy.' The article continued, 'The Germans are going through a crash course in being a leading power.'

Their new-found influence was based on *Wirtschaftswunder*, an 'economic miracle'. The Germans had developed an economic model that was the envy of others. Unions were willing to forgo pay rises in order for businesses to become more competitive. Whilst other countries were seeing their companies battered by emerging nations like China, with their low costs, the Germans retained their long list of global brands: BMW, Mercedes, Volkswagen, Siemens, Bosch, Beyer and Allianz to name but a few. When the value of the euro dipped it only boosted their exports. The German finance minister, Wolfgang Schäuble, said the economy 'was a source of pride' but he felt compelled to add 'not smugness'.

This more confident Germany was visible at its most famous festival, *Oktoberfest* in Munich. From a distance it seems like a giant fairground. The neon lights. The wailing sirens from the rides. The sideshows. Taking aim at the ugly monster's mouth; firing pellets to win a cuddly bear. Tents with names like Hippodrome. *Oktoberfest*, however, is about beer. It cannot be rebranded or shaded. It is total immersion in amber. It is Europe's largest festival, but it is a time to revel in being German.

Inside one of the tents, hundreds of people sit at long wooden tables. Many of the young men are in lederhosen and the women in dirndl, peasant blouses and country skirts with aprons. The numbers who dress traditionally are increasing each year. The waitresses serve the beer, fistfuls of litre glasses resting on push-up bras. Some are almost caricatures: the blonde plaited hair, the full cleavage. Others have nurtured their own legends: the woman who carried eighteen glasses at one time and entered beer-soaked history. Others strap their wrists, like iron-pumpers, before lifting the beer steins. Everyone is bunched in, close and sweaty. To drink is to belong, to feel connected, to be part of a tradition that stretches back 200 years.

'A toast, a toast, to happiness!' the cry rings out. 'One, two, three, drink!' The oompah band stamps out its drinking songs as the *würstl* sausages, the giant pretzels, the pork knuckles, the *schweinshaxe* are carried on trays that swirl above the heads of the drinkers.

An important part of the festival is the Costume and Riflemen's Parade. Thousands of performers, some with animals, parade through the streets in ancient costumes. There are men in tails and top hats with bonneted ladies on their arms. Some troupes wear grey military uniforms. Some, in peasant clothes, carry craftsmen's tools. There are women in Black Forest *bollenhut* hats topped with bright red pom-poms.

Others ride in carts clutching carnations with the skins of dead foxes hanging from the cart's sides.

These are the costumes of a past that until recently had been stored away. The clothes are immaculate. The parade is taken seriously. There is a waiting list to be part of it. The uniforms have to be spotless and authentic. The modern must not intrude. Wristwatches and sunglasses are forbidden. For this is about memory, reminding Germans of who they are, where they come from and what they share.

'Twenty years ago there would have been nothing like this,' said a young woman from Munich. 'This is the first generation not to be embarrassed to be German,' she said, with a nod of certainty. For a while, after the Second World War, the new Germany found its identity in being model Europeans. In 1954, when Germany won the soccer World Cup, almost no German flags were waved. Time, European integration and the single currency have changed that. In Germany, many people find their identity in their region. 'I am Bavarian first, then German, then European,' said the woman.

So, a newly confident Germany found itself, at the moment of Europe's greatest recent crisis, in a position of leadership. To those nations facing bankruptcy, the Germans preached austerity. Redemption lay in discipline. Initially, Berlin set its face against rescuing any of these countries. When it did support a bail-out, it insisted on spending cuts: nations had to slim their deficits by a brutal winnowing of their welfare states. Some detected a creeping arrogance, accusing Germany of trying to remake the rest of Europe in its own image. Countries like Greece and Spain were condemned to years of grinding austerity. A prominent German commentator, Ulrike Guérot, warned, 'This will backfire on us terribly in two or three years.'

And so old wounds reopened. The German paper *Die Welt* noted that 'our new power is triggering rejection and resentment'. Some Greeks responded by bringing up the war. They argued that Germany had not fully paid reparations for the atrocities during the German occupation. Banners with swastikas began appearing at demonstrations. A group of off-duty Greek policemen even went to the German embassy in Athens with signs that said that modern Germany still owed Greece money. A Greek shop-owner displayed a picture of Angela Merkel in Nazi uniform. The currency that was intended to bring countries together was sowing new divisions and resurrecting old stereotypes.

The European project began with a dream, a dream born out of the ashes of war. It was a noble vision: the determination to make conflict on the continent impossible ever again. European institutions evolved into a union of states. Over time, this union proved a beacon for democracy, encouraging the countries of eastern Europe to shed their communist past. There would be three outstanding pillars of the European project: a single market, the free movement of people and a shared currency.

The European Union enjoyed years of great confidence. Europeans were able to travel across much of a continent with scarcely the wave of a passport. The modern stag and hen weekend grew out of budget airlines operating in a Europe without frontiers. Hundreds of thousands of eastern Europeans seized the opportunity to move freely abroad and follow the scent of work. Then there was the quality of life: paid holidays, maternity leave, paternity leave, child care, sick leave, unemployment benefits, pension schemes and affordable health care.

The crisis, however, raised fundamental questions about the European way of life. Over the past sixty years, Europe had developed a strong welfare state; it was one of the features that distinguished it from America. The safety nets were stronger. The entitlements greater. Life in Europe was less fragile. The French, in particular, had made sure that the EU helped preserve their way of life by robust funding of its rural life and farms.

Suddenly, in 2010, all of this was thrown into doubt as nations began trimming, then cutting, then slashing, their social programmes. As the continent peered into the future, its old ways seemed no longer sustainable. 'Without reform,' said Jesus Banegas Nunez, President of the Confederation of Employers and Industries of Span, 'Europe will not be able to maintain its welfare state.' As it struggled with its debts, a deeper problem was revealed: an absence of growth. Europe had some world-beating companies but, without growth, its influence would decline. No longer could there be the certainty that the continent would be a global player. Energy and dyna-mism were migrating to the emerging nations.

From the beginning of monetary union there had been deception. Figures were massaged to allow countries like Greece to join; later, rules were bent to allow countries like France and Germany to run up large deficits. Objections were ignored. Critics who warned of the dangers of such different countries sharing a monetary union were dismissed as being anti-European. The gathering storm, however, was debt.

The American economist, Paul Krugman, said Europe's leaders engaged in 'magical thinking'. 'No, the real story behind the euro-mess,' he wrote, 'lies not in the profligacy of politicians but in the arrogance of élites, specifically the policy élites who pushed Europe into adopting a single currency well before the continent was ready for such an experiment.' In September 2011, the British Foreign

Secretary William Hague said, 'It was folly to create this system. It will be written about for centuries as a kind of historical monument to collective folly.'

It is the biggest political drama in Europe for sixty years, with the outcome uncertain. Old assumptions are being torn up. The crisis will leave Europe a changed place. It may prove the catalyst that catapults old nation states into a much closer union. It may force democracy into retreat. For the moment the continent is lost, absorbed in its own turmoil.

This, then, is the story of the dream that turned dangerous and came to threaten Europe and the global economy.

Chapter 1
The Dream

In the late afternoon of 9 November 1989, in a hall in East Berlin, a communist party official, Guenther Schabowski, baffled and intrigued his audience. 'If you want to go,' he said, 'you are free to leave.' Journalists who were present huddled together, trying to unravel what the official meant, but the implication was clear: the people of East Germany, penned in behind walls and barbed wire, could travel.

By mid-evening there were cries echoing through the streets of East Berlin. '*Freiheit*,' 'freedom' was shouted over and over again. People, couples, groups tumbled out of apartment buildings. Many were young, their faces alive, daring to believe. They surged through dimly lit streets towards Checkpoint Charlie, one of the crossing points to West Berlin.

At the checkpoint, the crowd slowed. From the West German side there was the buzz of a party, of celebration. In that moment, defined by a distant sound, some sensed their world had changed and they embraced, their tears running onto the shoulders of friends.

Ahead of them were guards, edgy and uncertain, standing back in the shadows. On the Western side of the crossing was a bear, a dancing bear. Someone placed an East German border guard's cap on its head and the crowd laughed and drank from the necks of bottles.

Then on the East German side, a middle-aged couple saun-
tered towards the security post and just kept walking. Two
ordinary, anonymous people. The crowd fell silent and
watched a slow, agonising walk into history. The guards did
not stop them. They just checked out. On the West German
side there was a roar, and the couple were swallowed up by a
crowd fêting them.

At the Brandenburg Gate there was a line of East German
police. A man in a black leather jacket and blue jeans climbed
on top of the wall. He stood there, legs apart, his arms
outstretched, his fingers shaped in a gesture of victory. Some
East German guards turned a fire-hose on him but they
appeared half-hearted enforcers, and soon others were on the
wall, stamping on it, revelling in their defiance.

Army trucks arrived and the disembarking soldiers stood in
groups, back-lit by orange street lights, waiting for orders.
Then some young men jumped off the wall, into East Berlin,
and walked towards the police lines. They were smiling and
offered their hands to the police, whose faces betrayed fear
and bewilderment. And in those gestures of hesitation, of
uncertainty, the authority of the German Democratic Republic, with its feared secret police the Stasi, crumbled.

It is the curse of authoritarian regimes that at the very
moment they embrace reform and relax their grip, they are at
their most vulnerable. The crowd sensed this and was no
longer afraid. A couple with a sparkler walked towards the
wall, shrugging off police requests to stay back, but the request
had been polite, more pleading than an order, and it only
encouraged others to follow. They showed no hostility to the
police; they just humiliated them.

The police attempted to hold their lines but the people
streamed through. They were pulled up onto the wall and

stood there looking down on the two sides of a divided city. A man was passed a pickaxe and began chipping pieces off the wall. It was the moment when force might have been used, but the crowd had tasted freedom and not without terrible bloodshed could it be wrested from them. So, in a long night, where every stranger became a friend, the curtain that divided Europe was lifted and the history of the continent changed.

The following day there was a great migration. Tens of thousands of people headed for the crossing points into the west. Most of them had no plans. They were driven by curiosity and the irresistible lure of liberty. At the border they bunched close together, urging on the person in front, as if they feared that at any time East Germany would be sealed up again. It was like a herd driven by a strong, compelling instinct. Many of them clutched Ostmarks, a currency that would be of little use to them. They window-shopped at KaDaWe, strolled down the Kurfürstendamm, and stared at the sex shops. It was a bright, shining, unknown world and wherever they went, they were fêted and embraced as fellow Germans.

As they crossed into West Berlin, most of them said that they would return that evening and most of them did. Many were cautious, mindful that the secret police had not been disbanded, but amidst all the exhilaration of that day the future of a divided Germany was sealed. It could not survive. The West German government was careful with its words, determined not to alarm Moscow. It was too soon to discuss reunification said officials, but on the streets, in casual encounters, everyone spoke of it. At the crossing points there was the occasional cry: 'We are one people.'

The world sensed history turn. It had been on 5 March 1946 that Winston Churchill had taken the stage in the small town of Fulton, Missouri and declared that 'from Stettin in the Baltic to Trieste in the Adriatic, an iron curtain has descended across the Continent'. Now it had been torn down. Not through war or violence, but because Moscow had lost the will to maintain its empire. Europe was no longer divided.

For forty-five years, West Germany had been a model democracy, firmly planting its identity in being European. Yet for all that, the fear of a united and powerful Germany had not disappeared. It lurked there in the minds of leaders like Margaret Thatcher. She was nervous. Helmut Kohl, who was the German Chancellor at the time, recalls her saying, 'We beat the Germans twice and now they're back.' One of her ministers, Nicholas Ridley, described reunification as a 'German racket designed to take over the whole of Europe'.

Mrs Thatcher was not alone with her fears. On 20 January 1990 she went to lunch at the Elysée Palace with the French president, François Mitterrand. He warned that reunification would result in Germany gaining more influence in Europe than Hitler ever had. He even expressed a concern that the 'bad' Germans could return. According to a British official, the French president said, 'They might make even more ground than Hitler.' The year before the wall came down, Mitterrand had said that 'the Germans are a great people deprived of certain attributes of sovereignty, with reduced diplomatic status. Germans compensate for this weakness with economic power. The Deutsche mark is to some extent its nuclear force.' Yet for all his doubts, Mitterrand understood there was a 'logic to reunification'.

During this period, the British prime minister dusted down old maps and pointed to names like East Prussia, Silesia and Pomerania and questioned whether the new Germany would want those places too. On 18 November 1989, she had had a furious row with the German Chancellor, who told her, 'You will not stop the German people following their destiny.'

For Germany, however, the most important European leader was the French president, François Mitterrand. He had developed a strong bond with Helmut Kohl. War to them was not a distant memory. It shaped their politics. On 22 September 1984, they had gone together to the Douaumont cemetery in Verdun. It was there, amidst the hilly terrain, that in 1916 nearly 800,000 French and German soldiers were killed or wounded in one of the fiercest battles on the Western Front. The two leaders stood in the rain in front of two wreaths and a casket wrapped in the French and German flags. Behind them were hundreds of veterans. Mitterrand reached out to Kohl and for minutes they stood there holding hands, remembering the sacrifices that had been made to feed the bitter rivalries between their two countries. Mitterrand had fought in the nearby hills in World War Two and had been taken prisoner. Kohl's father had fought in the same area in World War One.

Both men were committed to a united Europe that made war impossible. Even so, there were suspicions and tensions between them. Over time, the French president softened his opposition to German reunification. In any event, he understood it could not be opposed: the German people wanted it. Helmut Kohl was wary of his French ally. He suspected that Mitterrand had become more relaxed because he believed that the Soviet leader, Mikhail Gorbachev, would block Germany becoming one nation once again. Thatcher, too, saw the Soviet leader as an ally. In early 1990 she told him that 'all Europe is watching this, not without a degree of fear, remembering very well who started the two world wars'. Gorbachev, however, had decided that Moscow neither had the means or the desire to hold the Soviet empire together with force.

Mitterrand believed the Germans needed to be bound more tightly into Europe, through deeper European integration. 'I believe,' he said, 'it is the EU, and only the EU, that can contain this German power.' Mrs Thatcher was less sure. She had told a French minister that European integration would increase Germany's dominance by giving Germany 'Europe on a plate'. The German Chancellor understood a price would have to be paid for German reunification, and that the rest of Europe would only be reassured by Berlin committing to a closer European union.

There was already a blueprint for the next stage of European integration. It was economic and monetary union, with a shared currency. Mitterrand and Kohl had already discussed it in 1987. No one underestimated the scale of the ambition. The French franc and the German mark had been linked, but not since the Roman Empire had a large part of Europe had the same currency.

Mitterrand now wanted urgent negotiations on creating this new currency. In 1991, at a summit in Maastricht, the two leaders committed themselves to an 'irreversible deadline for the start of monetary union' and the introduction of a single currency. They set a target date of 1999, with the new notes and coins in circulation by the start of 2002. The French leader understood the trade-off. At the time it was described as Mitterrand saying to Kohl, 'You get all Deutschland and I get half the Deutsche mark.'

For the Germans there could be no greater commitment to the future of European unity than giving up their currency and reducing the power of their admired central bank, the Bundesbank. There was such pride in the Deutsche mark that it was seen as a substitute for the flag – history having left Germans wary of flag-waving. Jacques Delors, the French politician, who was one of the architects of the euro, said that, 'not all Germans believe in God, but they all believe in the Bundesbank'.

There were many obstacles. Europe's economies were very different and so were the political cultures that guided them. Some were wary of debt; others more relaxed. Some ran tight accounts; others had a tradition of easy spending and tax evasion. Some, like Italy, had taken refuge in devaluations. In order to qualify to use this new currency, states had to pass economic tests and to bring their economies closer together. Deficits had to be lowered, budgets tightened and debt reduced.

From the very start there were doubts that this could be done, and these doubts would only deepen as the launch date grew closer. As early as 1990, the Central Council of the Bundesbank had questioned whether a monetary union, with a European central bank setting interest rates, could survive on its own. It believed that political union was needed to control economic policy. Monetary union, it said in a statement, 'is an irrevocable joint and several community, which, in the light of past experience, requires a more far-reaching association, in the form of a political union, if it is to prove durable'. There had been two European reports in the seventies and the eighties, which had concluded it would be rash to set up monetary union without political union.

There were many other warnings that the design of the monetary union was flawed. How could you have monetary union without central control of budgets and spending? How would states that violated the limits on debt and deficit spending be disciplined? Even the German Chancellor said that monetary union without political union would be a 'castle in the air'. Much later, when the currency was in operation, Helmut Kohl said that, 'Recent history, and not just that of Germany, teaches us that the idea of sustaining an economic and monetary union over time without political union is a fallacy.'

In July 1998, a poll conducted by 34 out of 42 economists found that the 'discipline needed to make the euro work was completely lacking'. That same year, 155 German economists signed a letter saying 'the euro is coming too early'. It said that insufficient progress had been made in improving public finances, and labour markets were too rigid so that wages could not adapt to changing conditions. Wolfgang Schäuble, the German finance minister during the euro-zone crisis, said in December 2012 that, 'If we had waited until we had achieved political union we would never have introduced the single currency. That is one of the basic principles of how European integration works. You always start with imperfect solutions. If you want to wait until you have the perfect solution you never go ahead.' There was a reason why they never sought political union; the people in Europe had shown no desire for it. However determined France's leaders were to bind Germany to Europe, they could not imagine selling political union to the French people. Schäuble said, 'We knew when we decided on the single currency that it would be better to have a political union ahead of it, but we knew also that we wouldn't get it.'

The president of the European Council, Herman Van Rompuy, said that for Kohl and Mitterrand, the currency was never, at heart, an economic project. 'The euro was not created,' he said, 'because there was an economic necessity. Not at all. The euro was created as a major step in European integration.' He believed that if you analysed this creation with only the eyes of an economist then you understood nothing. The trouble was that the dream, so enticing to a European élite, obscured flaws that were starkly obvious.

Those countries that planned to use the euro were told to bring their deficits down, and targets were set. In the event, the criteria for joining the new currency were fudged. There was creative accounting. Countries used the proceeds of privatisations and profits from the sale of gold to boost their accounts. There were numerous warnings that Italy was not ready to join the euro. Italy's figures, it was suspected at the time, were based on a fraud: the country was selling gold reserves from one branch of government to another. The German Chancellor, Helmut Kohl, was told but he did not heed the warnings. He felt, he said, the 'weight of history' and insisted the project could not go ahead 'without the Italians'. His closest adviser said at the time, 'We all shared a certain love for Italy.' Reunification gave urgency to the introduction of the new currency, but the leaders were caught up in the romance of their ambition. Some hoped the euro would prove a match for the dollar and that, in time, it would propel Europe into being a global power. It was a project driven not by the dreams and hopes of the people, but by an élite that believed that destiny lay in building an ever-closer European union.

Greece, too, caused concern. On 3 May 1998, the European Commission judged that Greece had not met the criteria for joining because the deficit of its public sector was too large. However, in the following year, the officials dropped their objections and the criteria were eased: it was enough for Greek public debt merely to be heading in the right direction.

Miranda Xafa was an economist working at Salomon Brothers in London at the time. She knew – and advised her clients – that Greece's economy was not ready; that the statistics its government was publishing did not reflect reality. 'I'd come to Athens from London with clients,' she said. 'We always saw the head of the statistical agency of Greece who compiled statistics on the debt, the deficit and so on. We'd call him the magician because he could make everything disappear. He made inflation disappear. And he made the deficit disappear.'

She used the example of the Greek state railway. Its accounts were impenetrable, as if a mist had fallen on its books. The suspicion was that there were more employees than passengers. A former minister, Stefanos Manos, said publicly at the time that it would be cheaper to send everyone by taxi. Manos said the railway company issued shares that the government would buy 'so that it was counted not as expenditure but as a financial transaction'. The whole point of the ruse, he said, was that it did not appear on the budget balance sheet.

Monetary union was launched on 1 January 1999. Otmar Issing, who would serve at the European Central Bank, said it was a 'milestone in history'. 'Never before,' he said, 'had sovereign states ceded their responsibility for monetary policy to a supranational institution.' In 2002, 8 billion new banknotes and 38 billion coins were put into circulation. It was a giant undertaking, performed efficiently. According to the financial analyst, David Marsh, the notes, if laid end to end, would have reached the moon and back two and a half times.

The moment itself was curiously flat. It was a historic day but with little sense of occasion. Eleven national currencies were being discarded. After over 2,500 years, the Greek drachma was no more. Other currencies that had helped define nations, like the franc, the guilder, the mark, the peseta and the lira were consigned to history. There were fireworks and music at the Brandenburg Gate in Berlin, and some Italians drowned their lire in the Trevi Fountain, but the celebrations were muted.

Most notably, the German public was unenthusiastic about the new currency: 60 per cent of them opposed it. One of their fears was that they would become responsible for the debts of other states. Others warned that one interest rate for such different economies would create havoc. To reassure the Germans, the European Central Bank – which would set the rate – would be modelled on the Bundesbank and based in Frankfurt.

Many of Europe's leaders, however, saw it as a foundation stone of the European dream. Gerhard Schröder, who would later succeed Helmut Kohl as German Chancellor, said, 'We are witnessing the dawn of an age that people of Europe have dreamed of for centuries – borderless travel and a payment in a common currency.' A former Italian prime minister, Carlo Azeglio Ciampi, saw the euro 'as a decisive step towards ever-closer political and institutional union in Europe'.

On the Champs Elysées, the EU's top monetary official, Yves-Thibault de Silguy, went shopping with his pristine new euros. He spent 141 euros on CDs and declared the occasion 'dynamic and full of gaiety' but, unlike others, he was more cautious with his dream. 'We can never be an American melting pot,' he said, 'even with a single currency . . . people here are firmly attached to national ideas.'

For some, the new currency was just a more convenient means of exchange; for others, it heralded a new Europe. None more so than the Portuguese prime minister, Antonio Gutierrez, who had declared in 1995 in a fit of exuberance that, 'When Jesus resolved to found a church, he said to Peter, "You are Peter, the rock, and upon this rock I will build my

Church."' Turning to the single currency he continued, 'You are the euro and upon the new currency we will build our Europe.'

It was the stuff of dreams, potentially dangerous dreams. The biggest myth was that these ancient and separate countries, fashioned and shaped by their own history, had become a cohesive economic and political bloc. They had not, but they could borrow on near identical terms regardless of the strengths and weaknesses of their economies.

There were other flaws too, which would be revealed later, but Europe's leaders had embarked on the giant undertaking – which would transform their continent – knowing that it was flawed. As one economist said, the currency 'offered every facility to a country to get into trouble'.

Chapter 2
Boom Time

The village of Vilanova d'Alcolea is tucked away amid the wheat plains in the province of Castellón. The business of this Spanish village, with 700 inhabitants, centres on olives and almonds, and tending the vineyards and carob trees. It has been that way for as long as anyone can remember; an undisturbed place, thirty-six kilometres from the coast and the frenzy of development.

In 2003, the people were informed that an airport was planned. The runway would pass two kilometres from their houses. They were told the project was essential to the development of the region but they were unconvinced, and not just because every take-off and landing would rattle their windows. They were baffled by the need for another airport. Valencia, which lay just an hour away, already had bustling terminals and runways.

The residents were up against a powerful local politician, Carlos Fabra. For much of the time since the nineteenth century, his family had been controlling the province of Castellón. Like him, his father, grandfather and great-grandfather had run the local government. Fabra was not used to being denied. With his swept-back hair and his penchant for wearing sunglasses even indoors, he was referred to as the Godfather. He tossed out promises; that the airport would attract 600,000 passengers a year, that 17 golf courses would be built and that jobs and money would flow to the region.

There were legal battles but eventually the airport, backed by public money, was carved out of the countryside. It was not an ideal location. It was a protected area for birdlife. There were hills, and two of them had to be dynamited to make way for the runway. The project was forced through at a cost of 155 million euros. There was, however, no demand from the airlines. In any event, the winds were in the wrong direction and landing was difficult.

Fabra was unabashed. The building provided more work for local construction companies. All across Spain, there were powerful networks linking politicians to local banks and building firms. At the entrance to the airport, Fabra commissioned a statue to himself. That cost another 300,000 euros. There was a gleaming new terminal. Roads were built connecting the airport with the *Autopista Del Mediterraneo*. A further 7 million euros were spent on advertising, including persuading the local first division football team to wear the airport's logo. Still no planes landed. There was not even a test flight.

When questioned as to the purpose of the airport, Carlos Fabra provoked ridicule when he tried to argue that this was not an airport for planes but for people who could come and visit and stroll around the runways. It was a unique opportunity, he said, to turn an airport into a tourist attraction by giving visitors full access to a non-functioning airport.

Maintenance cost hundreds of thousands a year. It included a contract with a local wrangler for his eight ferrets and falcons to control the birds and rabbits that might endanger the aircraft. But still no aircraft came. In any event, its airstrip would have to be widened to take commercial jets.

Later there was a mocking headline: 'News flash. Plane is seen at Castellón airport.' It turned out to be the story of an aluminium model plonked on top of the seventy-nine-foot statue at the entrance. It was the finishing touch, the final tribute to Fabra, who liked the fact that the statue was called 'the plane man'. He has been placed under judicial investigation. Among the questions being asked is how he so regularly appeared to win the El Gordo Christmas lottery. He denies any wrong-doing.

It is impossible to go inside the airport. A security firm patrols the terminal and runway and blocks access to visitors. Local people, like Paco Gonzalez, are helpful. They guide you to the point where the control tower can be seen and where you can gaze down on the 8,856-foot runway. The locals feel vindicated but it brings them no satisfaction. They take you to a mothballed desalination plant beside unfinished and half-empty apartments. They shake their heads at the madness but their protests were swept aside. They were denounced as backwoodsmen, standing in the way of development at a time when concrete was king.

Castellón airport, in its wind-scarred emptiness, is not alone. Rising up from Spain's arid plain is the airport of Ciudad Real. It sparkles in the sunlight, all glass and brushed steel. It boasts one of Europe's longest runways. Its vast, airy, light terminal is designed to handle 5 million passengers a year. It cost nearly a billion euros. Yet there are no planes. It is a white elephant funded by tax-payers' money. There are still other 'ghost' airports. All over the country are half-finished projects, testament to the politicians who used public money to slake their ambition.

These airports became the symbols of the construction boom that took hold in the years after Spain joined the euro.

The fiesta was fuelled by local government officials selling building permits. Many of the same officials had links with the property companies, and funding was easy. Spain, in a monetary union, could borrow at the same interest rate as Germany. The risks were judged equal but the rates set by the European Central Bank were too loose for a country like Spain. They stoked demand and fuelled the bubble. The same German officials who later would demand austerity had remained silent when German banks were lending the Spanish money; as they grew richer, the Spanish were importing more and more German luxury goods. The American economist, Adam Posen, said, 'It was as if Germany had been running a scheme in its own interest.'

Much of the Spanish boom was based on developing the country's infrastructure. Between 1999 and 2009, Spain added 5,000 kilometres of highway, the biggest road construction ever undertaken in Europe. It expanded its high-speed rail network to over 2,000 kilometres, more than France. Castellón was just one of twenty-four new regional air terminals. Not all were wasted; some were beneficial, opening up remoter regions, and the rail network is one of the best in Europe.

There was no restraint, however. Spain had become intoxicated by its new-found wealth and the EU stood in the wings applauding. After all, this was what the single currency was intended to do: stimulate trade and development. As with other booms, the nay-sayers were ignored. Local governments indulged themselves with vanity projects. The administration in Valencia was one of those with soaring ambitions. It built a City of Arts and Sciences with a Sydney-style opera house, a futuristic science museum and the biggest aquarium in Europe. It was completed in 2005 at a cost of 1.1 billion euros.

The architect alone collected fees of over 100 million euros. Another 2.4 billion was spent on a new harbour in order to host the America's Cup yacht race in 2007. It is now almost empty. The city wanted to lure Formula 1 to Valencia and paid out 20 million euros each year to stage the event there. The city ran up debts of over 25 billion euros and when the bubble burst, austerity followed. Children were told to bring their own toilet rolls and soap to school along with their exercise books. When, later, Valencia struggled to pay outstanding bills to healthcare suppliers, an official said bitterly, 'We are becoming beggars in a city of expensive wonders.' When it was far, far too late and the party was over, the Spanish prime minister said, 'We can't have twice as many airports as Germany. No one understands that. Nor can we have sports pavilions all over the place or conference halls and exhibition centres . . .' The debts by then were embedded in regions, cities and even small towns. The head of the Spanish Central Bank, Luis Linde, said that at the height of the boom, 'there was a sort of euphoria . . . which meant people did not see and did not want to see the risks that were building up'.

Construction consumed the Spanish economy. It reached 17 per cent of GDP. In just ten years, house prices doubled. In 2006, Spain started building more homes than the UK, Germany, France and Italy combined. Over ten years, wages in Spain rose 20 per cent faster than those in Germany. For a while it did not matter. The housing boom generated more revenue than expected for the government and between the years 2005 and 2009, it increased spending by 7.5 per cent. In Germany, over the same period, government expenditure grew by just 0.8 per cent.

In 2008, the financial crisis exploded in America, and credit dried up. Banks and other financial institutions were exposed as having aggressively sold mortgages to poorer people even when they knew there was no realistic chance of the money being repaid. Once the deal had been done, they passed on the risk. The mortgages – known as subprime – were sliced and diced and re-packaged and sold to worldwide investors. The exposure of these rotten deals undermined confidence in some of the world's best-known banks and financial institutions. On 15 September 2008, in America, Lehman Brothers crashed and credit became tight. Large banking institutions, whose names were seen as guarantors of trust and stability, went under.

Spain was dangerously exposed. Gradually, the funding for its glittering projects stopped. Construction companies went bankrupt and unemployment soared. The country, by now, had an unbalanced economy. Property prices fell and the debts piled up. What the country needed was growth. In a monetary union, countries share the same currency and the same interest rates; there was not the option to devalue and become more competitive. All the country could do was to reduce wages and cut government spending, and that would tip Spain into recession.

In the first seven years after joining the euro, the Spanish revelled in being European. Life had never been better. They felt rich, and the shadows of the past were fading. The dictator, General Franco, had only died in 1975. For the Spanish people, the answers lay not in looking back and examining the days of the *Generalissimo* but in embracing being European. The philosopher, José Ortega y Gasset, had expressed a widely held view that, 'Spain is the problem, Europe the solution.' Europe was seen as saving the country from itself, from its weaknesses, from its political culture. Spain in the first decade of the twenty-first century was young, vibrant, and confident.

The boom had also drawn in 4 million migrants. When the cranes stopped turning and the construction sites lay idle, they were the first to lose their jobs. Many of them, however, had settled in Spain, investing their future there. Some had bought property that, without work, they could no longer afford. Many were caught up in the struggle to avoid eviction; some of them found themselves part of a wider cause.

The activist sat alone amidst the cheap tables and plastic chairs. Outside the sky was leaden blue, before dawn. The Madrid street was deserted. Seated near him was an old man with a worn face in a faded denim jacket. He sipped his morning brandy. A night-shift worker came in and pushed a euro into a fruit machine without expectation. The activist gazed at the faded black and white photos of Murillo and Toledo on the walls before turning up his collar and heading for the Abrantes metro station. A few others were waiting. They nodded to him but at that hour there was little conversation. Sometime later, they started walking past squat five-storey apartments with grills on the ground-floor windows. The balconies were cluttered with drying jeans, plastic flowers and discarded air-conditioners.

The group was small. An older man with crinkly blond hair walked with a crutch. Another, much younger, had a stubbly beard and hid himself under a hood. Another wore a loosely wound Palestinian scarf. There was a woman who had dropped a megaphone into her shopping basket, almost as an after-thought.

They stopped outside an apartment block on the main street. Someone slapped a poster on the door. 'Stop *desahucios*' it read, 'Stop evictions'. Others began joining them, forming a human chain across the door. The morning traffic was stirring now. The activist, unprompted, grabbed the megaphone and started shouting, 'Neighbours, wake up! Someone is being evicted.'

The door to the block opened and there were stifled cheers. Luciano Chancusig seemed to recoil from the attention, then smiled and stepped outside. The protestors were there for him. This was the day he could be evicted and put on the street. He was in his forties. He wore a black corduroy jacket with a white woollen lining. His hair, still jet-black, was swept back. He stood there, his hands thrust deep inside the front pockets of his jeans.

The small crowd became agitated when they spotted a van across the street. Three men had got out. One of them pulled a white baseball hat tightly over his head, half obscuring his face. The other two just stood there, rubbing their arm muscles against the morning chill. They were the lock-changers; the men who would go inside the apartment once the police had cleared it. Some of the protestors detached themselves from the group and tried to appeal to the locksmiths, but they only shrugged. Work was too precious to be compromised by appeals to solidarity.

A window opened and a woman called at the crowd to stop the noise. 'You could be next,' shouted back the activist.

Luciano had never imagined he would be at the centre of anything. Certainly not a protest. He looked along the street. He knew the sequence of these events. Everyone did in this neighbourhood. He had been served notice to leave his apartment. Sometime during the morning, a magistrate would arrive with the police and they would decide whether his dream was over.

Upstairs in the smallness of the apartment, all he owned had been squeezed into black plastic bags. They were piled in a corner with a few jackets, the microwave and an old TV.

His journey had begun in 1998 in Quito, Ecuador. He had been a civil servant. When the government changed, he found himself on the outside: he no longer had the connections and was made redundant. It stayed that way for three years; a daily struggle to feed three children. One day in 2001, he left his family behind and headed for Spain. His brother was already there and told him there was work and a future. Luciano, like so many migrants before him, promised he would send for his family as soon as he got settled.

In Spain he was an illegal, without documents. Madrid surprised him. Its raw energy. The thousands of people from South America and from elsewhere in Europe. Everyone jostling for work. There were corners you would stand on before dawn and you could almost guarantee someone would hire you. Luciano got a job stacking boxes at the Mercamadrid, the vast fruit and vegetable market on the edge of the city. He was paid under the table. Fifty euros a day. He had no rights. One mistake, one wrong word, the foreman told him, and he would be out.

After a year he got documents. Other jobs followed. Bus driver. Truck driver. Then working in construction. There were cranes everywhere. No other country had built so many houses and apartments in such a short space of time. The years of cement, as they were called, needed an army of migrants.

Luciano was sending back money to Ecuador but he wanted to bring his family to Spain. Five years after having landed in Madrid, he bought an apartment. It had seemed the realisation of an impossible dream. He had built a life from nothing and had become a Spanish national, and he had immense pride in that cramped two-room space.

The bank had made it easy for him. Although he had no permanent job, no contract, they offered him a loan of 228,000 euros. At the time it seemed without risk. Everyone was buying, from single-room apartments on vast anonymous estates to second homes by the coast. You could not fail with property, he had heard time and again. And there was plenty of work. Initially, Luciano paid back the bank 1,000 euros a month. He was often earning double that amount and, at first, did not find the repayments difficult.

His children were now teenagers. They came to Madrid for a holiday and loved it. Old Europe for them was the new world. He planned for them to become Spanish nationals too. It was the greatest gift he could give them: to be Europeans and to escape poverty.

Then in 2009 Luciano lost his job. Dismissal came suddenly. The construction industry was no longer hiring. There was talk of a financial crash in America but he knew little about that. A few part-time jobs came and went. The bank suddenly wanted 1,500 euros a month. He fought to keep making the payments. He managed to sell a property in Ecuador for 6,000 euros. He sold his car. His brother loaned him money but he could not repay him and the relationship soured. By 2012, the apartment was worth 100,000 euros, less than half he had paid for it. Luciano could not pay any more and his children returned to Ecuador. Over time, the bank reclaimed the apartment and told him to leave. They wanted to rent it. They still, however, wanted money from Luciano. He would lose the apartment but he would not be free of the bank loan.

He decided to resist. He had heard about activists who were fighting the evictions, staging protests, blocking doorways;

using social network sites to thwart the police, the courts and the lock-changers. He sunk his anger into a cause and discovered he was not alone. Across the country, 300 people a day on average were being evicted. Most were too ashamed to protest. They slunk away and moved in with friends and family. Some of the migrants returned to countries they had long forgotten. Others curled up in blankets on the streets or in the city squares.

All over the capital there were desperate attempts to raise a few cents. In the Plaza Maya, one of the city's main squares, it was like a circus, a parade of people in absurd costumes doing cheap tricks. There were grown men who put a small box in their mouths so that they squawked instead of spoke and hoped, somehow, they would earn twenty cents. There were others dressed as goats, covered in colourful foil strips, who clapped their jaws together and hoped the kids would throw them a coin; if they did, they would clap noisily again. Others were pretending to be headless men. Some were dressed as Elvis or Puss in Boots. One woman was draped in plastic fruit. Some of them were from Ecuador, whiling away their days with an outstretched plastic cup.

All of this Luciano knew as he waited for the police to arrive. They had with them a man from the court. A discussion started on the streets. Outsiders listened in. There were some shouts of encouragement, for everyone in the neighbourhood had seen these scenes before. The court agreed he could stay for another two weeks. The small crowd cheered him as if he had won some minor victory, but he had no doubt it had only postponed the inevitable. Luciano could not stand the humiliation and what he called the 'psychological torture', the daily pressure of living without a future. His resentment changed him. What he feared most was ending up in the

Galiana, a vast shanty town of tin and wooden shacks on the edge of this European capital. They called it the slum of shame. It was a place of wrecked cars, rubbish, no sewage system and home to 30,000 people.

'If someone told me it could make a difference,' he said at one point, 'I would go to the Bank of Spain or anywhere else and set myself on fire.'

Luciano bridled at what he felt was the lash of injustice, and struggled to understand it. It was not just Spain, however, that was shaken up by Europe's big dream.

In a single generation, Ireland had gone from being one of the poorest countries in Europe to one of the richest. It was not long before – and certainly within memory – that in towns like Limerick and Galway, in western Ireland, cars had jostled with pony and traps. By 2005, the country was the largest exporter of software in the world. Dublin was no longer the 'dirty old town' with the 'sniffy Liffey' running through. It was the capital of the Celtic Tiger, and other countries despatched their young and ambitious to learn from the Irish. It had almost as many millionaires per head as the United States. In time, however, the boom would threaten the very foundation of the state.

Ireland needed a face for its boom and its bust and found it in a banker, Sean Fitzpatrick. On 24 July 2012, he stepped off the overnight flight from Atlanta and was arrested on the tarmac of Dublin airport. The time was 5.37 a.m. The details were precise, such was the man's importance. He was driven to Bridewell police station, held in a cell, and charged with taking part in a plot to ramp up the share price of the bank he once ran. Later, he was squeezed into a police van with the morning's petty offenders and driven to the Dublin

District Court. This was the nearest Ireland came to the American perp walk, where the accused are cuffed and marched to the court house. It was what the people wanted. 'In the US,' said one Irish politician, 'we have seen white-collar criminals being led out in handcuffs. I want to see the same regime in this country.' Fitzpatrick managed to slide a coat over his handcuffs.

Even in his humiliation he appeared rich. The patina of comfortable living stuck to him. He said he was bankrupt but he had not shed his appearance of affluence. Someone observed that he looked as if he was arriving for early evening drinks at a marina. He was aged sixty-four, tanned, with a full head of grey hair. He wore a blazer, a deep blue shirt, a pink tie and chinos.

The court, which smelt of stale beer, heard twenty cases before his: the daily parade of shoplifters, drug addicts and those who somehow had ended up in an overnight donny-brook. Eventually, the banker, who had once been worth 150 million euros, sat amongst the other defendants. They were curious about him, even though none seemed to know him. One eyed him up and said, 'He's rich, isn't he?' The man lingered with his own question and then asked, 'How much is he worth?' Fitzpatrick hardly said a word and in eight minutes was gone, to appear in court another day. As part of his bail conditions, he had to report regularly to his local police station.

Sean Fitzpatrick had grown Anglo Irish from a small Dublin bank into a lender with loans of 73 billion euros. He had been heaped with praise, flattered and courted, and nominated as Ireland's best chief executive. In time he would be hated: they even held an online auction to determine who would have the privilege of destroying his repossessed BMW. The auction was advertised on eBay with the words, 'This is your chance to crush this cursed car, which is the symbol of all that was wrong with the Celtic Tiger.' Fitzpatrick was despised and mocked. They wrote a musical about the bank he ran featuring puppets belting out song lines like, 'Because all it takes is a few Muppets to screw an entire country.'

Fitzpatrick believed in the power of the club, the golden circle. He had played rugby and golf and those were the roots of his network. He socialised with the property developers, the bankers, the money men, the financiers, the regulators and government ministers. He even played golf with the prime minister. He was at the heart of the tightly wound nexus that ran Ireland.

Most of the bank's money was made from commercial property deals. Two-thirds of its loans were invested in hotels, offices and shopping malls. Anglo became a real-estate bank. When it came to loans, Fitzpatrick trusted his instincts and he backed those he knew. He said, 'The real thing in life was not to be bright; it was to be lucky. I was lucky.' Huge loans were nodded through after just a few days' diligence. If his favoured clients did not have the funds for a project, he loaned it to them from the bank. Crucially, there were always friends in government. This was crony capitalism.

Fitzpatrick and the Anglo Irish Bank were not alone. Other Irish banks became aggressive players internationally. In just one year, they put £5 billion into commercial property in the UK. Hotels like the Savoy were snapped up by a new breed of Irish buccaneers.

Even before Ireland joined the euro, its economy had been booming. The interest rates, set by the European Central Bank in Frankfurt, were too low for Ireland, as they had been for Spain. After joining the single currency, Ireland found its interest rate was halved from 6 per cent to 3 per cent. In

Europe, money became cheap and capital flowed into countries like Ireland. Between 2003 and 2007 the Irish banking system imported funds equivalent to over 50 per cent of GDP. The German banks were only too willing to lend to the Celtic Tiger. They invested over 200 billion euros, fuelling the appetites of the Irish developers. The governor of the Central Bank of Ireland, Patrick Honohan, said afterwards that foreign borrowing had financed the bubble. In just a few years, the indebtedness of Irish banks to the rest of the world jumped from 10 per cent of GDP to over 60 per cent.

The banks were caught up in what an official report described as a 'tidal wave of uncritical enthusiasm'. People were offered forty-year mortgages. The loans were frequently seven or eight times a person's income. Salaries often went unchecked. Sometimes, no deposit was required. A quarter of first-time buyers were offered 100 per cent mortgages. In the ten years up to 2006, property prices doubled. By 2005, with the Irish property boom at its peak, interest rates, set for the euro-zone as a whole, had fallen to 2 per cent. They needed to be at least 6 per cent to rein in Ireland's spending. The bubble was further inflated by corruption in the planning system: at the height of the boom, so much land was zoned for residential building that it would have needed the Irish population to double to fill the empty properties.

The government in Dublin seemed in awe of the bankers and developers: the wizards who had delivered the economic miracle. There were warnings but they were dismissed. In 2005, the government even extended tax relief for property developers. Later, the governor of Ireland's Central Bank said the construction boom had been driven by a myth that the Irish economy would keep growing.

In 2008, the winds changed as the ominous storm clouds gathered in America and prestigious financial institutions crashed. In Ireland there was an immediate flight from risk and that left the country vulnerable. Governor Patrick Honohan was clear that the collapse of Lehman Brothers had not caused the Irish crisis. 'This had been driven,' he said, 'by excessive overseas borrowing . . . to support a credit-fuelled property market and construction frenzy.'

In Ireland, the doubts that had been growing about the Anglo Irish Bank could not be stifled. The country's richest man, Sean Quinn, had been speculating heavily in Anglo's shares. Some of the money was borrowed from the bank itself. Bank officials say he ended up owing Anglo nearly 3 billion euros. There were rumours that nearly half the bank's loans were bad. Investors took fright and in just one week deposits of 5 billion euros were withdrawn. There were desperate meetings with the government. Anglo Irish was going bust, but the frightening truth was that the bank that had been the Celtic Tiger's brightest star was too big to fail. If it went down, it would take the other Irish banks with it, and threaten the state itself.

Even before all the details had emerged of Anglo's toxic assets, the Irish government had responded with extraordinary measures. They guaranteed all the deposits and loans of Ireland's six largest banks and financial institutions. It was an immense gamble. The government had taken on potential liabilities of 440 billion euros. Private debt had become public debt.

Some in the Irish government judged the guarantee to have been unwise. Patrick Honohan believed it was a 'mistake' in the way it had been done. The two worst banks could have been isolated. Some of the bank's bondholders could have shared the costs, and not just the Irish tax-payer. Ministers in Dublin, however, were faced with a determined campaign from the European Central Bank. Jean-Claude Trichet, the ECB's president, was on the line to the Irish finance minister and was most insistent: bondholders had to be repaid in full. If they took a hit in Ireland then he feared that investors would abandon Europe and that would set off a chain reaction, with other banks struggling to finance their debts.

For a long time, Morgan Kelly had been the scourge of politicians and their financial friends. He was professor of economics at University College in Dublin. He was a local Cassandra, unheeded and resented. He had warned in 2008 that it was, 'No longer a question of whether Ireland would go bust, but when.' After the bank guarantee was announced, he said it would 'sink us, unfortunately, but inevitably'. There was a brief respite but the good times were over. Money was tight. Companies laid off workers. Some of the new housing estates were abandoned, half finished. Others were just left unsold, monuments to wild and reckless borrowing.

In the space of ten years, 553,000 houses had been built. Nearly 300,000 of them lay empty. The estates were built for the burgeoning middle classes who had wanted to swap the cramped accommodation of the city for newly built and spacious homes. A sadness fell across many of these estates like a shadow.

Paul Mangan-Ebbs and his wife, Geraldine, walk their dog in the evening. They cannot avoid noticing the faded 'For sale' signs of their neighbourhood, and the families gone, unable to find a buyer. It's a depressing round, counting the houses that lie vacant. The street has lost its children, its energy and the promise of a future. Building materials have been left behind, as if the workers departed in a hurry. Paul had worked in the construction industry but lost his job. Geraldine is a civil servant but her income has been reduced. Public service jobs that had once seemed iron-clad have become fragile. They bought their house for just over 200,000 euros but its value had shrunk to 120,000 euros. Many people they know have left the country but, like many couples, are trapped by negative equity. 'I think,' says Geraldine, 'we got very greedy in this country. Just spend and spend and spend. People were just going crazy spending, because they never had it before.'

In 2012, Ireland sent in the bulldozers to demolish some of the estates. The land will be returned to farming.

In December 2008, Sean Fitzpatrick resigned as chairman of Anglo Irish Bank. It had emerged that he had personal borrowings from his bank of 87 million euros and had hidden them from shareholders. The commentator, David McKittrick, wrote that, 'The charge against him is he virtually bankrupted Ireland, wrecking the living standards of generations to come through a mixture of economic illiteracy, vanity and, above all, greed.'

Ireland witnessed one of the sharpest declines in a western economy since the Great Depression. It found itself at the centre of the euro-zone crisis. But all of that lay ahead. In 2008 and early 2009, Europe's leaders still believed and celebrated the success of their currency.

That was to change suddenly, not with Ireland, but with Greece.

Chapter 3

'We ate the money together.'

A blood-red pencil line marked the first stirring of dawn as the patrol boat headed back to the flickering lights of the harbour. It was October 2009 and for the Greek island of Samos, the holiday season was over; the port of Vathi was already easing back into the slowness of winter. Most of the small fishing boats with their brightly painted wooden wheelhouses were tied up. During the morning, a lone fisherman sat by the waterfront calling out the names of fish for sale, his voice competing with the whine of the occasional scooter. As the day wore on, the cafés pounded out their techno beat but their plastic chairs remained empty.

The Samos prefect looked at all this with deep, thoughtful eyes. There was a mournful air about Manolis Karlas. It was not just the post-season blues; his island was sinking into debt. It was having to shelter the hundreds of migrants who had made the short crossing from Turkey. They needed food, clothes and shoes. The local administration had gone shopping on credit, running up huge debts with local merchants. Millions of euros were owed to local clothing and catering companies.

Most nights the coastguard plied the waters that separated Greece from Turkey. The migrants did not try and flee.

Rather, they punctured their inflatable boats as the Greek vessel approached and jumped in the water, certain of rescue. Floating away were their identity cards and documents, discarded in order to conceal their country of origin and to make deportation more difficult. More than 600 migrants were currently being held in a camp on the edge of town. Central government had pledged 4 million euros in assistance, but it had not arrived.

Sitting watching the charcoal smudges in the morning sky, the prefect said that a new government, a socialist administration, was coming to power in Athens and he hoped it would save his island. Even so he had a regret: the knowledge that something had been lost. He loved the islands but they were no longer timeless. The young were leaving for university or for the cities and most did not return. The town was changing. It was not just the migrants, but the outsiders who came: Russians and wealthy Greeks. They bought properties but only dipped into the island. They did not belong. He was curious about the money and the people who so carelessly forced up local prices. These were just early morning quayside thoughts but at least, there was the prospect of a new government hearing his pleas for help.

All, however, was not what it seemed. A few months earlier, in 2009, an economist from the IMF had visited Greece. Bob Traa wrote a draft IMF country report No. 09/245. He was brutally clear. Greece was living beyond its means and the economy was spiralling out of control. He concluded the country could no longer pay its bills and needed to cut its debt drastically. Greek officials were outraged and complained to the IMF. The report was quietly sidelined; Greece was heading for elections and none of the political parties wanted to discuss cuts.

Even earlier in 2009, one of the big credit ratings agencies had downgraded Greece. It prompted the European Commission to begin proceedings against the country for running up an excessive deficit. There were warnings but no sanctions. Despite the rules having been broken time and again, no country in the euro-zone had ever been penalised.

During the election campaign, in the autumn of 2009, the socialist candidate, George Papandreou, tried to unearth the true state of the economy. 'I had asked in a public debate with Karamanlis (the then prime minister) "What is the deficit?" I didn't know.'

'Well, you know the numbers,' was the evasive reply. On the day before polling, the out-going government sent an official document to the European Commission declaring a deficit of 6.5 per cent. 'They were fudging the numbers,' said Papandreou.

The scale of the fudge only became clear as the new government took over. George Papaconstantinou was appointed finance minister. He was an economist who had studied at the London School of Economics and had worked at the Organisation for Economic Co-operation and Development. He was in his late forties, intelligent, softy spoken and urbane. He had scarcely settled into his office on Syntagma Square when he received a visit from the governor of the Bank of Greece, who told him the deficit was double what had been revealed publicly.

Greece was a modern European country anchored in the European Union, but it was not keeping proper accounts. The new government decided the truth could not be concealed and, a week after assuming power, announced that the 'economy was in intensive care'.

Papaconstantinou took his findings to the monthly meeting of European finance ministers. 'They were frustrated and angry,' he said. They demanded to know how it could happen. One minister turned to him and asked, 'Shouldn't someone go to jail?' In fact, the situation was worse than had been disclosed. 'In my first week in the job,' said Papacon-stantinou, 'I got handed letters from the pension funds saying there was no cash to pay for pensions in October, November or December.' Then he discovered that state hospitals had not been paying their bills. 'The suppliers were screaming they would shut down the hospitals if we did nothing,' he said. The bills amounted to 6 billion euros – and did not show up in the accounts. During the year, tax collection had all but disappeared because there had been an election. There was a tradition in Greek political culture that at election time, the government pulled the tax collectors off the streets.

Suddenly, Europe's leaders were confronted with a night-mare for which they were ill equipped: a country in the euro-zone struggling to pay its debts.

Not only was its deficit much higher than had previously been reported, but Greece had accumulated debts of 300 billion euros, equal to more than 120 per cent of its GDP. Europe's leaders were also dealing with the reality of a political and economic culture that they had been so willing to ignore ten years earlier, when Greece joined the euro-zone.

For a time, Greece's most famous businessman had been Aristotle Onassis. He was a Greek-born Argentine shipping magnate who married Jackie Kennedy on his private Greek island of Skorpios. He had summed up his philosophy this way: 'To be successful, keep looking tanned, live in an elegant building (even if you're in the cellar), be seen in smart restaurants (even if you nurse one drink) and if you borrow, borrow big.'

That is what the Greeks had done. They had borrowed big. Like the Spanish and the Irish, they had used the low interest rates of the euro-zone to buy property. Between 2000 and 2008, house prices more than doubled. Cheap money encouraged people to buy homes, second homes and investment property.

Paying tax was regarded as almost a lifestyle choice. Kifissia is one of Athens wealthiest suburbs. It is tree-lined, dotted with designer boutiques and home to some of the richest people in the world. There was a tax for having a swimming pool. According to the official records, Kifissia had just 324 pools. The finance ministry decided to put up a helicopter and counted thousands of pools.

The state was fair game, to be ripped off if the opportunity arose. The island of Zakynthos has a population of 39,000. An official noticed that 1.8 per cent of the population was claiming benefits for blindness. A further investigation discovered that among the claimants was a local taxi driver and a bird hunter. The police unearthed over 600 cases of bogus claims using fake medical certificates. Some of the local doctors were complicit in the scam.

Millions of euros a year were wasted on retirement payments to long-dead pensioners: it was discovered that 500 of those receiving pensions would have been over 110 years old. The new government made daily discoveries. 'We found one pension was paid to someone who died in 1999,' said the deputy labour minister, Giorgos Koutroumanis. There was an army of 'phantom' workers receiving generous benefits.

Politics was built on favours. A party campaigned for power with the promise that, once in office, they would reward their supporters with much-sought-after public sector jobs. All parties did it. The socialist party doled out jobs to trade unions and other interest groups. 'On a vast scale, party supporters benefitted from political appointments to the public sector,' said Jason Manolopoulos, the author of Greece's *Odious Debt*. It resulted in the public sector having nearly a million workers: almost 20 per cent of the total working population. These were secure jobs that paid much more than the private sector. Even as Greece began to confront its debts, the hiring continued: 29,000 public sector workers were taken on in 2009 and 2010.

Votes bankrolled the political machines. For every vote cast in their favour, the parties were able to claim 10 euros from the state. Not only were there no incentives to prune the public sector, there were actual benefits in packing it with party supporters.

As the new government struggled to compile accurate accounts, they realised they did not even know how many people worked in the public sector. It would not be until the summer of 2010 that they began drawing up a record.

Andreas Georgiou had spent twenty years working for the IMF. He was now invited back to Greece to run the agency responsible for compiling statistics. He made an early discovery: 'The National Statistical Institute of Greece needed to make changes in many areas,' he said. He found what he called a 'battered institution'. Even the language used by the staff betrayed a culture where records were adjusted to suit the demands of politicians. Staff would tell him they were 'wrestling' with the figures. He sensed they believed they had an obligation to minimise the numbers for both the debt and the deficit. 'To me,' he said, 'it was unacceptable to wrestle with anything except accurate statistics.'

What Georgiou found was shocking: there was no documentation for hundreds of entities that were already classified as part of general government. Very importantly, a number of state-controlled bodies, like the Greek National Tourism Organisation and the national radio and television network were not included on the books of the government as they should have been. Among others, a major government enterprise that did not feature in the accounts was the Hellenic Railways, which was experiencing heavy losses: its sales were a fraction of its production costs.

Georgiou was evangelical in following the facts and the numbers and in his zeal made enemies. He was accused of exaggerating the figures for the Greek deficit in order to justify further austerity measures, including the selling of Greek assets. Some questioned whether he stood to benefit from this. He was accused of treason, with one MP suggesting re-introducing the death penalty for people like him.

Robert Kaplan, writing in the *New York Times*, said, 'Modern Greece is far more the child of Byzantine and Turkish despotism than of Periclean Athens.' Under Ottoman rule, it was a badge of honour to avoid paying tax; for three centuries, the Greeks had been expected to pay *haratzi*, which was a tax levied on Christians.

When the euro-zone was created, there was scant regard for the reality of political culture. The eyes that viewed history were romantic. In 1980 a British Foreign Office minister said of Greece's entry into the European Union that it was a 'fitting repayment by the Europe of today for the cultural and political debt that we all owe to a Greek heritage almost three thousand years old'.

Like other countries, Greece took advantage of the euro and its low interest rates to spend freely. Other countries were only too keen to lend the money. By June 2009, Greece owed the French banks 76 billion euros and the German banks 38 billion. The easy money went on bolstering the system of political patronage. What it did not finance was modernising the Greek economy. Much later, Jens Weidmann, the president of the German Bundesbank, reflected that the 'many years of wrong developments' in countries like Greece, Spain and Italy 'were caused by homemade errors, principally a failure to use initially lower interest rates to channel funds into productive investment'. For many countries, it was as if membership of the single currency had given them access to a cash machine; what it did was to expose the political culture of much of Southern Europe.

During the first decade of the euro, Greece became the highest purchaser per head of Porsche Cayennes, cars that cost 60,000 euros. Sales doubled in just four years. By 2010, the car loans outstanding in Greece were valued at 8 billion euros. The deputy prime minister, Theodoros Pangalos, went on television and declared, 'We ate the money together.' The people were furious. They would not be blamed and pointed the finger at the politicians. They regularly stood outside the Parliament buildings and denounced the MPs as thieves.

Greece's recent history is spiked with lies, deceit and wishful thinking. In 1993, the country was already in trouble. Its debt was 114 per cent of GDP and its economy was declining. At the same time, it was lobbying to join the euro; it even argued that the new currency should be embossed with both Latin and Greek letters. In April 1997, in Brussels, the then German finance minister, Theo Waigel, turned to the Greek finance minister and said, 'You are not part of this, and you will not be part of this.' Yet such was the ambition of their dream that Europe's leaders could not say 'No' to Greece. The same finance minister later said that Greece's acceptance into the euro was a 'mortal sin'.

In late 2001, Athens had hired Goldman Sachs. They carried out a financial manoeuvre which helped mask the extent of the deficit. It was completely legal but secret and 2.8 billion euros disappeared off the books. German Chancellor Angela Merkel said it would be a 'disgrace if it turned out to be true that banks that already pushed us to the edge of the abyss were also party to falsifying Greek statistics.'

In 2004, in a flash of candour, the Greek government admitted its accounts were misleading. A new budget minister had urged his staff to tell the truth. 'Don't worry about persecution or anything,' he told them, 'just tell me the true story.' What emerged was that the real deficit was 8.3 per cent, compared to the published figure of 1.5 per cent. One of the conditions for joining the euro was that deficits had to be kept below 3 per cent of GDP. The new minister – Peter Doukas – suggested they take the axe to the budget, but the answer he got from other officials was that 'we have the Olympic Games in a few months and we cannot upset the whole population and have strikes and everything just before the Olympic Games'. So Greece borrowed, and Europe's banks lent it the money.

Even in government circles there was a belief that if the country got into difficulty, the EU would ride to its aid. The credit ratings agencies, which later would prove to be harsh judges of many euro-zone countries, for a long period treated Greece as if it carried the same risk as Germany. Later, the president of the European Council, Herman Van Rompuy, said: 'The euro became a strong currency with very small interest rate spreads (on government bonds). It was like some sleeping pill, some kind of drug. We weren't aware of the underlying conditions.' It was a rare admission that Europe had been blinded by the romance of its project.

In late 2009, the prime minister, George Papandreou, went to Brussels and spoke to Europe's leaders. Speaking in fluent English, he played his audience cleverly. He came clean about the accounts in Greece. He struck a confessional note. Greece was riddled with corruption, he said. The other leaders were shocked. They had rarely heard a presentation like it. He promised to make tough cuts. Spending would be reduced by 10 per cent the following year. The German Chancellor, Angela Merkel, was among those impressed. She said that Papandreou had shown 'great resolve'. There were lots of calls for Athens to 'take the courageous measures required' but most leaders thought that a dose of self-imposed austerity would solve the Greek problem.

In the final weeks of 2009, Greece embarked on what would prove to be the first of many austerity plans. Pensions were frozen and the pay of civil servants was cut. VAT was increased, as were taxes on cigarettes and alcohol. The aim was to cut the deficit by 4 per cent. The markets were calm. In fact, the interest rates for Greece were lower at the end of the year than they had been at the start.

There were, however, the first rumblings of a much greater crisis. In London the Treasury was not just looking at Greece. 'No one in the Treasury had believed the Greek figures anyway,' said the Chancellor of the Exchequer, Alistair Darling. He was warned that Greece was not the heart of the problem. 'There is a well-developed storm coming,' he was told by his advisers, 'and it is only going to get worse.'

The Greek finance minister, George Papaconstantinou, harboured doubts about whether the measures would be sufficient, and what would happen if they were not. 'I remember at the end of 2009, going to see my German counterpart and saying "What if–?" and he said, "Do your job. Reduce the deficit and everything will be fine."'

By early 2010, investors and the markets had turned negative on Greece. The Greek prime minister attended a meeting of world leaders and financiers in Davos, Switzerland. 'I was chased around, followed upstairs by TV crews asking whether I had come on borrowed money to Davos,' recalled George Papandreou. He spoke to bankers, to politicians, to hedge-fund managers, and detected a deepening fear that Europe itself was facing a crisis. 'I came away believing that whatever Greece did – even a somersault – and we completely cut our deficit, that the markets would not respond positively without a wider European response.'

Europe still saw it as a Greek problem but in 2010 its leaders would face the threat of the entire European project collapsing.

Chapter 4
The Night they Almost Lost the Euro

Brussels is a company town. Its business is servicing Project Europe. Not just the 30,000 people who work for the European Commission but the 10,000 lawyers and lobbyists who come to argue and plead. Brussels likes to present itself as the capital of Europe. Sometimes a visiting American politician will call it that and leave a warm glow.

Despite the glass and concrete canyons of the European quarter, it remains a provincial town, insecure in itself. It is not a town for dissenters. It subtly grades and assesses, teasing out who is and who is not with the project. The town lacks the cut and thrust of party politics, where the powerful are challenged and held to account. It is an enclave that thrives on deal-making and compromise: the Commission's headquarters is known as the 'fudge factory'.

Until recently, the European élite had basked in the continent's narrative. Modern Europe had defied the barbarism of its history. It was not just at peace: it had helped spread democracy to a swathe of nations that for more than half a century had known only oppression. Oxford professor Timothy Garton Ash said, 'In terms of European history this is the best Europe we've ever had. It is an extraordinary achievement.' Some Americans, too, doled out plaudits. The economist Paul Krugman looked across the Atlantic and saw the European experience demonstrating that 'social progress and justice can go hand in hand'. The academic Steven Hill, lifting his head from his Washington think-tank, waxed lyrical. 'Europe,' he sighed, 'is a beacon for humanity's future.'

Europe's political élite had bought into the success story. They saw the continent as a benchmark of civilisation and, buoyed by their belief, they yearned for recognition and power; the power that would guarantee them a seat at the world's highest tables. Some were so convinced by the European model – where sovereignty was shared – that they saw it as a template for an increasingly global world. The president of the European Commission, José Manuel Barroso, said, 'The European Union has had almost sixty years as a laboratory for cross-border supranational co-operation, making it a natural champion of global governance.'

As 2010 dawned, Europe's officials were brimming with confidence, certain that the continent's destiny was ever-closer union. A new treaty had been ratified deepening integration. The euro-zone was seen as a safe haven from the financial currents swirling around the United States. In early February, President Barroso described the euro as 'a protective shield against the crisis'.

Greece was seen as a little local difficulty. Its GDP accounted for just 2 per cent of the euro-zone economy. All that was needed was for Athens to implement rigorous cuts, reduce its deficit and straighten out its accounts. 'Cooking the books must be stopped,' said the German Chancellor, Angela Merkel. The Greek government dripped out a list of new austerity measures but by February the financial markets were growing sceptical. They found the spending cuts unconvincing. The country needed to raise 53 billion euros just that year in order to meet its commitments. That was looking increasingly difficult as the markets insisted on a higher return for investing in Greece. The country's borrowing costs moved inexorably higher.

The Greek people were at first baffled and then angry. They did not understand where this crisis had come from. Their instinct was to blame their own venal politicians but they resented, too, that the fate of their country seemed to be in the hands of markets and European officials. As the government started to prune the public sector the response was instinctive: doctors, nurses, teachers and civil servants prepared to strike.

Costa Katarachias was a young doctor and highly educated. He was determined to resist the cuts. When not on shift, he got up early and squeezed himself onto an Athens bus and headed for his hospital to agitate, to stir up support for a strike. He was more resentful than political. He was proud of being a professional in public service but felt undervalued. After tax, he earned three euros an hour. That was not, however, what drove him. He did not accept that ordinary workers should pay a price for what had been done by previous governments and, particularly, international bankers. The fact that Greece had to live by the rules of the currency union it belonged to made no impression on him. These were not his rules and he could not remember voting for them. Greece, in his view, should leave the euro.

The country was already in recession. Further austerity was a hard sell. Vaso Mamali was a leather worker. All she knew was that the shoe factory where she worked could not pay her wages. She, too, resented how Greece was being muscled from abroad. Her bitterness was directed at the European Union. 'The EU,' she said, 'didn't turn out to be the paradise it was supposed to be.' So she and countless thousands decided to protest and join the workers' struggle. Over time, Athens would become a cock-pit of riot and protest, of police lines being pelted with rocks and petrol bombs, of people clutching masks to their faces against the clouds of tear gas.

The Germans were outraged by the Greeks. They were offended by their cheating and dismissive of their protests. They struck a harsh tone. 'Greece has to realise,' said the German finance minister, Wolfgang Schäuble, 'that when you break rules over a long period of time, you have to pay a high price.' Chancellor Merkel said, 'There are rules and these rules must be adhered to.' The Greeks simply had to accept austerity. A member of Chancellor Merkel's coalition said, 'We don't help an alcoholic by giving him another bottle of schnapps.' The former French finance minister, François Baroin, said for Germany, the problem with Greece was 'not economic or strategic but moral'.

Merkel struggled to accept what Greece had done. Its government had lied about its figures. It agreed to reforms but failed to implement them. To the German Chancellor this was unacceptable.

The hard, unforgiving message beamed out from Berlin prompted the Greek prime minister to remind Germany that it still had obligations arising from the war. On 26 February, he said: 'The issue of German World War Two reparations has not been finally settled. We have never given up on our claims. The issue exists in the framework of our bilateral relations with Germany.' He said he would not use the issue but he had raised it nonetheless. He wanted everyone to know, particularly the Germans, that it was there, like some dormant but live electricity cable.

The markets were probing. They demanded answers to difficult questions and were always ahead of the politicians. They wanted to know what would happen if Greece could not finance its debt. Would lines of credit be made available? Would existing loans be honoured? Would the EU come to the rescue? These were difficult questions, not least for Germany. In early 2010, Chancellor Merkel understood she and the rest of Europe faced a dangerous dilemma. If Greece could not fund itself, it would either be left to default or have to be bailed out.

Both options were fraught with risk. A default would do lasting damage to the credibility of the euro, and German and French banks would take heavy losses. A bail-out, particularly for Germany, was equally sensitive. It touched on one of the most fundamental guarantees underpinning the single currency; rules that had persuaded the Germans to abandon their beloved Deutsche mark. Article 103, paragraph 1 of the Maastricht Treaty was clear: 'The community shall not be liable for or assume the commitments of central governments, regional, local or other public authorities, other bodies governed by public law or public undertakings of any Member State.' In other words, countries were not responsible for the debts of others. That article had been a safety blanket to the Germans and, in their view, it ruled out bail-outs.

Faced with such difficult choices the Germans pondered another option: expelling Greece from the club. The idea was floated by the German finance minister, Wolfgang Schäuble. 'We need tighter rules,' he said, 'that means, in an extreme case, the possibility that a country that does not get its finances in order at all leaves the euro group.' Chancellor Merkel said it would be an action of the last resort and would only apply to a serial offender that broke the rules.

European officials were appalled. It was an article of faith for them that the European Union and the euro-zone only expanded. It never contracted. Destiny was a United States of Europe. The project was irreversible. Under no circumstances could it be allowed to fragment.

The French President was increasingly irritated with the Germans. Their reluctance to embrace bold solutions was, in his view, a mistake. Nicolas Sarkozy told an official at the Elysée Palace that if the Germans 'do not move fast enough, the crisis will spread and that at the end of the day we will all be dead, including the Germans'. According to one of the French president's friends, 'He pushed Merkel very strongly. "You cannot take the responsibility for making the euro explode," he told her, "not a German statesman or woman could do that."'

In the face of a hostile and sceptical public, the Greek prime minister, George Papandreou, railed against the financiers. Greece, he said, had become 'the weak victim, the guinea pig. We stand unprotected before the markets' wild appetite'. He told the Greek people that their country had become 'a laboratory animal between Europe and the markets'. Others, too, preferred to ignore Greece's debts or the flaws of the single currency. The Spanish public works minister, José Blanco, said, 'None of what is happening . . . is coincidental or innocent.' Spanish papers reported that the country's National Intelligence Centre was looking into 'speculative attacks on Spain', including the 'aggressiveness of some Anglo-Saxon media'. French commentators were drawn to this scenario: it was the Anglo-Saxon banks and hedge funds who were behind the euro crisis. One writer warned that 'those who played against Greece will pay dearly. The European Union now views this as direct aggression against them.' In Britain, the MP Denis

MacShane said that 'the Anglo-Saxon club of anti-Europeans was on the rampage.' The prime minister of Luxembourg, Jean-Claude Juncker, became so agitated by the power of the markets that he spoke darkly of torture. 'We have to strengthen the primacy of politics,' he said. 'We have to be able to stop the financial markets. We have the instruments of torture in the basement. We will display them if it becomes necessary.'

Privately, the Greek prime minister did not believe the strategy was working. At the end of February at a summit in Brussels, Chancellor Merkel had turned to him and told him to announce new measures from Brussels. Papandreou said it would be politically unwise to do this from the Belgian capital, but he agreed to further austerity. 'I said I will make another deep cut in the budget but I will need another strong statement from the EU which will support us.' Papandreou thought he had won that assurance from Angela Merkel. What he wanted was a statement that Greece was part of the euro-zone and its debt obligations would be honoured. Papandreou went home and came up with what he regarded as a very harsh budget. 'That evening,' he said, 'I was in Berlin and I said (to Merkel) "Now I want a statement." Her response was, "Listen, the markets will understand. You do your work and the markets will understand." That was not my view.' Papandreou felt badly let down.

Statements were made but they failed to calm the markets. Both Chancellor Merkel and President Sarkozy said that the European Union stood behind Greece but were not more specific. They both used the same phrase: 'We have sent a very clear political signal.' The markets believed they were being spun. Greece's borrowing costs were reaching the point where it would be effectively shut out of the market and unable to finance itself.

In late March 2010, the Europeans tore up their own rule-book. President Sarkozy and Chancellor Merkel agreed in principle to bail out Greece with loans of up to 40 billion euros. Brussels believed the crisis had been averted. The following morning, as the elevator rose to the thirteenth floor of the European Commission building, two colleagues smiled at each other. 'I hear Greece has been saved,' said one. The other man said it was 'great news' before disappearing into the vastness of the bureaucracy. 'The relief of Athens' felt like news from some distant front line. The president of the Commission, José Manuel Barroso, sat down to breakfast and declared himself 'extremely happy'. 'Common sense,' he declared, 'has prevailed,' and he exhaled, an official satisfied. The president of the European Council, Herman Van Rompuy, spoke of the 'courageous act' that had given birth to the deal.

Two-thirds of the money would come from the other countries in the euro-zone; one third would come from the IMF. Merkel had fought for that. It lessened the burden for the Germans. President Sarkozy, who felt the involvement of the IMF was humiliating for Europe, insisted that the euro-zone remain the dominant partner. He was extremely sensitive to the involvement of the IMF and its ambitious managing director, Dominique Strauss-Kahn, who was expected to be a candidate for the French presidency. 'Sarkozy did not want Strauss-Kahn coming into Europe and sorting it out,' said Chancellor of the Exchequer, Alistair Darling. 'Strauss-Kahn with his economic experience at the IMF,' he said, 'was already seen as the potential saviour of France ... so the (Elysée) was very keen on a European solution.'

It was hoped that the size of the war chest for Greece would see off the speculators. The Greek prime minister, George

Papandreou, said: 'No one, any longer, can play with the euro, no one can play with our common future.' A gun is on the table, he said, and it was about to be loaded. The target was the speculators. What both Athens and the rest of Europe hoped was that investors who had been testing the will of the euro-zone's leaders would back off, knowing there was now a wall of money behind Greece.

The markets were not so easily persuaded: they were increasingly wary of the Brussels fudge factory. The credibility of Europe's leaders had been undermined. There had been too much weaving and revising. There were too many details missing. What precisely would trigger a Greek rescue? Would 40 billion be sufficient? What would be the terms of any loans?

Investors could not see Greece surviving without a rescue. They doubted Greek statistics. It did not help that it was disclosed that the figures for the deficit in 2009 were worse than had been previously revealed. The economy was contracting with unemployment rising. Greece was caught in a downward spiral: as it fought to slash its deficit, the economy began shrinking, making it even more difficult to reduce its debt. There were almost daily strikes and protests. The markets shunned Greece, and its borrowing costs continued to rise. The uncertainty was damaging confidence beyond Europe.

On the night of 22 April 2010, some of the world's most powerful finance ministers and central bank governors gathered for dinner in Washington at 501 Pennsylvania Avenue. Their concerns went way beyond Greece. They believed that other European countries had high debts and were also vulnerable. They warned that the entire euro-zone could break up. The same searching questions about Greek debt were now being asked of countries like Spain and Portugal. If

Greece went under, other countries could follow, and quickly. They spoke of contagion, of the crisis spreading to other vulnerable countries with large debts. The Americans and the Canadians believed that the rescue package offered to Greece was far too small. One of those present was the British Chancellor of the Exchequer, Alistair Darling. The Americans were showing growing alarm, he said. He recalled the United States Secretary of the Treasury, Timothy Geithner, saying that 'if Europe goes down, we'll go down with it'.

'You can't overstate the fact,' said Darling, 'that America, with increasing incredulity and anxiety, was watching Europe's inability to act.' The German finance minister was not present, but the North Americans continued pressing the point, saying the Germans had to realise that this was not going away. They demanded of other Europeans, 'Why can't you take action?' If Greece defaulted, they said the global financial system was at risk.

Shortly after, Greece was bailed out. What, until that point, had been provisional and theoretical became reality and the sums were much higher than had been agreed just weeks earlier. The country was loaned 110 billion euros; 80 billion of that would come from the euro-zone and 30 billion from the IMF.

It was a moment of surrender, a day the architects of the single currency had never envisaged. Europe's leaders were forced to concede that a country using the euro had needed rescuing. In doing so, the EU broke its own rules, and justified it in the name of European unity. The fear in Germany was that this was only the beginning; that the country had signed up to bankrolling a series of fragile economies. German leaders tried to sell the rescue as 'in the national interest'. The German finance minister, Wolfgang Schäuble, said: 'What we are talking about is the destiny of the whole of Europe.'

Increasingly, rescues would be justified as necessary to save the entire European project. Merkel told the Bundestag (the German Parliament), 'We're at a fork in the road. This is about nothing less than the future of Europe and, with it, the fate of Germany in Europe.'

On 2 May, Greek ministers turned up for a Sunday cabinet meeting to learn the terms of their salvation. The country had become, in effect, a protectorate of the European Union and the IMF. In Athens, the bail-out was treated with suspicion. There was widespread unease at the involvement of the IMF. They were regarded as the 'men in black', hard-faced officials who had slashed spending elsewhere. The Greek finance minister, George Papaconstantinou, said the choice had been 'between collapse and salvation'.

The IMF and the EU, however, set a hard bargain. In exchange for bailing out Greece, they demanded 30 billion euros of new budget cuts over the following three years. The economy was predicted to shrink by 4 per cent in 2010; now it had to cut spending further and increase taxes. Many public sector workers had already seen their take-home pay fall by 20 per cent. The annual holiday bonuses – such an important part of public sector pay – would be capped. The Greek prime minister went on television and said, 'I want to tell Greeks very honestly that we have a big trial ahead of us.'

In the first week of May, the markets were rattled again. Their anxiety was no longer directed at Greece: they feared the whole euro-zone could collapse, sparking a global financial disaster. No European leader had addressed what would happen if other countries needed rescuing, or where the funds would come from to do so: they were still struggling to fund Greece, let alone other, larger economies. Prominent commentators started delivering grave warnings. Joseph Stiglitz, the

Nobel Prize-winning economist, said, 'the very survival of the euro is at stake'. The US economist, Nouriel Roubini, said the euro-zone was in danger of breaking up. Ominously, borrowing costs began rising for countries like Spain and Portugal. The Portuguese foreign minister, Luis Amado, acknowledged his country had been drawn into a fight. 'We are not in such a critical situation as Greece,' he said. 'We did not cheat.' The markets did not care. The investors had an over-arching question: how would countries like Portugal be rescued if they got into trouble, or would they be left to default?

On Friday 7 May a new, more dangerous, more apocalyptic mood was coursing through the financial markets. Investors saw sentiment turn against the euro. Borrowing costs for many euro-zone countries were being forced up. The crisis that the Americans had predicted was now imminent.

Angela Merkel was in the Chancellery in Berlin preparing for a campaign event in Dusseldorf. One of her advisers, Jens Weidmann – who would later go on to run the Bundesbank – was alerted to the atmosphere in the markets and sent a note to Merkel. The president of the European Commission, José Manuel Barroso, called her. His advisers had told him that big funds were on the verge of pulling out of Europe. It was a full-blown crisis and could bring down the single currency.

At 2 p.m. that afternoon the seven most powerful finance ministers in the world held a conference call. The mood was gloomy. The US Treasury secretary, Tim Geithner, spoke of the apprehension in the markets. Interbank trading was seizing up, he said. He spoke of panic and a crisis more serious than the collapse of Lehman Brothers. Investors, he said, sensed there was no plan, no safety net if other euro-zone countries got into difficulty. Within days, the single currency would be in free fall. The German finance minister, Wolfgang

Schäuble, issued a statement saying, 'We must defend the common European currency in its entirety.' Words, however, had lost their power to move markets.

That evening, Europe's leaders gathered in Brussels. Some were unaware of what was building in the markets. The word was spread that 'things were coming to a head'. Before the dinner of asparagus and turbot, the president of the European Central Bank, Jean-Claude Trichet, pulled out some charts. He believed he was fighting to save the euro. 'I was quite strong,' he said. 'I told them we are in a very grave situation which is of a systemic nature. It is not about Greece. It is not one country in particular.' The leaders were ashen as he told them, 'We have the worst financial crisis since World War Two.' He did not spare those around the table. He said 'we had rules in Europe' but even the major countries did not obey them. They had allowed debt and deficits to grow. It was absolutely dramatic what had happened in Greece, he told them, but 'you did not control what was going on'. Referring to his charts, he said that since 2005, he had circulated the details of labour costs. 'We all could see,' he said, 'that a number of countries were going in a direction that was not sustainable. We are responsible individually and collectively,' he told them. Indirectly he also took aim at countries like Germany that were resistant to using their economic power to save the euro. He said it was 'benign neglect'.

One of those present said some of the leaders were numb. President Sarkozy was white with shock. Later, he began screaming, 'Come on, come on, stop hesitating.' Trichet also demonstrated how the borrowing costs of weaker euro-zone nations were surging to unsustainable levels. It was impossible to bail them all out. There were not the funds. The single currency, which was one of the pillars of European unity, was in danger of collapsing. The situation was deteriorating with extreme rapidity, he said. A crash could be days away.

Sarkozy suggested introducing Eurobonds, where the debts of one nation would become the debts of all. That, in his view, would eliminate the difference in interest rates that countries had to pay to fund their debts. The German Chancellor pointed out it would also eliminate any penalty for irresponsibility.

The French president also urged the ECB to buy the bonds of troubled countries and force down their borrowing costs. Angela Merkel intervened to say that it was not the job of politicians to tell the bank what to do.

Trichet and others said what was needed was a very large bail-out fund 'for the rest of the world to understand we might have problems in Greece, but they could not start a general speculation against other countries'. President Sarkozy eagerly seized on the idea of a giant fund for the euro-zone. Angela Merkel, as is her way, was cautious. She wanted to know who would control the fund and how it was to be used. The Italian prime minister, Silvio Berlusconi, backed the French president. 'When a house is burning,' he said, 'it doesn't matter where the water comes from.'

The leaders left Brussels at 12.30 on Saturday morning. They had agreed that a solution had to be found that weekend and that the EU's finance ministers would meet on Sunday. President Sarkozy stepped before the cameras and announced that a 'rescue umbrella' was being planned for the euro. No such umbrella had been agreed, but the French president wanted to make it harder for ministers to go soft on the idea. As they returned to their capitals, all the leaders understood they needed a plan in place before the Asian markets opened on Monday morning.

On Saturday 8 May, Alistair Darling was in his garden at his home in Edinburgh when he received a call from a senior European official. He said that there would be a meeting of finance ministers the following day in Brussels and that he needed to attend, 'because we're about to take a momentous decision'. Britain had just had an election and it was clear there would be a change of government. Darling spoke to George Osborne, the man who would be his successor as Chancellor of the Exchequer, and they agreed there could not be an empty chair in Brussels. 'Osborne hoped I wouldn't commit the UK government to anything it couldn't get out of,' recalled Darling.

On Sunday 9 May, the president of the German Bundesbank gathered his advisers together at 12 noon. He updated them on the meeting in Brussels and the plan to set up a rescue fund for the euro-zone as a whole. He was curious to know how much funding would be needed to support those weaker – mainly southern European countries – over the next two years. The answer was that some 500 billion euros in debt would mature during that period. It was a huge figure, but if the markets were to be reassured that the euro-zone could and would protect its own, then it would need a fund of that magnitude. The European Commission, too, had been working on a draft proposal. It was ready by the time the finance ministers met in Brussels.

Mid-afternoon and before the meeting got under way, there was an interruption. The powerful German finance minister, Wolfgang Schäuble, had complained of feeling unwell during the drive from Brussels airport. He was rushed to a medical emergency room but his condition failed to improve and he was put into an ambulance and taken to the Cliniques Universitaires Saint-Luc and admitted to intensive care. The

French finance minister, Christine Lagarde, said: 'We can't carry on without Germany.' Chancellor Merkel was called. She phoned Thomas de Maizière, her interior minister, who was walking in the woods near Dresden with his wife. A bodyguard handed him the phone. The Chancellor told him to go to the meeting. An official aircraft was diverted to collect him, and by early evening he was in Brussels.

Darling noticed a different atmosphere amongst the finance ministers. 'Something,' he said, 'had put the fear of God into them.' The person most exercised, in his view, was Christine Lagarde. French banks were heavily exposed to Greece. The ministers knew, said Darling, that 'unless they came up with something by Monday morning, the risk was there could be a complete meltdown and not just in Greece. It was obvious people were scared.' There were only a few hours before the markets opened in the Far East. During the afternoon, President Obama and Angela Merkel talked on the phone. The American president wanted to exert pressure, to remind the German Chancellor of what was at stake. As the president understood it, a collapse of the single currency could bring down the global economy. He said it was vital for a 'convincing' response that truly impressed the markets.

Everyone knew what was needed: shock and awe. They had to establish a rescue fund of such size that it would convince the markets that Europe could support any euro-zone country in difficulty. Bizarrely, considering the urgency of the occasion, the ministers became distracted over whether Britain would contribute to the fund. 'For at least six hours,' said Darling, 'they were mucking about trying to get us to contribute to it, despite the fact that we couldn't, and almost certainly there would be another government . . . We were being blamed as ever,' said Darling, and the muttering was that the 'Brits were being difficult'.

The Americans made repeated calls. For two hours, central bank governors were on the line waiting for a decision. The governor of the Bank of England, Sir Mervyn King, passed the time providing a detailed analysis of the weekend football results. As Monday broke, Christine Lagarde began calling out the names of markets as they opened. First up was Sydney, Australia. She was particularly fearful of the opening bell in Tokyo. If there was no agreement, the Asian markets would set the tone for the rest of the day with a massive sell-off.

Eventually, Angela Merkel phoned President Sarkozy in the Elysée Palace and said that she supported the creation of a giant fund. At 2 a.m., it was finally agreed. It would be called the European Financial Stability Facility and would be backed by 750 billion euros: almost a trillion dollars. The final figure had been influenced by the German research on what might be required over the next two years. The euro-zone countries guaranteed up to 440 billion euros; the rest came from the IMF. It was intended to demonstrate, once and for all, that Europe's leaders had the will and the means to stand behind any euro-zone country with funding problems. Anders Borg, the Swedish finance minister, said the firepower was aimed at stopping the 'wolf-pack behaviour' of the speculators. The German Chancellor had shown her flexibility as she would time and again when faced with the prospect of the euro breaking up.

Sometime during that long night, the European Central Bank agreed that it would buy the bonds of countries under pressure and so reduce their borrowing costs. The bond buying would start that day. Everyone understood it was a potentially dangerous step. The decision meant that the bank was close to supporting governments, which was against its rules. However much it was denied, the bank had come under political pressure to act and that diminished its independence. On a plane back from Brussels, Axel Weber, the head of the Bundesbank and a member of the ECB's governing council penned a resignation letter. He believed the bank's independence had been compromised.

It was the night they almost lost the euro but it involved a sleight of hand. One of the most powerful people present said, 'The trillion dollars was not there. It was advertised. It was a very nice communication, a very impressive communication, but unfortunately it did not correspond to what our democracies were really able to deliver.' A commitment made did not prove the same as delivering the funds. In time the markets would realise that the new fund was not as powerful as it was first sold on that Monday morning in May.

For Britain, the night ended with a legacy of bitterness. It had made clear it would not be held liable for the defaults of euro-zone countries and it would not contribute to the fund. The accusation was that at a moment when the European project was in danger, Britain chose to watch from the sidelines. The moment would not be forgotten.

The Germans, having made concessions, were even more determined that the weaker countries should implement austerity. They began floating the idea that the euro could only be saved with stricter rules on borrowing, enforced by sanctions.

The French drew another conclusion. An official at the Elysée Palace said, 'For the French, the key was contagion; for the Germans, it was moral hazard. We were obsessed by contagion and I'm sorry to say, we were right.'

For Greece, the bail-out only piled debt on debt. The financier George Soros, said: 'The situation was eerily reminiscent of the 1930s.'

No one could remember a country that had been forced to cut its spending so quickly. It destroyed the fabric of the society, and the rage flowed on the streets of Greece.

Chapter 5
Greek Rage and German Resentment

Stadiou Street in Athens is drab and frequently shuttered. It used not to be that way, but it has become a street of protest, of the clenched fist; a long road that rises slowly to Syntagma Square, the country's theatre for the angry, across from the Greek Parliament. Every store on Stadiou has its shutter operator, a security man who stands with a finger on a button ready to lower the shutters as the demonstrators file past. Within seconds of the first banner appearing, the grills and the metal barriers, with their graffiti signatures, slide down and the street retreats, locking the doors upon itself.

On 5 May 2010, the Greek unions called a general strike. The mood was sour and resentful. The government had just agreed to an international bail-out. The people did not feel rescued but humiliated. To Greeks the sums were unimaginable. The country had been loaned 110 billion euros to save it from bankruptcy. This lifeline had come with a price. The bonuses that boosted pay at Christmas, Easter and over the holiday season were sharply reduced. There had been no negotiation; they had just been signed away at the insistence of outsiders. Public sector wages had been cut and pension payments frozen.

Greece was being punished. It was what the German Chancellor wanted. 'She said that very clearly to me,' said the Greek prime minister. 'Someone has to be seen to be punished so others don't do this in the future.'

It hurt because it felt imposed; it wounded because many Greeks believed the crisis was caused by greedy bankers and venal politicians. Time and again the people on the street insisted they were being punished for the sins of others. Now the continuum of their lives had been snapped, or that was how it seemed. There were no longer any guarantees, any certainty, not even with a public sector job. So the unions summoned their members for a massive protest: the rumours, the street talk and the tweets predicted violence.

Angeliki Papathanasopoulou worked on Stadiou Street in the Marfin bank. She was a financial analyst who put in long hours. She was used to hunkering down over her computer while the chants of the protestors seeped through the windows. She understood their anger but did not share it. She had lived and worked in a bank in London and had nearly settled there, but she knew Greece needed to change and she wanted to be part of that. The previous September she had married Christos Karapanagiotis. They had decided together to build their future in their homeland, a country they both regarded as beautiful.

On the day of the strike they had discussed the protest. Angeliki was unconcerned. She had lived through countless marches and demonstrations and had no intention of stepping outside the bank until she went home. She would stay hidden away as she had done many times before. Christos drove her to the bank: he did not want her walking because she was four months' pregnant with her first baby. They were due to learn that afternoon the sex of their child, and Christos said that he would pick her up between 3 and 4 p.m. Afterwards, she planned to go and see her elder sister and to share the news with her.

When they arrived at the bank the street was quiet; many workers were either on strike or had stayed away.

Not far from the bank was the university and the polytechnic. Students and anarchists were planning to join the main demonstration. There was a ritual to these events. The unions would march into Syntagma Square first and stand in front of the Parliament buildings. The anarchists would infiltrate the crowd and take up positions on the four corners of the square. They would co-ordinate their plans by phone and text message. When they had sufficient numbers, one of the groups would start throwing rocks at the police.

On this occasion, the anarchists were soon fighting the riot police, who responded with volleys of tear gas. The gas canisters left an arc – like a vapour trail – as they were fired into the square. Many of the crowd had come prepared for violence; they carried motorcycle helmets and masks. Some were just small surgical masks that covered the nose; others had full gas masks with detachable filters. Athens was probably the only city in Europe where informed conversations were held on the effectiveness of filters, with the Israeli charcoal filters judged the best protection against gas.

Some of the protestors leaned into the alleys and lit their petrol bombs and hurled them at the lines of white-helmeted police guarding the Parliament. For a time the police held their defensive positions, then they charged forward and the protestors retreated. So it see-sawed.

The Greek Presidential Guard, with their skirted tunics and red clogs topped off with pom-poms, stood in front of the Parliament. They were one of the symbols of the country but, amidst the clashes, they were forced to abandon their sentry posts beside the Tomb of the Unknown Soldier. Then some of the more radical protestors tired of the square and began looking for targets that were unprotected by the police.

Inside the Marfin bank, at around 11 a.m., Angeliki picked up a phone and spoke to her mother and then to her sister, who she was meeting later. She was not alone in the bank. There were two other colleagues with her.

Just after 1.30 p.m., about fifty protestors ran along Patission Street. They were hooded, and wearing masks and plastic gloves. They turned left into Stadiou and stopped in front of the bank. Their shoulder bags were heavy with petrol bombs and rocks. They urged each other on with chants of, 'Burn them, burn the rich.' They took hammers from their rucksacks and smashed the front window. Others hurled rocks at other windows. A small crowd watched, knowing what was planned. Banks in Athens had been burned before. Some of the crowd warned that there were people inside. Others pleaded with them not to fire the building, but the protestors were caught up in the blind certainty of their cause. The banks were their enemies.

After the windows were smashed, they poured gasoline inside and then threw in the petrol bombs. At 2 p.m., Angeliki phoned her husband. The bank was on fire, she told him. There was smoke in the building. They never spoke again.

The three employees inside were trapped. During the riots, the heavy main doors of the bank had been locked. There was no access to an emergency exit. There were no ceiling sprinklers and no fire hoses. There was a fire extinguisher but it was ineffective against the smoke filling the building. Angeliki tried to make it to a front window, which is where she was found. She had been killed by toxic fumes. The police and fire fighters arrived later, after the rioters in black had left. A fire fighter could be seen on the first floor. The bank's blue shuttered doors were ajar, the windows blackened. On the floor lay the curled-up body of a woman in a red dress.

For a while Greece paused in its anger. The rebellion against the state lost its appeal. Nothing, in the view of most people, could justify the killing of the innocent. The following day, crowds gathered outside the bank and stared into its charred interior. Some were just curious. Others struggled to understand. Some left flowers, messages, candles and toys for a baby that would not be born. In their faces there was shame. Some shook their heads as if they no longer understood the mood that was tearing away at the heart of their country. Someone scrawled on the wall: 'Traitors' and 'Killers'. International financial markets dipped, fearing there would be further attacks on Greece's banks, but the deaths had weakened the protests, if only for a time.

George Papandreou went and put some flowers on the doorstep of the bank. Many people regarded the death as murder, but the government was wary of giving a tough response. Its authority was weak and ministers feared more violence. 'Even though things looked quite violent,' said Papandreou, 'what I tried very much to avoid was for the state to be seen repressing people, so we tried to restrain the state's response, which was not easy.'

Those who had torched the bank withdrew into the sanctuary of their campuses. Since 1974, police had been forbidden from entering university grounds. It was off-limits to them. In 1973 it had been students and anarchists that had resisted the 'regime of the Colonels', and the junta had sent tanks crashing through the gates of the Athens polytechnic. The date of their defiance – 17 November – remains an official school holiday. So history had given radical groups a base where they could pack their bags with bottles and petrol bombs undisturbed. No one has been arrested for the attack on the Marfin bank.

Greece has a long tradition of protest. Anarchist groups have taken root, with cells like the Thieves in Black, the Conscientious Arsonists and the Revolutionary Nuclei. They are forever disbanding and forming and falling out over splinters of ideology. Occasionally they fight each other; the anarchists pitted against the KKE, the communist party of Greece, because they regard them as 'Stalinist bourgeois'.

The groups were united, however, in opposing the world of international finance and bankers. Globalisation benefitted élites at the expense of ordinary people. The European Union was seen as on the side of international capital. As the debt crisis unfolded, the focus of their anger shifted to Germany and its powerful industries. They resented Berlin for its insistence on austerity and for trying to remake the rest of Europe in its own economic image. Greece, they believed, had become a laboratory for global capitalism, with Europe's southern rim earmarked as a zone of cheap labour for Germany; that idea chimed with the suspicions of many ordinary protestors.

Mihalis rides a powerful motorbike, has an open, intelligent face and is an anarchist. He is steeped in his country's history and reels off the damage done to the country by outsiders. He blames the British for helping Nazi sympathisers take power in 1949. He blames the Americans for backing the rule of the Colonels. He seeks revolution and the destruction of the system. Greece needs to be remade. It is, in his view, run by fifty rich families who care little for development.

After the burning of the Marfin bank he said, 'There was a big conversation in the movement.' Some were ready to find the people who carried out the attack and hand them to the police. At one meeting, a man had said, 'We are being told we are killers and that we are against the people.' For all the doubts and all the self-examination, they never reached a conclusion. 'Nobody talks about it today,' said Mihalis. 'The crisis is so overwhelming.' In less than a year, buildings in Athens were once again being fire-bombed.

Economists such as Hans-Werner Sinn, president of the Institute for Economic Research in Munich, were among those to question whether austerity would work. 'This tragedy,' he said, 'does not have a solution . . . it is impossible to cut wages and prices by 30 per cent without major riots.' Privately, Greek ministers believed the social fabric of the country was being stretched to breaking point. The Greek prime minister, George Papandreou, tried to encourage people by telling them that their place in Europe had been protected. A majority wanted that, but they were not prepared to endure years of hardship. The prime minister reached back into the past to appeal for patience. 'We know the road to Ithaca,' he told them, 'and we have charted the waters,' but modern Greeks, unlike Odysseus, did not want to embark on some epic voyage with an uncertain destiny.

So, Europe's leaders and officials embraced a radical experiment in austerity. It was the new mantra. Officials who had previously been relaxed with government over-spending now delivered stern lectures on the dangers of countries living beyond their means. Some called the new orthodoxy 'debt fetishism'. Greece had been rescued in order to give the country time to reduce the size of its state. The experiment was to defy the long-established beliefs of economists. Greece was being ordered to slash spending whilst in the midst of a recession. Some, like the financier George Soros, believed the

approach was dangerously misguided. 'They didn't understand the problem,' he said. 'They applied the wrong remedy;
you cannot reduce the debt burden by shrinking the economy,
only by growing your way out of it.'

Mikis Theodorakis was the country's most famous songwriter
and composer. He had scored the film *Zorba the Greek*, which
had helped shape Greek identity. Theodorakis had a lifetime of
resistance. He had stood up to the Colonels when they took
power in 1967 and had gone underground. The Colonels retaliated with Army decree No. 13, which banned the playing of his
music. Later he was interned. For many, he was a Greek hero.

In May 2010, Theodorakis believed his country was slowly
being strangled on the altar of austerity. The conditions
reminded him of reparations imposed after a war had been
lost. In front of a crowd of 10,000 people, he called for revolution. For him, the price of the EU bail-out was that Greece
would be 'bound hand and foot on a stake of debt and interest
for the next 150 years'. In his view, this was debt servitude.
Over time his anger was directed at the Germans. 'If one
considers,' he said, 'that the German occupation cost us one
million people dead and the total destruction of our country,
how is it possible for us Greeks to accept Mrs Merkel's threats
and the Germans' intention to impose on us a new *Gauleiter*,
wearing a tie.'

In their rage, their resentment, their bewilderment, many
Greeks turned on Germany. It was not forgotten that during
the Second World War, whilst under German occupation, the
country had lost 13 per cent of its population. They were
intensely proud of their resistance. Winston Churchill had
paid tribute to them: 'Hence we will not say that Greeks fight
like heroes, but that heroes fight like Greeks.'

Although the bail-out had been arranged by the EU and the IMF, the Greeks felt the orders came from Berlin. At the very highest levels of government there was a stiffening against the old enemy, with the deputy prime minister, Theodoros Pangalos, reminding the people that, 'They (the Nazis) took away the Greek gold that was in the bank of Greece. They took away the Greek money and never gave it back.'

Germany was appalled. It had worked hard to escape its past but was never allowed to forget it: history lay there just beneath the surface and most Germans knew that. The horrors of the war were frequently recalled to serve the cause of further European integration. What Germany deeply resented, however, was the ease with which Greece fell back on old stereotypes, rather than owning up to and addressing the flaws in its economy. Sharing a currency was supposed to bring countries closer together. For a period it had worked, but the debt crisis was sowing division and highlighting the differences in culture.

The German papers portrayed the Greeks as 'lazy, profligate and irresponsible'. The Germans were particularly incensed at the number of Greeks retiring at the age of fifty: in Germany, they worked until sixty-seven. The German writers were in full cry as they unearthed how Greeks played their own retirement rules. The Greeks could retire early if their work had been particularly hazardous. Over time, almost 500 jobs were deemed to have been fraught with risk. A hairdresser could leave at fifty because she had been handling hair dyes, which were judged hazardous materials. Trombonists could also retire early because of the perceived risks from puffing. Even broadcasters could head off for a long retirement, their microphones suspected of storing dangerous bacteria. The Germans were incredulous. Neither could they believe that

Greece had four times the number of teachers as Finland and that some Greek islands had more registered teachers – drawing salaries – than inhabitants. Every day, the Germans were learning new details about a country they were in a monetary union with.

As early as April 2010, the German tabloid *Bild* was remarking that 'supposedly we have no more money for tax cuts, no money for school upgrades, no money to maintain parks, no money to fix our streets . . . but suddenly our politicians have billions of euros for the Greeks, who have deceived Europe'. One German MP, Frank Schaeffler – a supporter of Chancellor Merkel's coalition – called for Greece to sell some of its uninhabited islands to cut its debt. Another German MP also wanted the islands to provide collateral for the rescue loan. One member of the German Parliament, Joséf Schlarmann, said: 'Those in insolvency have to sell everything they have to pay their creditors.' He foresaw a fire-sale of monuments and buildings. *Bild* summed up the policy: 'We give you cash, you give us Corfu.' The paper bellowed its advice with the headline: 'Sell your islands, you bankrupt Greeks. And sell the Acropolis, too.' One German magazine stuck the Greek marble statue, the Venus de Milo, on its front cover. In the picture Aphrodite's arm was intact and the Greek goddess of love was giving the reader the finger. Underneath the caption read: 'Swindlers in the Euro family.' The Greeks were outraged; the magazine cover was condemned by the Greek president. The national fury clogged up the radio stations. One pensioner phoned in to say that when Greeks were carving beautiful statues, the Germans were living 'in caves and growling like dogs'. The country's consumer federation called on Greeks to boycott German cars and supermarkets. One Greek paper printed a picture of Berlin's victory column in the *Tiergarten*. The goddess Viktoria was depicted holding a swastika.

So insults were traded. The Germans felt betrayed. Promises made on joining the euro were being shredded. In rescuing Greece they had taken on the debts of another country, an undertaking that had been expressly excluded when the euro was launched. Guarantees given had not been honoured. The senior and influential German MP, Peter Altmaier, who is a close ally of Chancellor Merkel, said, 'When the euro was introduced by the Maastricht Treaty in 1999, there was a historic compromise. Firstly, the strong Deutsche mark would be abolished and secondly, German stability culture would be implemented across Europe. The first part was implemented. The second part is still written and binding in the treaty, but it hasn't yet been implemented.'

History had taught the Germans and the Greeks different lessons. The Germans have a deep aversion to unsound finance: the inflation of the Weimar Republic is seared in the collective memory. In 1923, monthly inflation reached a scarcely credible 32,000 per cent. In the history museum in Berlin, a queue forms to take a photo of a small item protected behind glass. It is a Reichsmark banknote for one billion marks. The Germans visitors do not hurry past; they stand there absorbing, in their view, one of the great object lessons of history. They study, too, the black and white photo of a procession of hand-drawn carts carrying the wages for a small firm. A kilo of bread cost 69,000 marks in August 1923. By November it cost 200 billion. Pay rises could not keep pace with the almost hourly rise in prices. By the end of the year, the currency had lost its role as a medium of exchange and millions of people saw their savings wiped out. The writer, Stefan Zweig, said inflation left Germans 'besmirched, betrayed and belittled' and vulnerable to Hitler's delusional fantasies of power. Even today, more purchases are made in Germany with cash than credit cards compared to other European countries. The memories of inflation and unsound money have left Germans cautious about borrowing. Only 36 per cent of Germans over the age of fifteen possess a credit card, compared to double that number in the United States. When the euro was being launched it was Germany that asked for a 500-euro note to be printed. Cash was still king. Those that use a credit card ensure that their debts are automatically paid off each month. The reluctance to borrow also ensures that home ownership is lower than elsewhere.

The Germans have rebuilt their country twice: once after World War Two, and then after reunification. They have made sacrifices. In the German mind they embraced painful reforms whilst the Spanish, Irish and Greeks were gorging themselves on debt. The labour market was freed up to boost jobs. Unions accepted changes to their way of working and costs fell. Companies poured money into research and development. Many of the reforms were introduced by Chancellor Gerhard Schröder, who told the German people, 'We shall reduce social benefits, promote individual responsibility and demand more from each and all.' After 2005, Germany was the only European country that actually reduced its labour costs.

The American Pulitzer-prize winning journalist Thomas Friedman said, 'The Germans pulled together. Labour gave up wage hikes and allowed businesses to improve competitiveness and worker flexibility, while the government subsidised firms to keep skilled workmen on the job in the downturn.'

Out of all this emerged a stellar economy with world-class manufacturing. German exports are almost as large as those of France, the UK and Italy combined. Around the globe, customers seek out the 'Made in Germany' label. No company summed up the *Wirtschaftswunder* – the economic miracle – better than Bayerische Motoren Werke: BMW.

From a distance, BMW Welt (World) looks like a stainless steel stadium. It is a bold, futuristic temple to the cars that are built close by. In part, BMW Welt is a delivery centre where new owners come to pick up their cars. Each year 15,000 people, brimming with aspiration, journey from across the world to take possession of a car. It is driven out for them on an automotive catwalk. The car is not sold to them as a means of transport. It is a brand, a badge of arrival, of inclusion; a mark of success. An American from Illinois stands in awe as his BMW emerges. He has built his entire vacation around this moment. For two weeks he will drive it on the *autobahns* before the company ships it to the United States for him.

Inside the delivery centre, a BMW G450 motorbike performs a twice-daily stunt, driving down the main staircase. The crowds cheer. Two million people a year visit this cathedral to the motoring dream. The young are nurtured: for those aged between ten and twelve there are over-night stays with a drive-in cinema. For older visitors the BMW Isetta – known in the fifties as the 'cuddle car' – makes an appearance.

It is a company, like so much of German engineering, which defies history. It was founded in 1913. Four years later, it was building aircraft engines. After World War Two the allies dismantled the plant. When production restarted, the company was only allowed to manufacture household utensils and bicycles. In 1950, BMW started building cars once again. Last year it sold over a million.

The key to its success is research and innovation. It has become the German way, holding on to its markets through quality. BMW has a research campus with a *designhaus* and *projecthaus*. Around 7,000 engineers, prototype builders and software designers study new materials, lightweight structures, nanomaterials, mechatronics, high-performance resins, thermoplastics – all the science of modern motor manufacturing.

The Germans are proud of their economy. Mrs Merkel has described it as 'a small miracle', although her finance minister has warned against German smugness. What it has done is to deliver Berlin immense influence. It is the engine for the entire European economy. Few important decisions in Europe are taken without consulting Germany. Its price for shouldering the burden of saving the euro is to insist that the rest of Europe becomes more German in the way it manages its budget and economy. The crisis in the euro-zone is changing Europe and Germany, and it carries great risks for both. As the former German Chancellor, Helmut Schmidt, said, 'If we let ourselves be seduced into taking a leading role in Europe, our neighbours will brace themselves against us.'

Jürgen Habermas is one of Germany's most influential philosophers. He has warned against it becoming a 'self-absorbed Colossus'. 'The country has awoken, ready to celebrate its economic ingenuity,' another commentator wrote. 'In many ways, large and small, Germany is flexing its muscles and reasserting long repressed national pride.'

The German finance minister Wolfgang Schäuble said, 'We don't want to dominate Europe, but if the German economy is weakening, everyone is complaining (to us). We will not be seen as the masters of Europe, but we have to bear in mind our responsibility for the entire European economy.'

The responsibility for managing Germany fell to France. It is the relationship that has driven and shaped the European project. General de Gaulle once described Europe as 'a coach and horses, with Germany the horse and France the coach-man'. At the time of Europe's greatest crisis in sixty years, the Franco–German relationship depended on the character and personalities of Angela Merkel and Nicolas Sarkozy.

Chapter 6
Opposite Twins

In the weeks that followed the Greek bail-out in May 2010 and the setting up of a giant rescue fund, the German Chancellor Angela Merkel was in reflective mood. In her view, the crisis in Europe was not over. 'We've done no more than buy time for ourselves,' she said. She was being warned by her close circle of advisers that the problems with the single currency were deep rooted and systemic. It was not just Greece that was running a dangerously high deficit on its budget: other countries might need bailing out. She was also troubled by the divide between northern and southern Europe: they might share the same currency, but their economies were worlds apart. The gulf between the so-called Club Med countries, the southern rim, the periphery, and Germany had widened during the euro's first decade. Many countries had become less competitive.

The German leader realised that battles lay ahead. She was already bruised from the Greek crisis. She had been criticised abroad for dithering, for putting the European project at risk. She was also under fire at home. German tax-payers were seeing their money loaned to governments they did not trust. If the currency was to survive, she was determined there would be no more cheating and deceiving. For too long she believed problems had been glossed over 'because we wanted to be nice to each other'. That time was over.

In previous times of crisis it had been the German–French relationship that had underpinned the European project. France saw itself as custodian of the European idea and, politically, the dominant partner. Germany, on the other hand, had the economic power. In the early years of European integration, Germany had deferred to Paris. No longer. Germany would work with France but it would also defend its national interests. As the crisis deepened, previous European leaders were troubled by the tension between Paris and Berlin. The former French president, Valéry Giscard d'Estaing, told an audience at the German Embassy in the French capital that 'Europe cannot move ahead without the Franco–German engine'. The partnership was heavily dependent on the personal chemistry between the French president and the German Chancellor: Charles de Gaulle and Konrad Adenauer respected each other; François Mitterrand and Helmut Kohl did not always trust each other but they were close allies; Valéry Giscard d'Estaing and Helmut Schmidt became friends; and Jacques Chirac and Gerhard Schröder had detested each other but they learnt to work together.

Angela Merkel and Nicolas Sarkozy, however, could not have been more different. There was an edge, an uncertainty to their relationship. She was cautious and analytical; he was hyperactive and impulsive. She disguised her ambition; he flaunted it. She was married to a chemistry professor who loved opera; he was married to a supermodel who loved the camera. Merkel would shop in her local convenience store near the Friedrichstrasse station; Sarkozy headed for Fouquet's on the Champs Elysées. He flashed his Rolex; she did not even wear a ring. She recoiled from showiness; he revelled in the full glare of political theatre. He loved the physicality of campaigning, the back-patting, the touching of strangers; she hated his Gallic embrace.

Sarkozy believed that Merkel's innate caution had damaged Europe. Sometimes in Cabinet meetings he would not even mention her by name, preferring to refer to her as 'the woman from the East'. Previous German Chancellors, in his view, would not have hesitated over the Greek debt crisis; they would have supported Athens. Angela Merkel seemed different. Appeals to solidarity did not settle the argument. She was more pragmatic, more calculating. Her fight was less the defence of the European ideal but more the protection of the German tax-payer. Her instinctive wariness, the French believed, had not just deepened the crisis but had ended up costing all of Europe much more money. 'In January,' Sarkozy said, 'this would have cost us 15 billion euros, but today we have had to come up with 750 billion.'

The differences in style and character between the two leaders stoked mistrust. At the May summit in 2010, President Sarkozy had arrived bristling with action and certainty. 'We must act,' he kept saying. He lined up other leaders behind the idea of a massive rescue fund that would bail out any other country that ran into difficulty. He had wanted to build an unstoppable momentum behind the fund before Merkel set foot in Brussels, and he was keen to take ownership of the plan. Later, he would claim 95 per cent of what had been agreed was a French idea. As he made his rounds of the other leaders, he was trailed by a posse of photographers and cameramen. When it came to the moment to visit Merkel, she threw the cameras out. She understood at once the political game: 'I'm not going to let you cast me as a stubborn old bag,' she said. Sarkozy was drawn to the grand gesture; Merkel had an eye for the detail.

Merkel and Sarkozy were the central actors in Europe's deepening crisis. Their differences were more fundamental than matters of style or their approach to power. Their idea of Europe was not always the same. Sarkozy sensed a new, more assertive Germany. The memory of war no longer defined German foreign policy. Ulrike Guérot from the European Council on Foreign Relations noted that 'Germany was moving away from a romantic view of its role in Europe that was driven by history and now wanted to strike a hard-headed deal with the rest of Europe about who pays what. The message from Berlin was that German history was no longer the driving force and the fuel for European integration.' This changed the Franco–German relationship in Sarkozy's view. He came to believe that the central mission of his presidency was to keep Germany committed to Europe. In the German Chancellor, he faced a leader whose background and instincts were sharply different from his own.

Angela Merkel was born in Hamburg in 1954. She was only a few months old when her father, a Lutheran pastor, moved the family to the parish of Templin in East Germany, which was under Soviet occupation. He was serious-minded and set high standards for work and study. As a pupil, Angela Merkel stood out. She was selected to visit Moscow as a prize for her mastery of Russian. Even at school she was cautious, assessing situations before committing herself. She once spent an entire swimming lesson hovering on a diving board. Only when the bell sounded did she enter the water. 'I am not spontaneously courageous,' she said much later. 'I am, I think, courageous at the right moment but led too much by my head.'

After school she went to Leipzig University to study physics. Later, she enrolled at the East German Academy of

Sciences as a research scientist. She wrote her thesis on the mechanisms and speed constants in atomic decay reactions. She never joined the communist party. She was asked to spy on her fellow students by the Stasi, the secret police, but she refused. 'I quickly said that it wasn't for me because I couldn't keep my mouth shut,' she said.

Just before the Berlin Wall came down in 1989 she became active in the democracy movement. On one of history's nights, when the Cold War ended and the gates to the West opened, she did not head for the border crossings like countless thousands of others. She kept an appointment and went to the sauna instead.

Aged thirty-five, she was increasingly drawn to politics. Before reunification, she joined the conservative Christian Democrat party, the CDU. Chancellor Helmut Kohl immediately saw her potential. She was an *Ossi* (from the east) and a woman. He referred to her as '*das mädchen*', 'the girl', which she found patronising, but he promoted her to minister for women and youth. It suited her to be underestimated, to disguise her intense ambition. Once, with a flicker of a smile, she conceded, 'I've never underestimated myself.' Later, the British prime minister Tony Blair would say, 'She was one of the easiest politicians to underestimate and it was one of the stupidest things any politician could do.'

In time, she would turn on her mentor. In December 1999, the *Frankfurter Allgemeine Zeitung* published a letter from her. It tore into Helmut Kohl, who had recently retired as Chancellor and was embroiled in a funding scandal. He had to be cut loose, she urged. The only way forward for the Christian Democrats was a complete break with the past. She urged the party to move on 'without its old war horse'. It was a clinical assassination that marked the end of Kohl's dominance of the party and set her on the road to leadership.

She plotted to lead a party that was conservative, Catholic, male-dominated; where all its senior politicians had learnt their political trade in the former West Germany. She was from the East, where survival depended on caution, on disguising your hand, on revealing your position at the final moment. By 2000 she was party leader. By 2005 she was Chancellor of Germany.

Her upbringing instilled in her the value of hard work. Most of her life she had studied. It was reflected in her style as Chancellor. She put in long hours pouring over policy papers. She consulted and then reflected. At meetings she asked for opinions without disclosing her own. She believed in analysis that was methodical and, on occasions, painstaking. She would not be hurried. The Americans saw her as 'circumspect' and 'unimaginative'. One of her biographers, Gerd Langguth, said she liked to 'sit problems out'. She was a pragmatist rather than a conviction politician.

The euro-zone crisis would make the pastor's daughter from East Germany the most powerful woman in the world. She became 'Frau Europe', a leader who intrigued not just because of her influence but because she eschewed the style of her time. She was not a celebrity politician – she was simply incredulous to discover that a Barbie doll had been made of her. There was nothing showy about her. It took much gentle pleading to get her to visit a prominent Berlin hairstylist. She guarded her privacy. In 1977, she had married a fellow student but it ended after five years. Later, she met and eventually married Joachim Sauer, a quantum chemist. They were rarely seen together in public, although she accompanied him to music festivals. His aversion to publicity led him to be referred to as 'the Phantom of the Opera'. She has never had children.

Like Angela Merkel, Nicolas Sarkozy was an outsider. She came from the East; he came from abroad. He was descended from Hungarian and Sephardic Jewish immigrants. His name set him apart. He was born Nicolas Paul Stéphane Sarközy de Nagy-Bosca. His father was a refugee from Hungary whose entrée into French society came via the Foreign Legion.

Sarkozy said there had never been enough money growing up; he liked people to believe he came from the rough side of the tracks. He earned degrees in law and business. Afterwards, he studied at the Institut d'Etudes Politiques de Paris. It was one of the *grand écoles* that bred the future leaders and administrators of France. He mistrusted and despised the élite, however, and they treated him as an outsider.

For nineteen years he was the mayor of Neuilly, just outside Paris. It was the eye for the grand gesture, for seizing the moment, that brought him to national attention. It became part of the Sarkozy narrative that he had not flinched from tackling the 'human bomb'. Whilst he was mayor, a man strapped with explosives walked into a kindergarten in Neuilly and took the children hostage, threatening to blow himself up. Sarkozy headed for the school and went inside. Over two days, he persuaded the man to release batches of children.

There was a swagger about Sarkozy, an impatience. He crackled with energy, a politician in perpetual motion. He had the style of an American politician, a country he admired. 'They call me Sarko the American,' he said. 'They consider it an insult, but I like it. It is a compliment.' He recognised himself in America's values and culture. It was President George W. Bush that dubbed him, 'Sarko L'Americain'.

As a boy, he had told his father he wanted to be president. His father had replied by saying, 'In that case, go to America

– because with a name like Sarko you'll never make it here.' Later, as president, he reflected on his journey to power. 'What made me who I am now,' he said, 'is the sum of all the humiliations suffered during childhood.'

So he fought his way up. The machine politicians mistrusted his drive, his ambition undisguised. They sneered at his French, which betrayed his background; they regarded him as unrefined, but they could not fault his determination and talent. President Chirac nurtured him as a protégé and promoted him, despite occasional fallings out.

Sarkozy was given several ministerial posts before he was elected leader of the conservative '*Union pour un Mouvement Populaire*'. In May 2007, he became the twenty-third president of the French Republic. He succeeded because he promised change. He sold himself as a moderniser, the man to re-invigorate France's sclerotic economy. He would shrink the state and wean France off its thirty-five-hour week.

Sarkozy, with his torrent of ideas, unsettled the French. The French people thought they wanted reform but when it came to it, their instinct was to hold on, to preserve the French way of life as they knew it. He was a head of state who lacked refinement. During an audience with the Pope he appeared to be playing with his phone. When a man refused to shake his hand at an agricultural show, Sarkozy snapped at him, '*Casse toi, pauvre con*,' – 'Sod off, asshole.' In an interview with the *New Yorker* magazine, the philosopher Pascal Brucker observed, 'He desecrates everything.' In his early days as president he summoned the journalist, Franz-Olivier Giesbert, to the Elysée Palace. He wanted to talk about his political opponents: 'You want to know the difference between me and all those people? It's quite simple . . . beginning in the cradle, they were pampered and coddled and repeatedly told, "You're the best, the most handsome, the most intelligent." And they studied at fancy schools. Look how much they love themselves. I'm a different type. I'm the bastard. But there it is, the bastard is president of the Republic.'

On the issue of Europe he was committed to defending it, but was jealous of French sovereignty. At meetings in Brussels he was the protector of the European project; at home, he was the defender of the French Republic. He was wary and at times hostile towards the European Commission. There was a part of Sarkozy that was drawn to de Gaulle's romantic view of France, set out in the opening paragraph of his *War Memoirs*. 'All my life,' said de Gaulle, 'I have had a certain idea of France. This is inspired by sentiment as much as by reason . . . in short, to my mind, France cannot be France without greatness.'

Sarkozy sought the leading role for himself and his country. He regarded France and Germany as 'opposite twins'. They were yoked together by history but in almost every way they were different. From the start, there was an undercurrent of tension between Angela Merkel and Nicolas Sarkozy. In 2007, whilst visiting the Airbus factory together in Toulouse, Sarkozy had joked that they would make a good management team for Airbus. 'You could look after the details,' he said, with a hint of condescension. 'You,' she quipped back, 'could look after the marketing.'

In 2008 Sarkozy, during a press conference, had revealed his irritation with the German leader over the issue of whether there should be a European plan to stimulate all their economies. 'France is working on it,' he said. 'Germany is thinking about it.' Merkel would not let the remark stand. 'We must be careful that we don't get ahead of ourselves,' she added.

'It was difficult at the beginning,' said François Baroin, the former French finance minister. 'At the start, Sarkozy had tried to forge an alliance with London.' He saw his natural allies as Britain and America.

The Greek crisis in 2010 exacerbated the differences between them. Merkel was offended by the over-spending and false accounting in Athens: it was an affront to her sense of good government. It became a morality play for her. Countries had to live within their means; 'deficit sinners' had to be punished. She praised the thrift and frugality of the *Schwäbische Hausfrau*, the Swabian housewife. Virtue and atonement lay in austerity. She wanted rules to be obeyed; Sarkozy wanted the euro to be saved.

For the French president, virtue lay in solidarity. That was the European way. The French papers were inclined to portray Greece and other countries as victims of speculation; Angela Merkel saw such thinking as absolving Athens from responsibility and opening the way to a transfer union, where disciplined countries like Germany bankrolled the rest. She believed that the answer lay in the strict enforcement of the rules that governed national budgets and was prepared to wait for the austerity medicine to do its work.

Sarkozy, however, complained that delay and indecision were undermining the euro. He could not get through to the German leader that time was not on their side.

Alain Minc, a close friend of Sarkozy, says that French presidents need two years to understand the limits to the power of the German Chancellor. The French president, he says, is more like a monarch. They tend to believe other leaders have the same influence as the British prime minister. Parliamentary democracy in Germany, however, is deliberately structured to make assertive leadership more difficult.

Sarkozy tells the story of how the German Chancellor took him to one side. 'Nicolas,' she said, 'you must understand. You are a man. I am a woman. I am from the north. You are from the south. I am a physicist. You are a lawyer. You are a king and I am managing a damned coalition. I cannot walk as quickly as you. You must walk as I do.' Xavier Musca, who was Sarkozy's chief of staff, said that the German Chancellor 'is extremely powerful and extremely weak' at the same time. This insight would eventually change Sarkozy's strategy in dealing with his German counterpart.

The summer of 2010, however, was a time of misunderstandings. The two leaders had planned to meet in Berlin and the French journalists had already arrived in the German capital. Sarkozy's motorcade was ready to depart when the Quai d'Orsay, the French foreign ministry, was informed the meeting had been postponed. A terse statement was issued by the Elysée Palace: 'At the suggestion of the Chancellery, the meeting has been rescheduled . . .' The French media was in uproar, with one paper saying, 'No one is being deceived here: there is a strong smell of fire between Paris and Berlin.'

From the start, Sarkozy believed it had been a mistake not to embrace bold solutions. For the French, their big fear was that contagion would spread to Italy. 'The moment Italy was touched by this crisis,' said Xavier Musca, 'the whole euro-zone would explode. It will be an awful catastrophe economically for us and for the rest of Europe and the world.'

The two leaders clashed over the involvement of the International Monetary Fund. Sarkozy was vehement in his opposition: inviting in the IMF was a sign of Europe's weakness, telegraphing to the rest of the world that the continent could not solve problems itself. He wanted a solution to the crisis to be home-grown in Europe. Merkel would not have it. She wanted the unsentimental rigour that the so-called 'men in black' from the IMF brought with them. Europe, she well knew, had a history of back-sliding.

Paris and Berlin disagreed over the role of the European Central Bank, too. As the crisis over Greece deepened, Sarkozy began putting subtle pressure on the ECB to buy up Greek bonds to lower the country's borrowing costs. Merkel said the independence of the bank could not be compromised. Sarkozy, time and again, wanted the bank to intervene in the markets.

In the event, however, it was Merkel who had to make the bigger concessions. Greek was not only bailed out, but there was now a vast fund to help others who had run into unsustainable debt. If the currency was to survive, she believed it needed fundamental reform. Treaties would have to be changed. Those countries that over-spent would have to be punished. There would be sanctions.

French–German discord did not just unsettle European officials: it troubled the markets. Investors questioned whether the will existed to defend the currency. In June 2010, the two leaders did what was expected of them and tried to display unity. It was the old courtship ritual: 'More than ever,' said the French president, 'Germany and France are determined to talk with one voice, to adopt common policies, to give Europe the means to meet its legitimate ambitions.' It was a display, and it did not entirely convince. One German magazine opined that in reality, 'they can hardly stand each other'. She called him 'the little Napoleon'; he called her La Boche. A French paper wrote that 'nothing is working any more in the German–French relationship'.

The partnership, however, was changing. Sarkozy saw grave dangers in Germany being isolated. His friend Alain Minc said he knew the relationship had altered when Sarkozy stopped saying, 'She doesn't want . . .' and began saying, 'She can't . . .' Sarkozy was beginning to understand that there were lines that the Chancellor could not cross, and she told him where the red lines were. The Elysée Palace also noted how damaging it was when the French papers praised Sarkozy for winning against the Chancellor. 'It created a backlash for her back home,' said Sarkozy's chief of staff. When she was accused in Germany of backtracking for the benefit of France, it made her more difficult in negotiations. 'When Sarkozy understood this,' said Musca, 'he decided not to say too much. We remained extremely silent. We were creating reaction in Germany and unease in the financial markets, creating conditions for investors to withdraw.' In time, Merkel would come to see Sarkozy as an indispensable ally, but that lay ahead.

During 2010, the mood in Europe darkened. John Kornblum, a former United States ambassador to Berlin, said the EU was facing its first 'existential crisis', with Europe's leaders facing the possibility of the whole project collapsing. The head of the ECB, Jean-Claude Trichet, said: 'Europe is undoubtedly in the worst situation since the Second World War, perhaps even since the First.'

Despite the chorus of concern there was, however, no urgency. During that summer, Europe's leaders believed that, with Greece, they had stopped the bleeding. The patient was in recovery. Elsewhere it was seen differently. The *New York Times* said, 'Today's complacency is so dangerous since none of the euro's basic problems . . . have been addressed.' The head of the IMF chimed in by saying, 'The whole world is watching . . . and is losing confidence in Europe.' The historian Simon Schama warned that the currency had become 'a sinkhole' which would lead to a 'lashing out at remote masters'.

Europe had signed up to a grand experiment. Austerity was the new religion. All over the continent, governments vied with each other to see who could sharpen the axe first. The daily news was peppered with announcements of cutting, of pruning, of scaling back, of bloated public sectors being squeezed. Spain cut public sector wages by 5 per cent. In Greece it was 16 per cent. In Portugal, the salaries of civil servants were slimmed by 5 per cent. Silvio Berlusconi spoke of 'heavy sacrifices' needed in Italy. Almost every European country now had its austerity package, including Germany. It was a cultural revolution that marked the end of an ever-expanding welfare state that partly defined the European way of life.

Europe had persuaded itself that Greece was facing a liquidity crisis, that it needed money flowing through its accounts. But the continent's problem's ran much deeper; there was little or no growth, debt was stubbornly high and there was a widening gap between some of the economies in the euro-zone. And, before the year ended, the crisis would snare another government.

Chapter 7
Ireland:
Hell was at the Gates

Over the summer and autumn of 2010, the fate of Greece haunted the Irish government. It feared that Ireland, too, would be forced into accepting a bail-out. Dublin had followed closely the humiliation of Athens, the capitulation and the protests. The financial markets had detected the black hole at the heart of Greece's finances and had not relented; they had pushed up the cost of borrowing to the point where the country could not finance itself. Greece was now an EU dependency, and Ireland was determined not to follow Greece.

The government in Dublin defined it as a fight for national dignity; an epic struggle to avoid having its destiny defined by others. Its campaign was run from the Department of Finance in Merrion Street, a heavy-set Edwardian building, erected under British rule. A team was assembled with the task of persuading markets and European officials that Ireland could manage its own finances and survive. They called the spacious office where the team met 'the war room'. 'I hadn't seen anything like the atmosphere,' said the governor of the central Bank of Ireland, Patrick Honohan. 'There was meeting after meeting, with sandwiches being brought in,' as officials tracked the markets and planned their defence. 'It was war,' said Dr Alan Ahearne, who was brought in as an adviser.

'There was a constant feeling of being in the trenches,' he said. 'Every day brought a new battle. We were a virtual war cabinet.'

The campaign manager was Brian Lenihan, the Irish minister of finance. Politics ran in his family. He came from one of Ireland's political dynasties. He had been educated by Jesuits and trained as a barrister. He had an easy manner and was plausible in debate, and that had been a factor in appointing him finance minister. It turned out to be the most controversial job in Ireland's recent history. Aged fifty-one, Lenihan was tasked with saving Ireland and its independence. Less than a year earlier, he had learnt that he was suffering from pancreatic cancer that was untreatable. The Irish prime minister, Brian Cowen, broke down in tears when he heard the news. Lenihan offered to step aside but the prime minister asked him to stay, despite periods when he would be unable to work. He was judged too valuable to lose, even though he was fighting for his own survival. Neither man, at this crucial moment in Irish history, had any background in the world of finance.

Ireland's problem was its banks. The government was weighed down by the decision taken in 2008 to guarantee the loans and deposits of its major banks and financial institutions. It now had the banks' debts on the government's books but no one in Dublin, however, had been able to settle on a figure for all the bad loans. 'It took ages to get information from the banks,' said Patrick Honohan, the governor of the central Bank of Ireland. 'It was not very well organised but by the end of March 2010 we got an indication of total losses. They were very large. Much larger than had been projected six months before.' Even so, officials thought in early summer that 'we might get through this'. They clung to encouraging

news. An article in *Newsweek* praised Ireland and its government. 'They've pushed through austerity packages drastic
enough to win the admiration of the international community,' wrote the American magazine. What caused amazement
in Ireland was that *Newsweek* named their prime minister as
one of the world's top ten leaders.

Ireland became the poster boy of austerity. It had not
flinched. It slashed spending and raised taxes. Nearly 3 billion
euros were cut from the social welfare bill. The minimum
wage was reduced, as were public sector pensions. The sales
tax rose to 23 per cent. Wages had fallen by 15 per cent in two
years. Such rigour earned Ireland friends and praise. 'I have
admiration for Ireland,' said Jean-Claude Trichet, the president of the European Central Bank. 'It is the country which is
exemplary in adjusting and recovering rapidly its competitiveness.' Through it all the Irish people had been stoical: it
was almost as if they knew a penance had to be paid for the
excesses of the Celtic Tiger.

Dublin promised more pain; there would be a further
hardship budget before the end of the year. Greek promises
had proved empty. Irish ministers flaunted their toughness
in the hope markets would reward their resolve. They
declared the deficit would be down to 3 per cent by 2014.
The truth was that whatever savings were made, the deficit
would remain stubbornly high. Cleaning out the bad debts
of the banks would be a formidable challenge for any small
country, let alone at a time when the economy was bordering
on recession.

By September 2010 the markets had turned sceptical.
Lenihan was defiant. 'We will have to hold our nerve through
this difficult period,' he said. Others around him, however,
had their doubts. Some officials in Dublin privately

concluded it was a lost cause. Ireland would be snared like Greece before it.

The government insisted it could finance itself until well into 2011. The assessments of some of the big international financial institutions were, however, damning. 'Ireland's economic difficulties are moving it into Greek territory,' concluded one bank's internal briefing notes. Since late summer, the rates for financing Irish debt had soared above 6 per cent. Ireland was seen as a risk; the investors wanted out, whatever the rates they were being offered. On 24 September, the government finally announced the price tag for fixing the banks. It was 45 billion euros and could even rise to 50 billion. That afternoon the newspaper sellers threaded through the Dublin traffic, waving the headlines: 'Black Thursday'. Even so, Lenihan and his 'war cabinet' believed they could hold out.

European leaders and officials in Brussels, however, had lost faith. They gasped at the figures. Ireland now had a budget deficit of 32 per cent of its gross domestic product. The EU limit was supposed to be 3 per cent. Ireland's national debt exceeded the amount that the economy produced each year and there was almost no growth. Privately, European officials spoke about an impending catastrophe. They feared that a sudden collapse in Ireland would be contagious. The markets would then turn their attention to Portugal and perhaps Spain, the fourth largest economy in the euro-zone. If Madrid needed help there were not the funds available. The country would face bankruptcy and the euro-zone would break up, bringing down with it many of Europe's banks. This was the doomsday scenario and, over the weeks ahead, Ireland came under relentless pressure not just to rescue itself, but to save the European project.

The Irish dug in, determined to resist. Senior politicians like Mary O'Rourke, who was related to Brian Lenihan, said that 'once again our sovereignty is at stake'. Irish papers wrote of the last throw of the dice to retain control of the country's finances. One minister said, 'It has been a very hard-won sovereignty for this country and this government is not going to give over that sovereignty to anyone.'

Ireland was a young country. It had fought a war of independence and only broke the British grip in 1922. Whilst under British rule it had lost half its population to famine and emigration. Now it faced, once again, having its economy run by outsiders.

Its prime minister, Brian Cowen, was a machine politician who owed his job to party loyalty. Many blamed him for not reining in the property boom while he was finance minister. The American ambassador summed him up as 'burly and brusque', with a reputation for not caring about his public image. His nickname was Biffo. At times he appeared over-whelmed by the pressure. His enemies accused him of 'running the country from a bar stool'. In an early morning radio interview in September 2010 he had slurred his words and was suspected of being hung over: at 3 a.m. he had been leading the hotel bar in a rendition of 'The Lakes of Pontch-artrain.'

On 18 October 2010, Ireland's prospects of survival were damaged further by a meeting at the French seaside resort of Deauville. President Sarkozy and Chancellor Merkel went for a stroll along the promenade, their collars turned up, looking out at an autumn sky streaked with sunset red. Merkel had come with a deal. She wanted to impose automatic penalties on the over-spenders, but she knew that Sarkozy would resist that. In exchange for her rowing back on sanctions, she wanted the French president's support in getting private investors to share the cost of future bail-outs: tax-payers alone could not be expected to pick up the tab. She wanted private investors like banks and hedge funds to share some of the losses. 'We cannot keep explaining to our voters and our citizens,' she said, 'why the tax-payer should bear the costs of a country's risks and not those people who have earned a lot of money from taking those risks.' It was for her a moral question. 'Why should dealing in government debt be the only business in the world that involves no risk?' she demanded to know. The injustice of it offended her, and President Sarkozy gave her his support.

In the short-term it proved a dangerous mistake. Investors were spooked; they believed they had been served notice that with future bail-outs they would take a 'hair-cut' and incur losses. Some of them withdrew their funds from Europe. The news from Deauville made holding Irish bonds more risky. Within days, its borrowing costs had soared above 7 per cent. The Greek prime minister, George Papandreou, thought the plan was a disaster and challenged Angela Merkel. She told him that 'we have to punish the banks'. Papandreou believed it was sending a message to investors that in future they would lose money. 'They will factor in that risk,' he said, 'and insist on higher returns. This is going to break the backs of some countries,' he argued.

The head of the European Central Bank thought the idea was 'seductive' but wrong. The Irish said that the Deauville agreement essentially slammed the door on them being able to raise money again in the markets. The Germans, meanwhile, have always insisted that the decisions of Deauville played no part in the Irish bail-out: the German finance minister Wolfgang Schäuble said, 'If you look at the debt and deficit figures of Ireland at the time, do you really think that was the reason?'

By early November 2010, the crisis had turned critical. Ireland's borrowing costs had reached 8.89 per cent. No government could borrow at those rates. Big businesses and financial institutions were withdrawing their deposits from Ireland. Confidence had snapped, and London became the safe haven for funds fleeing Ireland. 'There was a lot of confusion, a lot of money was leaving the country,' said the governor of the Bank of Ireland. 'There was a bank run on.' No institution was willing to lend to Irish banks, which had become dependent on borrowing from the European Central Bank.

Uncertainty over Ireland was putting other countries at risk. Portugal was struggling to raise funds. European officials feared a replay of the Greek crisis, when indecision had threatened the entire euro-zone. The pressure on Ireland was relentless. On 8 November the EU's economics commissioner, Olli Rehn, came to Dublin and was mockingly described 'as the most important man in the country'. His presence was widely resented, with the papers reporting how he dined at L'Ecrivain, a Michelin-starred restaurant, whilst the country faced years of hardship.

By Sunday 14 November, the tension between Dublin and European officials could no longer be disguised. European officials were blunt. One of them phoned Brian Lenihan from a G20 summit in Seoul and told him 'the situation has changed'. The international financial community had lost patience with uncertainty. No one in Europe had ever anticipated a situation where a country would openly resist a rescue. It was assumed that countries would be grateful, but they underestimated national pride.

The weekend had been marked by phone calls, leaks and denials. The BBC reported that it was 'no longer a matter of whether but when' Ireland agreed to a bail-out. Irish ministers were exasperated. At a critical moment in their history, they felt sidelined. One of them walked around with a briefing paper. In big capitals at the bottom of the page were the words, 'WE CAN WORK THROUGH THIS OURSELVES'. The Irish prime minister was furious in his denial that a rescue was imminent yet, that day, some of Ireland's most senior officials began talks in Brussels.

Dr Ahearne, who was working in the 'war room', said the 'tension was awful'. 'I remember going in on the train thinking "What will happen today?"' On Monday 15 November, however, prime minister Brian Cowen fought back. He went on Irish television and declared that, 'Ireland is making no application for the funding of the state because clearly we're pre-funded right up to the middle of next year.' The words were intended to counter the expectation building in Brussels. The following day, he took on the leakers directly by going before the Irish Parliament and denouncing 'ill-informed and inaccurate speculation'.

In the space of five weeks, beginning on 15 October, three letters were sent from Jean-Claude Trichet, the president of the European Central Bank, to Brian Lenihan, Ireland's minister of finance. There was also at least one phone call. It was a steady turning of the screw, increasing pressure on Ireland to apply for a bail-out. Trichet pointed out that the ECB was under-writing the Irish banking system to the tune of 150 billion euros. He doubted such levels of support could continue. The exposure was too great and some at the ECB feared there were risks to the whole European banking system. The underlying message was clear that continued support for the banks was dependent on Ireland agreeing to a bail-out. Some officials who had been in the 'war room' believed the messages amounted to a threat to withdraw funding for the banks. One of the letters was so sensitive that its contents have never been revealed: the ECB, without explaining why, said publication was not in the public interest. Certainly, Mr Lenihan felt that the unelected officials of the ECB were not just briefing against Ireland but were trying to dictate policy.

The messages from other parts of the European establishment became less and less coded. The president of the European Commission, José Manuel Barroso, whilst accepting that Ireland had not requested a bail-out, reminded everyone that there were rescue mechanisms available 'to deal with the problems as they come up'. The Portuguese finance minister, Teixeira dos Santos, said he did not want to lecture Ireland and then did it anyway. 'I want to believe,' he said, 'they will decide to do what is most appropriate together for Ireland and the euro. I want to believe they have the vision to take the right decision.' A similar line was taken by the governor of the central bank in Spain who said, 'It's up to Ireland to make the right decision – I hope it makes it.'

The Irish government, however, did not accept that Europe knew best and that there was only one right decision and that was to submit to a bail-out. Ireland's minister for European affairs, Dick Roche, hit back: 'It is not just a question of national pride,' he said. 'It is very important that any sovereign nation retains control over key issues. It would not be a good thing for us to go running to the IMF when it is clear that there is no need to so do.'

On Tuesday 16 November 2010, there was a meeting of the euro-zone's finance ministers in Brussels. Brian Lenihan flew from Dublin. The tone had hardened. Ireland was being accused of standing in the way of the wider European project. Leaders were signalling that Europe had reached a dangerous moment. The president of the European Council, Herman

Van Rompuy, said, 'We're in a survival crisis . . . we all have to work together in order to survive with the euro-zone because if we don't survive with the euro-zone, we will not survive with the EU.' Chancellor Merkel said, 'I'm telling you, everything is at stake. If the euro fails, then Europe will fail. And with it fails the idea of European values and unity.'

Lenihan was cornered. One by one the other finance ministers leant on him. It came close to verbal bullying, said one Irish official. There was a real touch of menace. The German finance minister Wolfgang Schäuble demanded that Lenihan leave the meeting immediately and go before the cameras and announce that Ireland was requesting a bail-out. Lenihan was incensed. He would not be 'dragooned' or dictated to. He pointed out that such decisions were a matter for his government. It was also apparent to the Irish delegation that the other ministers who were urging Ireland to accept a rescue had little or no idea how it would work. As one Dublin economist put it, this was by now a game of 'geo-political hardball. Brian Lenihan from Castleknock versus the heirs of Bismarck and Cardinal Richelieu'. Even while Lenihan was flying home, European officials were briefing that they expected a definite decision 'within the coming days'.

On Thursday 18 November, everything changed: Ireland's defences were breached by one of its own. The governor of the Central Bank of Ireland, Patrick Honohan, was in Frankfurt at a European Central Bank meeting and decided to give an interview to the Irish radio programme, 'Morning Ireland'. He was asked why IMF officials were in Dublin. He did not hesitate: they were there to work out the details of giving our state 'a very substantial loan'. He spoke of tens of billions. So the Irish learnt from an unelected official on a radio programme that their government was in the midst of negotiating a bail-out that would significantly reduce Ireland's sovereignty over its own economy.

'I talked to Brian Lenihan the night before,' said Patrick Honohan, 'and I knew he wasn't going to ask for a bail-out.' He did not tell him that he was going to give a radio interview. 'For me it was an over-night decision,' he said. 'It didn't occur to me to tell the prime minister.'

The prime minister Brian Cowen was outraged. 'The governor gave his view,' he said. 'I am entitled to give the view about the decision the government will take when the necessary discussions are over.' Only the previous day, Cowen had insisted yet again that there was no question of negotiating a bail-out. Privately he believed that officials from the European Central Bank had pushed Honohan into making his statement, but Cowen's credibility and that of his government was now threadbare.

Three days later, a humiliated and broken prime minister conceded defeat. He told Brian Lenihan to apply for help. In his letter to Trichet the finance minister wrote 'there comes a point at which negative sentiment starts to feed on itself.' The move had been long predicted but it hurt Ireland. It undermined the country's sense of itself. John Bruton, a former Irish prime minister, said: 'It was a very sad day for Ireland.' Government ministers felt betrayed. The minister for justice, Dermot Ahern, said, 'There were people from outside this country who were trying to bounce us, as a sovereign state, into making an application – throwing in the towel – before we even considered it as a government.' Ireland's Europe minister, Dick Roche, found the whole episode 'sinister'. Ireland, in his view, had been sacrificed. 'They (ECB officials) believed,' he said, 'that the rot could be halted if Ireland was thrown to the wolves.'

Shortly after, Brian Lenihan went to Brussels to learn the terms of the country's rescue. One senior European official had warned that the rescue would come with 'drastic conditions'. Lenihan was forced to deny that the forthcoming budget would be dictated by the EU and the IMF. The December budget, he said, 'will be our budget and nobody else's'. When it was announced, payments to the blind, the unemployed, the disabled and carers had all been scaled back. The opposition said the government had become 'puppets' of Brussels.

The price of the rescue was that Ireland would not be able to make any major decisions about its economy without reference to the European Commission.

Later Brian Lenihan described his feelings while waiting for the plane: 'I've a very vivid memory of going to Brussels on the final Monday to sign the agreement and being on my own at the airport and looking at the snow gradually thawing and thinking to myself, "This is terrible. No Irish minister has had to do this before." I had fought for two and a half years to avoid this conclusion. I believed I had fought the good fight and taken every measure possible to delay such an eventuality. And now hell was at the gates.' He died a few months later.

Ireland was loaned 85 billion euros. The majority of that came from the EU. Some came from the IMF. Britain contributed 7 billion. The Irish prime minister said, 'I don't believe there's any reason for Irish people to be ashamed and humiliated,' but quietly they were. It stung. One paper asked whether Ireland's Republican fighters in 1916 had died for a 'bail-out from the German Chancellor with a few shillings of sympathy from the British Chancellor on the side?' The *Irish Independent* said, 'The ghosts of the Easter Rising are abroad in Ireland at the moment, and they are shaking their gory locks with some relish.'

*   *   *

Europe's leaders saw the bail-out as cause for celebration. The German finance minister Wolfgang Schäuble called it 'a big success for Europe'. His French counterpart said it revealed 'the absolute determination in Europe – of France and Germany – to save the euro-zone'. In late November Chancellor Merkel said, 'I am more confident than in spring that the euro-zone will make it out of the current turbulence.'

Within a short period the Irish voters took their revenge on Brian Cowen's party. Just before the election in 2011 he had stepped down as party leader. He knew what other European leaders had discovered before him that the voters were unforgiving. They could not eject European officials but they could remove their governments. And time and time again they did.

For all that, the Irish did not take their anger to the streets. A senior Irish official in Brussels said one word explained the calm, and that was 'guilt'. For almost a decade the country had been living high off the hog, and that always came at a price.

In the roaring years of the Celtic Tiger, Ireland had seemed to slip the leash of its past. The country had attracted immigrants. The new unoccupied estates had been built not just by Irish labour but by Poles, and that had been a badge of pride. Now the workers from Eastern Europe had packed their bags and emigration had returned.

Within days of the bail-out, 25 engineering students gathered in a lecture theatre at the college in Tallagh. They were ambitious and articulate and had gathered to be interviewed about Ireland's future. Unprompted, a young man said he was heading to Canada. When asked whether they were all considering emigrating, every hand shot up bar one, and he was a mature student with a family. In those eager, bright faces lay a brain-drain that Ireland could ill afford. Like generations before them they would follow the call of work and that would take them west, to the new world. An official at the college said she had found all the hands going up intensely sad. The government estimated that over 100,000 young people would emigrate in the coming years.

The governor of the Central Bank of Ireland, Patrick Honohan, later reflected on what had happened. 'Politicians are normally thought to be running the country. That's what was taken away. It was an indication of failure and a disaster for politicians.'

Ireland had been hustled into a bail-out to save Portugal, on Europe's far western edge. It had avoided Ireland's greedy ambition. Its banks had not stoked a construction bubble: funds had flowed into the property market but on a minor scale compared to its neighbour, Spain. Adopting the euro, however, had changed behaviour. The low interest rates gave the Portuguese the illusion of affluence and they shed caution. They borrowed and spent, particularly the government. The public sector expanded to the point where nearly one in five of the labour force worked for the government. Between 2000 and 2009, average wages grew by 37.9 per cent. Productivity, however, was just 5.9 per cent and well below the average for the euro-zone. It meant that labour costs were way above countries like Germany. Portugal became uncompetitive and priced itself out of the market.

Like the leaders of Greece and Ireland, the Portuguese prime minister, José Sócrates, put up a stout defence. 'We will not go for a bail-out,' he insisted, 'we don't need one . . . and we will not be pushed into a bail-out.' He vowed to remove Portugal from the evil eye of the markets. He, too, reined in state spending. Public sector pay was reduced. Spending cuts were announced. However, in the first half of 2011, the country had to repay 12 billion euros and its borrowing costs were hovering around 7 per cent. By now, said one official, it was like watching the slow dance of death, the European spiral. A country, under pressure, would try and cut its way out of trouble. Demand fell and unemployment rose. Tax revenues declined and overall debt increased. Investors watched the spectacle unfold from the stands and turned away.

Portugal had steep debts and an uncompetitive economy with little or no growth. The government rolled out its fourth austerity package in twelve months. It made little difference. Portugal lost access to the capital markets. Prime Minister Sócrates bristled as his options narrowed. 'We are not going around begging,' he said. 'We have money. We have dignity.'

By now the bail-out script was unfolding: the long defence, the frantic cost-cutting, the rising borrowing costs, the humiliation and the terms of surrender. Sócrates wanted no part of it and, in any event, he knew the next election was lost. If he had to appeal for help he would resign, he said. Support from elsewhere in Europe was lukewarm. Chancellor Merkel said, 'It is up to Portugal to decide if it needs help.'

By April 2011, Portugal was the third country in the euro-zone to have requested a bail-out and the prime minister stood down. The painful truth was that Portugal was a sideshow: it had been written off by European officials. Like Ireland before it, it was sacrificed for the battles that mattered: Italy and Spain. It received a loan of 78 billion euros. The country's economy was now in the hands of a troika: inspectors from the EU, the IMF and the ECB. They would descend on Lisbon regularly to check that the patient was following the programme. Pensions and health spending were cut, state assets sold off and the cost of dismissing workers reduced.

Portugal accepted its bail-out with resignation. On the day of the announcement there had been no gatherings on the streets: people had preferred the company of families or friends. There was not the history of street protests and violence – their dictatorship had been overthrown in a Carnation Revolution. Some hoped that a new, more modern and competitive economy would emerge but in the short-term, confidence drained away.

In Lisbon, on the banks of the wide-mouthed Tagus, stands the Monument to the Discoveries. It is a weather-worn concrete prow, facing west, crowded with earnest-looking men full of serious intent. At the front stands Prince Henry the Navigator, a student of mathematical sciences, who prised open the unknown world. Tucked in behind him are great explorers like Vasco da Gama. With him are scientists, priests, poets and chroniclers, faces taut with strain and endeavour. There are Franciscans with rosaries swinging from their belts, ascending standard-bearers holding crosses before them and artists with palettes. They are all certain of their mission: to explore, to conquer and to civilise. The monument, with the wide-open sky beyond, is one of Lisbon's symbols. It is testament to an era, a moment in time. The sculpture is packed with ambition, hope and the challenge of a great enterprise. On occasions a bride and groom step out from a car and pose to be photographed, linking themselves in some way with the greatness of their country's past.

Sometimes, these days, a solitary figure stands there in the bright light, looking at the monument, as if for the last time, then moves to the banks of the Tagus and turns towards the open sea. They are there to say goodbye. The Portuguese are returning to the lands they once colonised, not as colonisers but as migrants looking for work. Unemployment has stayed stubbornly high at over 14 per cent. For many, the future is stalled. Hope lies not at home but in faraway places like Angola; around 150,000 have obtained visas for the West African country. Some will go for months, wiring money back to their families. Others emigrate and begin a new life outside Europe, uncertain of their return. Head hunters from Brazil, Angola and Mozambique make camp in Lisbon's hotels, ready to scoop up the best and brightest. The European Union had helped countries like Portugal shed authoritarian rule with the promise of democracy and a civil society, but now its eager and ambitious were turning to the continents of Africa and South America.

Mozambique had been ruled by the Portuguese since the sixteenth century. Thousands had been forced into slavery and the country had not gained its independence until 1975. Now, over 20,000 Portuguese are living in and around Mozambique's capital. Whilst Lisbon stagnates, Maputo bustles beneath its cranes. Some African countries now have growth rates that Europe can only dream of, and so the sons and daughters of colonisers return as guest workers.

In a bid to save its currency, Europe had embarked on an experiment in which the remedies were only dimly understood. The Irish bail-out did not stop contagion. Portugal fell as was widely predicted, and Italy and Spain found themselves at risk. Economic orthodoxy was being stood on its head. Wages, pensions and jobs were being cut as countries headed into recession. Economies shrank and unemployment rose. Several leaders spoke of a European Great Depression. The entire strategy was proving a giant gamble.

As 2010 drew to a close, Europe's leaders tried to rally their people behind the sacrifices ahead. Germany's finance minister, Wolfgang Schäuble, said, 'It's our common currency that is at stake.' Angela Merkel said, 'We find ourselves in an extraordinarily serious situation.' President Sarkozy said, 'Mrs Merkel and I will never – do you hear me, never – let the euro fail. The euro spells Europe. The euro has spelled sixty years of peace on our continent, therefore we will never let the euro go or be destroyed. For us it is simply not an economic issue. It has to do with identity as Europeans.' They turned on the doubters. 'Euro-scepticism leads to war,' said the president of the European Council, Herman Van Rompuy. 'A rising tide of nationalism is the EU's biggest enemy,' he went on. 'In every member state there are people who believe their country can survive alone in the globalised world. It's a lie . . . the time of the homogeneous nation state is over.'

So the crisis became a battle for the future of the European dream. Some officials began to see an opportunity to push for ever-closer integration. The will to defend the European project was not in doubt. For many of Europe's leaders it had been the defining political idea of their generation, and they were determined not to let it fail. They believed that to save it, a new set of rules and institutions would have to be agreed. It would be a slow and painful process, with more power moving to Brussels at the expense of the nation state.

It would be the markets that would continue to drive events and to shape the arguments. What Europe's leaders feared most was that Spain and Italy would need rescuing. There was not the bail-out fund big enough to save them. And Italy was regarded as the killer domino.

Chapter 8
The Shadow of Silvio

It was on a Saturday in November 2010 during the stirrings of dawn that the stone house collapsed. It spread its rubble over what had been one of the main streets of Pompeii. It was believed to have been the House of the Gladiators: its frescoes portrayed contest, battle, trophies, lances and shields, overseen by a goddess of victory. It would have been where the gladiators prepared for their ordeal in the nearby amphitheatre.

Vesuvius erupted in AD 79 and the Roman city of Pompeii was buried under ash and lava. Much later, 250 years ago, it began to be uncovered, layer by layer. The town of 20,000 people slowly re-emerged, as if having been preserved in one shuddering moment in time. There were the bodies curled up against the heat and the gases, the wall paintings, the temples, the baths and fountains, the mosaics and the olive presses. All as it was. A living Roman town.

It was not clear why the House of the Gladiators collapsed. There had been no heavy rain. Most likely it crumbled from neglect. Funding had been promised and some donated, but Pompeii was poorly protected. Another wall surrounding the House of the Moralist had also buckled. The ancient city was unkempt and uncared for. A third of it lay unexcavated. There were mounds of scaffolding, roofs that leaked and bogus tour guides who had bribed their way inside to hawk their dubious fragments of history. One Italian MP described the site 'as torment without end'. The president of the Republic said the fall of the Gladiator's House was 'a shame for Italy'.

Then chunks of mortar fell from one of the arches in the Coliseum, the 50,000-seat amphitheatre that had hosted games for Imperial Rome. Where animals and gladiators once began their entrance parade, pieces of plaster peeled away from the roof. At the Trevi Fountain, where Anita Ekberg had waded through its waters in *La Dolce Vita*, part of a gargoyle's head crashed from the frieze. At Nero's Golden Palace, a roof caved in.

Italy's historic remains were trembling. In ancient times, no doubt, the augurs would have been consulted. As 2010 drew to a close, the Roman *cognoscenti* were searching for signs. Even the Italian president Giorgio Napolitano opined that you would need a crystal ball to know whether these were the last days of the great impresario, of the one-time cruise ship crooner who had become Italy's prime minister, of *Il Cavaliere*, the self-styled knight who had done so much to cast Italian society in his own image.

As Silvio Berlusconi's hold on power weakened, the country drifted. The country's debts stood at 1.9 trillion euros, 120 per cent of GDP, and no rescue fund could cover that. Italy's persistent flaw was that for ten years its economy had barely grown and that, troubled investors.

In December 2010, Berlusconi faced a vote of no confidence in the Chamber of Deputies. Rome was awash with intrigue: that MPs had been offered government jobs or even help with their mortgages in exchange for supporting the Italian leader. One opposition politician complained that the halls of the Parliament reeked like a cattle market. Another senior MP watched potential defectors weaken. They were, he said, like 'Judas selling themselves for 30 pieces of silver'. One opposition leader boldly declared that 'a crime was being committed' in Palazzo Montecitorio, where the Parliament sat. It was a world of deal-making and horse-trading in which Silvio Berlusconi excelled. If everyone who said they would vote against him actually did, he would be finished, but Roman politics had never worked that way and late-night alliances would suddenly blossom and the crisis would pass. During the vote – which Berlusconi survived – the Parliament had been ringed by police wagons with protestors calling out, 'You have bought the votes like you buy your women.'

The Italian leader himself was brazen, immune to outrage. Even as the ancient stones were tumbling, he slashed the fine arts budget by 40 per cent and stood accused of endangering Italy's heritage. His new-found parsimony did not, however, extend to the entrance to Palazzo Chigi, his official residence. Visitors passed a marble statue of Venus and Mars, two naked gods. Sometime over the past 1,800 years they had been disfigured: Venus had lost a hand and Mars his penis. Berlusconi wanted the perfect nude, and the statue was booked in for what amounted to plastic surgery. It cost over 70,000 euros. There might not be funds for Pompeii, but there was money for a new penis. Berlusconi shrugged off the criticism and made a joke of it. That was always his way.

As Europe struggled to save its currency, Italy had become a place of spectacle and diversion; a kind of daytime-TV show where the line between image and reality was increasingly blurred. Its new stars were *veline*, the scantily clad showgirls who handed scraps of paper to TV hosts. In interviews, young girls picked *velina* as a career choice: a touch of glamour and the chance to snare a footballer. Presiding over all this was Berlusconi, the owner of three TV networks. He combined politician with showman, quipping, telling stories and making gaffes. He jokingly suggested that his party *Forza Italia*, which had been named after a football chant, be rebranded '*Forza Gnocca*', 'Go pussy.' As he left hospital after being hit over the head in Milan with a metal copy of the Duomo, the city's cathedral, he quipped, 'Replicas are so cheap these days they're throwing them at you.' President Obama was referred to as 'handsome, young and also suntanned'. Without any sense of irony, a former topless model and *velina* was appointed as minister for equal opportunities. Normal public life was paralysed.

Into this arena had stepped Colonel Gaddafi. In August 2010, he had arrived in Rome with an entourage that filled four planes. He brought with him dozens of thoroughbreds and Berber riders who would entertain the Romans with their charging horses and flashing lances. Most of the time these two great showmen, Berlusconi and Gaddafi, vied with each other for attention. Here was the Libyan leader out in Piazza Navona downing a cappuccino and *gelato* before buying a fistful of rings from African street-traders; there was the Italian prime minister telling the Libyan leader over dinner, 'If you behave well, I'll sing you a song.' Gaddafi bowed out before the dessert.

A modelling agency was found to recruit several hundred young women to attend a Gaddafi lecture on Islam. They were paid between seventy and eighty euros to sit there. A handful of women apparently converted to Islam and were given bound copies of the Quran and tickets to Tripoli. Gaddafi shocked his Italian hosts by declaring that, 'Islam should become the religion of Europe.' One Italian paper, *La Repubblica*, described the whole episode 'as a humiliating circus'.

Berlusconi believed he could survive anything. He had faced countless accusations and court cases and had emerged largely unscathed. He had come to power promising to remake and modernise Italy. It had not happened, but many still believed he was the only person to run the country. The opposition was weak and divided and Berlusconi knew how to talk to ordinary Italians. They admired him for being self-made, for his wealth and for his disregard for rules; but slowly the drip-drip of revelation undermined his ability to implement change.

In 2008, an escort girl from Bari had attended two candle-lit dinners at Palazzo Grazioli, his private residence. Patrizia d'Addario, aged forty-two, found herself surrounded by much younger women. Silvio Berlusconi had sung Neapolitan love songs to them. On her second visit, he asked her to stay the night. She decided to tape-record her encounter, although it was never clear why. Maybe she saw an opportunity to make money or even to blackmail Berlusconi. Maybe she just wanted to prove to herself that she had been with an Italian prime minister.

In her home town, Patrizia had been waiting for a building permit for a bed and breakfast lodging but the paperwork had fallen through. She hoped that the prime minister would intervene on her behalf with the town council. Nothing, however, came from her night at Palazzo Grazioli and she resented it: there had been hints that she might be appointed to the European Parliament but those, too, faded away. When, later, Berlusconi visited Bari she waited outside his hotel but she was ignored, muscled away by the prime minister's security detail. She decided to go public with her tape.

Many Italian people treated it like a script for a soap opera:

Silvio: 'Are you going to wait for me in the big bed if you're done (taking a shower) before me?'

Patrizia: 'What big bed? Putin's?'
Silvio: 'Yes, Putin's.'
Patrizia: 'Oh, how nice . . . that one with the curtains.'

Patrizia got herself an agent, wrote a book and had her snapshot of fame. Berlusconi's aides dismissed the transcripts as trivia. The prime minister never commented directly but he said, 'Italians like me the way I am. I'm not a saint. You've all understood that.' There was truth in that. Many Italians said it was a personal matter; some rather admired him.

Many in the diplomatic community, however, saw it differently. They could not help but notice that the night with Patrizia had also been the evening that changed American history, when Barack Obama became the first African-American president. They believed that the leader of Italy should have been watching such a significant moment. The diplomats increasingly saw Berlusconi as a man of waning energy, unable to address the crisis facing his country. In cables, which were published by Wikileaks, the US Chargé d'Affaires in Rome described him as 'physically and politically weak', while his 'frequent late nights and penchant for partying hard means he does not get sufficient rest'. The diplomat also concluded he was 'feckless, vain and ineffective as a leader'. The leaks also raised concerns about his close relationship with 'the alpha dog, Putin'.

For the rest of Europe most of this was background noise – the gossip and chatter that accompanies the powerful – but the revelations were to become much more serious and, within a year, would convince other European leaders that Berlusconi had to be removed from power. In May 2009, his wife, Veronica Lario, had given an interview to the Italian news agency, ANSA.

In it she explained why she had asked for a divorce from him. 'I cannot be with a man who consorts with minors,' she said and added, 'I close the curtain on my married life.' She had been prompted to speak out after Berlusconi attended the birthday party of an eighteen-year-old. Veronica said that she could not go 'hand in hand with this show'. She said some regarded it as the 'Emperor's fun' but she spoke bitterly of 'figures of virgins that are offered to the dragon to chase success . . .' Later in the interview, she hinted that her husband was suffering from a sickness. 'I tried to help my husband,' she said. 'I implored those who stand by, to do the same as when you are next to a person who is not well.' Many treated the interview as the outpourings of a spurned wife, but the revelations from Berlusconi's parties were to over-shadow one of the most dangerous periods of the euro-zone crisis.

In February 2010, a young woman had been taken into custody at a police station in Milan. She was suspected of having stolen some jewellery and 2,000 euros in cash from an acquaintance. Her name was Karima El-Mahroug. She had just turned eighteen, and described herself as a dancer. To the surprise of the police she announced she was a friend of the prime minister and asked to contact him. Sometime later, the officers received calls from the prime minister's office and from Berlusconi himself. He (mistakenly) identified Karima as a niece of the then Egyptian president, Hosni Mubarak. To the further curiosity of the police, Berlusconi despatched another woman to come to the police station and arrange Karima's release.

The police wanted to know who exactly this young woman was and why she had the private number of the Italian prime minister. They soon discovered that Karima was in touch with other girls who were being investigated for under-age prostitution. Some of the girls were wiretapped and, later, the police picked up the voice of Berlusconi. What they heard convinced them they had enough evidence to build a case against him for having sex with Karima when she was seventeen years old and under age, and for abusing the power of his office by intervening to get her released. The police passed the file to investigating magistrates.

The wiretaps raised the curtain on the world of Silvio Berlusconi's parties. He had a small circle who would invite young women to 'elegant dinners'. They were told, 'I know someone who can change your life' and that there was much money to be made. Some of the women were prostitutes; others were performers from reality-TV shows; some were former weather girls; some were just wannabes with an eye for an encounter that might spin the wheel of fortune.

Karima described herself as 'Ruby Rubacuori', 'Ruby the heart-stealer'. She had been spotted at a beauty pageant in Sicily by one of Berlusconi's cronies. There were later stories that her Moroccan father had tried to marry her off to an older man when she was only twelve. She attended thirteen Berlusconi parties. She also mentioned a game called 'bunga-bunga'; a term apparently used by Colonel Gaddafi to describe a group of women who were lined up to have sex with him. The parties were held at Arcore, Berlusconi's residence outside Milan. Some of the girls who attended were paid between 10–15,000 euros. One former TV weather presenter said she received nearly 100,000 euros.

Added to this, between twelve and fifteen women were put up rent free in an apartment block not far from the prime minister's Milan residence. They stayed there on stand-by for parties. The investigators listened to the prime minister boasting that, 'Last night I had a queue outside my door, there were eleven of them. I only managed to do eight of them. I couldn't manage any more. You just can't get round to all of them. But this morning I feel great, I'm pleased with my stamina.' Girls were described as 'parcels' to be delivered. Returning from one official trip, he phoned a friend and declared, 'I need something fresh.'

One of those who attended the parties, Nadia Macri, said, 'The girls were young and it didn't sit easy with me.' The magistrates were amazed at the scale of the parties. They judged that between 2–3,000 girls at one time or another had attended evenings with Berlusconi. One businessman alone supplied over 130 prostitutes. The turnover of women was constant and the costs immense. Many of the young women were given cheques signed by Berlusconi's accountant. There were gifts of jewellery and even cars. The investigators believed Berlusconi may have spent 10 million euros on supporting this lifestyle; a running tap of payments for parties, for entertainment, for girls, for fixers, for house rents, for pay-offs and for legal bills.

As these revelations tumbled out, Berlusconi turned on the magistrates. He described them as leftists and politically motivated. It was, he said, the twenty-eighth time in seventeen years that the Milan judges had pursued him. The charges against him were 'groundless' and 'a farce'. He presented himself as the victim of a political assassination. 'I am the most accused man in the history of the universe,' he said.

In public, *Il Cavaliere*, as he liked to be known, exuded confidence. On official visits jokes flew like chaff. Whilst on an island off Sicily, he told the crowd that a pollster there had enquired as to how many women on the island would sleep with him. Apparently 30 per cent had said 'Yes', he told those listening, while 70 per cent said, 'What, again?' And so he continued to laugh off accusations that would have destroyed the premiership of any other leader in Europe.

His case was helped by Ruby's testimony: she denied that she had had sex with him. In police interviews she said. 'I meet him. He gives me 7,000 euros and he doesn't put a finger on me.' She was also being wire-tapped and the world exposed by the tapes was far from glamorous: it showed an old man cynically being used as a kind of cash machine. In their private calls, which were recorded, the women were unflattering towards him. 'He's fatter than before,' said one of them, 'more dead than alive.' The Italian paper *Il Fatto Quotidiano* described it as 'the tragedy of a ridiculous man'.

The Catholic Church, itself mired in scandal, described the revelations as a 'damaging tornado'. One Catholic paper said Berlusconi was 'sick and of unsound mind'. The Italian president, Giorgio Napolitano, called for the investigation to be settled quickly, fearing it was damaging Italy. There were signs that, internationally, Italy was losing its influence. Other world leaders declined to be photographed with Berlusconi: when she met the Italian prime minister, Michelle Obama pointedly stuck her hand out to avoid any embrace. When Berlusconi arrived at the Elysée Palace for the meeting that would launch the campaign against Libya, his arrival was met with open laughter from the waiting reporters and photographers, while the British prime minister would joke about the three lessons he had learnt in office: Never be late for an audience with the Queen. Always say 'yes' to an invitation to one of her parties. And if the Italian prime minister asks you to a party it is 'safer to say no'.

Even in the past, Berlusconi's actions had attracted suspicion. When he arrived at a NATO summit he had left the

German Chancellor Angela Merkel standing while he took a call on his mobile phone. Initially, she was faintly amused as the Italian prime minister paced up and down speaking on his phone but as the call went on, she was clearly irritated and insulted. Those close to Berlusconi insisted he was speaking with Prime Minister Erdoğan of Turkey, urging him not to veto the nomination for NATO Secretary General. The German press speculated that he was talking to a girlfriend.

By the start of 2011, the Italian Foreign Ministry believed the scandals were damaging Italy, although those loyal to Berlusconi insisted he remained focused and committed to reform. Italy withdrew inside itself and waited. For some it was like watching the last days of an emperor. They recalled Commodus with his harem of 300 girls, or Tiberius who had moved to his palace on Capri and held dinner parties and invited prostitutes, a leader of whom it was said that 'he would have sex with people of all ages and sexes'.

Berlusconi had come to believe that normal rules did not apply to him, that he was a man apart. In the garden of the house where he hosted his parties he had a large sarcophagus built. It was hewn out of white carrara marble by a well-known sculptor. A flight of stairs connected to an underground passage, which led to a burial chamber. There were thirty-six niches for family and *collaboratori*, for his business friends and cronies to join him in the after life. Terracotta bas-reliefs lined the passage way. There were no Christian motifs. It reminded a visitor of the Valley of the Kings, the final resting place for a pharaoh or an Etruscan king. Italians – steeped in history – have a long understanding of power and human weakness, but many of them did not like the shame and the mockery of the man elected to represent them.

In early 2011, it was widely assumed that *Il Cavaliere* could not survive. Beppe Severgnini, the writer, said: 'It is an old Italian tradition that the tenor is idolised until people start booing him.' One of the most powerful businessmen in Italy, Luca Cordero di Montezemolo, the chairman of Ferrari, announced 'the one-man show is over'. Berlusconi, however, was impervious to the criticism. Even whilst he was under investigation the parties continued. It was an addiction for him.

Italy was under scrutiny. It was regarded as holding the fate of the single currency in its grasp. The country defied easy definition. It was still the land of *la bella figura*, of style, of image, of easy elegance and world-class brands. Prada shoes, Fendi handbags and Gucci belts. A stroll down Via dei Condotti testified to the country's continuing influence on international fashion: Bvlgari, Armani, Valentino, Ferragamo, Brioni, Zegna all clustered together. Domenico Dolce and Stefano Gabbana had drawn on the 'whole religious gorgeousness of Sicily' to build a global business. Thirty years before, Renzo Rosso had launched ready-to-wear clothes for young adults. Diesel now had annual sales of over a billion euros. The super luxury car market was still dominated by Italian names: Maserati, Ferrari, Lamborghini and Bugatti – although Volkswagen had snapped up that label. Alpha Romeo, Lancia and Fabbrica Italiana Automobili Torino (Fiat) were distinctive Italian marques. Bologna produced the iconic Ducati motorbike, although it is now owned by Audi. Pirelli invented the wide radial tyre. Many an evening began with a Peroni or a Cinzano or Campari *apperitivo* with a bottle of San Pellegrino at the table. Luigi Lavazza had begun producing coffeemakers in 1895 in Turin; the fourth generation of the Lavazza family transformed coffee-making worldwide. Barilla had become a world giant in pasta sauce. Alessi brought style into the kitchen by turning utensils into highly designed products.

But for all of that dazzle and energy, the country had stagnated. In 2012, Italian GDP was lower than it had been ten years before. No other rich country had such a damning record. The only economies that have grown more slowly in the past twelve years have been Zimbabwe, San Marino and Portugal. Growth had been negligible. Productivity had remained stubbornly flat. Spending on welfare and, in particular, pensions had risen inexorably. In 2010, 15 per cent of GDP had gone on providing pensions.

Public life and politics remained unreformed. Two journalists from *Corriere della Sera* discovered there were 72,000 official cars, costing 1.85 billion euros annually. Italian MPs were the best paid in Europe: they received, with expenses, 16,000 euros a month. After thirty months' service, they qualified for a full and generous pension. They were awarded free travel tickets and discounts at Roman designer stores. They were cocooned with perks and privileges. In the parliamentary restaurant, a plate of spaghetti and anchovies costs 1.60 euros, a swordfish fillet 3.55. Many Italians believed their political culture cried out for reform.

Italy had escaped the property bubbles of Spain and Ireland. Its banks were healthier. Private savings were strong. Yet for all of that its debts had risen to 1.9 trillion euros. The country needed to raise massive amounts of money just to service its debts, and the markets questioned how it could be done if the costs of borrowing increased. Italy was the country that scared Europe's leaders. They met incessantly but they could not agree on a strategy that would convince the markets they had fixed the crisis. There were piecemeal ideas, many of which came and went. Nearly all of the plans involved, in some way, a transfer of funds from northern Europe to the south. No plan could survive without Germany.

The Germans believed they were already shouldering a mighty burden; they had taken on the lion's share of the liabilities involved in bailing-out Greece and Ireland. What the Germans would not accept was the euro-zone evolving into a transfer union, where they bankrolled the weaker countries of southern Europe. Some European officials believed, however, that the crisis would only be solved if Germany accepted that it had done very well out of the single currency and that, in return, it must deploy its financial power to stand behind the so-called 'Club Med' countries. Investors needed to know who or what, in the last resort, stood behind the single currency. In May 2010 they had set up a massive fund to bail-out troubled countries but all those billions were not sufficient to save Italy and Spain if they could not raise funds on the markets.

Towards the end of 2010 there had been a push to adopt Eurobonds or common debt. The bonds would be jointly offered to the market by euro-zone states. The advantage for debt-prone countries was that their interest rates would come down. All debt, be it German or Italian, would be treated equally. Germany's borrowing costs would edge up, while those of southern European countries would fall. The Germans were dismissive. They saw it as a way of allowing the weaker countries to escape the judgement of the markets. 'Each country needs to be held responsible for its own debt,' said Jürgen Stark, a former chief economist at the European Central Bank. The German paper *Bild* saw it as a way 'to make the euro soft'.

The chairman of the euro group – the seventeen countries that shared the single currency – turned on Germany. The prime minister of Luxembourg, Jean-Claude Juncker said, 'They are rejecting an idea before studying it . . . this way of creating taboo areas in Europe . . . is a very un-European way of dealing with European matters.' It was a stinging criticism. It recalled the committee in Washington in the fifties that went on the prowl for Un-American Activities: a paranoid search for disloyalty, for the dissenter, which led to a political witch hunt. Nobody believed that Juncker was doing that, but he was beginning to ask and define who were the good Europeans and who were not. What Juncker feared was Germany turning away from the binding European creed of solidarity. The concern was not only that Germany was bracing against taking on further liabilities, it was that it had become selfish, abandoning the European ideal in favour of its national interests. The Germans were insulted. One German paper asked pointedly: 'Is it European to bend the EU treaties and break the bail-out rule?' Angela Merkel's spokesman was equally robust. 'It is exactly this talking against other people and about other people,' she said, 'that should stop.'

The talking did not stop. Time and again suspicion of Germany would surface. It would be the unspoken undercurrent to many a conversation: sixty years of European co-operation had not exorcised old fears. They lay behind much of the criticism. Juncker accused the more assertive Germany of 'losing sight of the European public good'. Many officials hankered after a time when France set the pace for the European debate and Germany was quiescent. Economic power had bought Germany new-found power, and the rest of Europe struggled to adjust to that.

The single currency was intended to be a building block towards closer European integration, melding countries together. The opposite was happening. The tensions were sharpening the divide between the countries of the north, which shared a similar economic culture, and those of the south. When the European statesmen were dreaming of the new currency, they were warned not just of the differences between economies but the differences in culture. They had brushed such objections away. Part of the belief that drove the project was that a single currency would foster a European culture and identity, a European *demos*. That proved elusive. People, as evidenced in poll after poll, stuck stubbornly to their national identities. European officials feared the crisis was pushing nations further apart. The EU's economics commissioner, Olli Rehn, said he was 'worried about the divergence in the public debates between the northern and southern countries'.

Slowly Europe began building its defences. It had set up a large bail-out fund – the EFSF. Later in 2010 Europe's leaders decided to create a permanent fund which would provide a safety net for countries that ran into difficulty in the future. It was called the European Stability Mechanism and would start operating in 2012. It was not agreed without argument. Germany believed that the fund required changes to the main European treaty. Most other countries did not. Germany was mindful of its Constitutional Court, which could challenge the legality of a permanent fund bearing in mind that the existing treaty had explicitly ruled out taking on the debts of others. A former chief economist at the European Central Bank, Otmar Issing, gave voice to German fears. He said that highly indebted countries could be encouraged to blackmail more solid member states and that can raise political anger which would eventually undermine support for the single currency. Issing understood the risk that countries in trouble could threaten to default knowing it would twist the arms of Europe's leaders to bail them out.

In the meantime, European officials were urging a boosting of the firepower of the existing bail-out fund. Again Chancellor Merkel stood in the way. 'The volume (in the fund) is far from being exhausted,' she said. But officials knew there was no answer to the question of who or what would stand behind Spain or Italy if they needed rescuing. That remained one of the euro's major flaws.

Behind the daily drama, a great struggle was unfolding that would change Europe. Germany believed it was doing everything to secure the euro but it was not prepared to become the pay-master for the rest of Europe: there were limits to the amount of German treasure they would commit to the project. Other countries questioned Germany's commitment to the European ideal. The French prime minister, François Fillon, warned that Europe was 'at a historic turning point'.

Europe was only fire-fighting, applying band-aid. Three countries, Greece, Portugal and Ireland had been bailed out to prevent bankruptcy. The various rescue funds did not address the currency's fundamental flaws. There was a monetary union but there was little or no control over tax and spending. If the currency was to survive, countries in the euro-zone would have to forfeit some of the freedom involved in setting their own budgets. So in 2011 Europe's officials came to believe that the price of preserving the currency would be greater integration and a weakening of national governments.

In the short-term, there were signs that the austerity medicine was not working. Greeks complained it was killing the patient. Greece and Ireland were both implementing steep spending cuts but growth was being squeezed from their economies. The task-master was Chancellor Merkel. 'Member states face many years of work to atone for past sins,' she said. Indulgence had to be followed by repentance. Germany would stand by the euro but, in exchange, the rest of Europe would have to become more like Germany. The German finance minister said that Germany did not want to be in a position of lecturing others, but would not shy away from moments when it would do some teaching.

An outline of future plans was emerging. Tougher discipline over tax and spending would be demanded and enforced. A debt brake would have to be written into national legislation. Angela Merkel saw solidarity and competitiveness as two sides of the European coin. Solidarity would come at a price. Other countries would have to reach for the hair-shirt and reform themselves.

Chapter 9
Disobedience

At first it was a slow unravelling. The traces were easy to miss in the bustle of a city, but they were unmistakeable nonetheless. In 2010 Greece's social fabric had been under strain. A year later the society was fraying.

It is five in the afternoon and a crowd of mainly men gathers in front of a narrow door to a building splashed with bright Caribbean colours. It is a soup kitchen, close to the centre of Athens. When the door opens they file into a courtyard and are handed plastic containers of hot food. They are hungry men. Some scamper across the street with their bread and pasta and squat beside the nearby railway tracks, untroubled by the graffiti-covered commuter trains that pass a few feet from them. Others scurry away almost furtively, as if fearful the food could be taken from them. Some prefer to eat alone and find a stoop in the side streets.

Ada Alamanou is a volunteer who has found her cause. She is short, with cropped hair; a bundle of energy wrapped in a large green scarf. She eyes the numbers waiting for meals. They are her barometer for the city. 'Half of those who come here,' she says, 'live on less than twenty euros a month.'

The food is handed out by Klimaka, a social services organisation. They get no support from the government and Ada is proud of that. She has watched the numbers needing emergency help grow. It was a few hundred at first. Then it became several thousand a day searching for food. Many were middle-class people who could never have imagined they would be standing in a food line. Some of them had been unable to keep up the payments on their apartments and at night they curled up on Athens's streets. In a year, homelessness had increased by 25 per cent.

At first, Ada said, Greek families had provided a safety net, but that had weakened. Some of the most vulnerable were the older people who lost their jobs just before retirement. 'Without support,' she says, 'they are forced to live lives of total misery.' Often they have no health insurance and are dependent on the medical charities that have started operating in Greece. She says the crisis was changing the country. People are more aware of the lives of others. 'There is much more solidarity,' she says. Many want to help. An older woman donated a half-opened packet of pasta. A supermarket passes on the food it can no longer legally sell. 'This is the optimistic side,' said Ada, 'but solidarity doesn't help you find a job or guarantee you food.'

In the private sector there had been a great shedding of jobs: 250,000 had been lost. Greece had been in recession since 2008 and for over a year had been tightening spending. 'I was cutting public salaries in a way which had never been done before, ever,' said the finance minister. As in Ireland and Spain, construction had ceased, taking down the businesses that depended on it. In five years, cement production had declined 60 per cent and the fall in steel production had been even greater.

Even so, in the closing months of 2010, the Greek government believed it had bought itself some space. The bail-out of the previous May protected the country from steep borrowing costs and the harsh verdict of the markets. The people seemed to be giving the government the benefit of the doubt. 'The society as a whole,' said the finance minister, George Papaconstantinou, 'knew deep down that it (the high-spending lifestyle) couldn't continue. They were ready for a correction.' At the end of the year, the governing socialist party actually won the municipal elections.

Europe's leaders were encouraged. 'I would go to meetings (in Brussels) and get patted on the back,' said the finance minister. '"Great! Fantastic stuff!" I was told. We had finished pension reform ahead of schedule.' Papaconstantinou was convinced that the decision taken by President Sarkozy and Chancellor Merkel to inflict, in the future, losses on private investors 'completely screwed us'. What it meant, he said, was that if Greek debt had to be restructured, private investors would be the last to get their money back, so many of them sold out and turned their backs on Greece.

The country faced a formidable challenge. It had to reduce its deficit and it had to become competitive again. Locked inside a monetary union, Greece did not have the option of devaluing; all it could do was to reduce wages and pensions. There were protests, but the government did not believe they reflected the view of the majority. Many Greeks understood the society needed a short, sharp shock. 'While people were demonstrating, it didn't mean that the majority of society believed we were completely crazy,' said the finance minister. 'But when it continued beyond where they thought it would stop was when things started getting really difficult for us . . . and that was the beginning of 2011.'

The middle class was trapped: they were paying 18 per cent interest on their houses and cars whilst jobs were being cut and wages reduced. Increasingly, the people resented the squeezing of their lives and they resented the fact that hard times were being imposed from outside. Some said it felt like the nation was in emotional shock. So they resisted noisily on the streets and in smaller stubborn refusals. Public servants were not prepared to see the unwinding of Greece's large public sector. These were the jobs for life and the safety they offered would not be abandoned without a struggle. Civil servants occupied offices. They blocked access to the Finance Ministry by sitting on the stairs. Every day another public sector group went on strike. 'There was resistance at every level,' said Papaconstantinou. 'There was resistance within the Cabinet. There was resistance in the party . . . there was administrative resistance.' It meant that the government could not deliver what Greece's creditors were demanding. 'If you're a tax official,' said the finance minister, 'and you're used to making money on the side and I've cut your salary, then you will not go out of your way to collect taxes and to do your job . . . so the machinery that was supposed to help us through all the reforms was the same as the one being hit the hardest.'

Government appeals that the savings and reforms were a matter of national survival went unheeded. Significant sections in society were determined to sabotage the new measures. They spilled out onto the highways and surrounded the toll booths and made it impossible to collect road charges. They lifted the red and white barriers and the 2.80 euro toll went uncollected. Some of the activists wore vests that carried the slogan: 'Total disobedience.' They chanted, 'We won't pay for this crisis.' On the subways they taped plastic bags over the ticket machines so commuters could ride for free. On the buses and trams the ticket readers were disabled. Some hospital doctors even stood in front of the payment counters, preventing patients from paying the 5 euros for a consultation. Little acts of resistance gradually evolved into an 'I won't pay' movement. By March 2011, polls indicated that more than half the population supported these protests.

Some union leaders depicted the movement as a people's rebellion, almost a crusade against injustice. It incensed the prime minister, George Papandreou, and he scolded his left-wing critics. 'You think,' he said, 'that lawlessness is something revolutionary, which helps the Greek people. It is the lawlessness which we have in our country that the Greek people are paying for today.'

The rapid shrinking of the economy was dividing society. One columnist in the daily paper *Kathimerini* turned on the protestors. 'Now, with the crisis as an alibi . . . the freeloaders don't hide. They appear publicly and proudly and act like heroes of civil disobedience like Rosa Parks or Mahatma Gandhi.'

The activists on the highways could shrug off the charge of being freeloaders because the entire political class had lost credibility. Politicians were widely reviled. They and their friends were accused of ransacking the country. The banners unfurled in front of the Parliament read, 'Thieves! Hustlers! Bankers!' When the protestors shouted 'Thieves!' their hands shot up together, pointing accusingly at the Parliament. The political system, built on favours, was broken and in Greece's hour of need it lacked the moral authority to demand sacrifice. It was widely believed that the people were being asked to pay for the greed of international bankers.

By the spring of 2011 doubts had set in at the highest level of the Greek government. Ministers did not believe the strategy designed by the EU and the IMF was working. The markets and the ratings agencies were losing faith, too. Greece's credit rating was ranked alongside Mongolia. On one level, such a judgement did not matter: the country did not have to raise funds in the financial markets. On another level, Greece's credit rating spoke a truth that Europe's leaders did not want to address.

The Greek economy was collapsing. The bail-out plan, so dramatically and painfully drawn up in May 2010, was failing. Greece's mountain of debt was rising. Government revenue was falling. Unemployment was increasing sharply. Even if Athens carried out all the reforms promised – including privatisations – the ratio of debt to GDP would be 150 per cent by 2013. In the event, it would be much higher. Austerity seemed to be paralysing the country. Further cuts could not easily be imposed in the face of determined opposition.

Slowly, Europe's leaders understood that far from having addressed the Greek crisis, it was in fact deepening. Promises made were not being kept. The government in Athens was struggling to deliver. Old practices endured. Tax revenues were less than expected. A former anti-terrorist prosecutor was drafted in to root out the tax evaders but it was only a gesture and it came too late. Only in May 2011 did a government minister talk of judging performance in the civil service. 'One of the many problems of the Greek state,' he said, 'was that there is no such evaluation system . . . so no one has any incentive to perform better.' Some of Europe's leaders had persuaded themselves that Europe's countries were one and the same and that they shared the same culture and values. They did not. History and occupation had taught Greeks to be stubborn and defiant. They understood resistance. In everyday life, rules were casually disobeyed. They rode through red lights; they ignored safety regulations about the wearing of crash helmets; they broke anti-smoking laws; they ignored the demands of tax officials.

In the space of a year, Greece had shown the limits of what could be achieved by austerity alone. Some international economists were openly sceptical of the entire strategy designed by Germany and implemented by the EU. Paul Krugman, the American economist, wrote of the 'austerity delusion'. Quite simply, he said that 'slashing spending in the face of high unemployment was a mistake'. Even one of the great proponents of austerity, the German finance minister Wolfgang Schäuble warned that 'we are facing the risk of the first uncoordinated state insolvency within the euro-zone'. One German paper said the euro-zone had to choose between 'a horrific ending and endless horror'. In Brussels, the mood was increasingly fearful. Once again they were battling events they neither understood nor controlled. The first bail-out had proved insufficient and, without further help, Greece faced bankruptcy.

There were voices within the Greek government that concluded that the country could not survive without some of their debt being written off, but they were minority voices. 'Even if people thought there was something in it they were saying, "This is not for now",' said the finance minister. An air of unreality hung over Greece. It was tasked with making repayments in 2014 that under no circumstances could it achieve. 'Everyone knew that,' said the minister.

By the late spring of 2011, the government had shed its reticence. It was openly being argued in the Cabinet that Greece needed to have a large chunk of its debt forgiven. It would reduce the debt pile and might lead to an easing up on austerity sooner rather than later.

European officials were hostile. They believed that a debt restructuring would do lasting damage to Europe's reputation: it would send a message that investors in European government debt could not guarantee getting their money back. The president of the European Council, Herman Van Rompuy, dismissed the option as 'catastrophic' and 'not on the table'. The ECB president walked out of a meeting when the idea was discussed. The bank had a simple message for the Greek government: 'You have to honour the signature (on the bonds)'. Christine Lagarde, the French finance minister, said a write-down of Greek debt was absolutely out of the question.

Europe's leaders had not lost their fear of contagion. If investors took losses in Greece they would most likely take fright from Spain and Italy, too. At the very least they would insist on much higher interest rates to buy Spanish or Italian debt. It could force up borrowing costs to the point where those countries could not finance themselves. In that event, there were not the funds to rescue them. The initial bail-out fund was too small and its permanent replacement would not be operational until late 2012.

So the message to Greece was to do more, to cut deeper. The Germans were losing patience. Angela Merkel went to the German town of Meschede and, addressing her party supporters, gave voice to German resentment. 'It is also important,' she said, 'that people in countries like Greece, Spain and Portugal are not able to retire earlier than in Germany – that everyone exerts themselves more or less equally. That is important . . . We have a common currency where some get lots of vacation and others very little,' she went on. 'That won't work in the long-term.' Solidarity would come at a price. Germany would help, but only when other countries made sacrifices.

In Brussels, the remarks were seen as only sharpening European divisions. European officials longed for the German leader to speak of one Europe, of burden-sharing, of standing together, of shared European ideals, of solidarity, but politically that was not yet possible.

Greece, by now, was no longer a little European difficulty. Its tentacles spread into the continent's banks and from there into the global economy. When Angela Merkel went to Washington, President Obama questioned her closely about Greece. She was surprised by the president's knowledge of what was happening in a small economy in the Aegean. He told her that it 'would be disastrous for us to see an uncontrolled spiral and default in Europe, because that would trigger a whole range of other events'. Greece, the president said, could not be allowed to 'put global economic recovery at risk'.

The pressure from across the Atlantic, however, gave the German Chancellor ammunition to fight political battles back home, to tell German voters that what was at stake was way bigger than Greece and that deeper commitments would have to be made.

The Greek leadership was increasingly isolated. 'We were under siege,' said George Papaconstantinou, the finance minister. 'We were alone as a party,' he said. 'Everybody was against us . . . the entire political class, the media was criticising us.' It led the Greeks to raise the question of the country leaving the euro-zone.

At a meeting with Europe's leaders, the Greeks said, 'Let's put all options on the table.' According to the Greek finance minister, 'We told them, "There is an option of us getting out. We don't want it but you have to tell us if that's an option for you." And they would say no that is not an option.' In the presentation, made by the prime minister, leaving the euro was called 'scenario zero'. The Greeks made it clear they absolutely did not want to leave the euro and to return to the

drachma, but they listed it as an option. Banks and governments began thinking the unthinkable. 'No, we didn't have a
plan,' said the German finance minister, Wolfgang Schäuble,
'but of course if that had happened we would have had to be
prepared.'

George Papandreou had raised 'scenario zero' out of frustration. The prevailing narrative in Europe was that Greece
was to blame: it had not carried out the reforms it promised
at the time of the bail-out. The accusations infuriated the
prime minister. 'We had cut the deficit by 5 per cent in the
first year and 6 per cent in the second,' he said. 'It was
phenomenal. No other country had done this.' Papandreou
would tell visitors that German officials had admitted that
equivalent cuts in Germany would have meant savings of
320 billion euros.

The government in Greece believed it had implemented a
raft of difficult measures but was still judged a failure. The
deficit was being reduced but the economy was shrinking,
and Greece's debts were mounting. So, in the early summer
of 2011, the ground began to be prepared for a second bail-
out.

It would come at a price, and that would be further austerity measures. The EU and the IMF said 28 billion euros of
extra savings would not only have to be found but approved
by the Greek Parliament. By the second half of May, those
leaders, who had been so dismissive of a debt write-down, had
tempered their opposition. They spoke of a 'soft restructuring'. Private investors, such as banks, could be asked to accept
losses voluntarily.

Greece was heading for a decisive moment. At the end of
June there would be a vote of confidence in the government
and then a vote on the new austerity package. Police from all

over Greece were summoned to the capital. In the weeks before, protestors began occupying Syntagma Square. They pitched blue and grey tents and hung their slogans from the orange trees. 'We got the solution,' declared one poster boldly, 'revolution'. Another urged the people to rise up. Their inspiration to occupy, to hold public ground was borrowed from elsewhere, from the Arab uprisings and from the indignant ones in Madrid. They were there to oppose further spending cuts. The encampment did not crackle with revolutionary fervour. It had the feel of an anti-globalisation village that had taken root alongside African migrants selling handbag copies and bright-rimmed sunglasses.

The prime minister, George Papandreou, was depicted as a capitalist stooge, a passenger on a plane from CIA/IMF Airways. The protestors called themselves pro-democracy activists but bickered about its meaning. 'We have no leaders here,' said one tousle-haired protestor. They went into contortions over giving interviews in case by speaking out they were judged to have assumed a leadership role. They spoke, misty-eyed, about the Paris Commune of 1871 and the European revolutions of 1848, but amongst the hammocks and tables piled high with pamphlets, there was no agreed agenda. They were united only by their hatred of the bankers and international capitalism. They were indignant but they lacked the will, the determination, the message and the zeal to shake Athens. Greek society was fractured and broken but it was not ready for revolution. It despised its leaders but it feared itself and its history more than the anonymous officials from the EU and the IMF that were mapping its future.

What the encampment did do was to serve as a rallying point. In the cool of the early evenings, families brought their children to see and perhaps remember the calls for revolution that tumbled from the loud-speakers. The crowds would sit cross-legged listening to open-air lectures about capitalism and its failures.

Away from the square was another mood: despondency. The economist, Yanis Varoufakis, said that, 'Above all, the people resented the loss of dignity.'

The mood was tinder dry. At times the city seemed on the edge of rebellion. There was a pervading sense of crisis. In the stifling heat of summer, electricity workers went on strike and triggered power cuts. A Greek paper said that 'never before in Greece's history has there been such a lack of leadership'.

In the coastal city of Piraeus, Roula stared from her apartment window as the weekly market outside wound down. She was middle aged and had been given notice that her job was closing. Littered on the street were discarded boxes and damaged fruit and vegetables. The street sweepers waited for the last stalls to be broken down. Roula watched until she spotted her neighbours scavenging for the food that had been abandoned. They scampered about, hoping to pass unseen. It told Roula which of her neighbours were losing the battle to survive. It made her sad and frightened. In her mid-forties, there was little or no prospect of finding new work. Her daughter Barbara, aged twenty-three, was thinking of emigrating. The young were leaving and Roula sighed, 'This will be a country of old people.' Barbara's friends dreamt of Canada and in particular Australia, where a previous generation had fled from the Greek civil war. The euro-zone had proved a terrible trap for so many countries. The low interest rates, the easy money, had led to property booms, speculation and piles of debt. Reducing the debt was now exacting a terrible toll on a new generation. There was creeping despair, injured national pride and perhaps ten years of austerity stretching ahead.

Improbably, a small country in the Aegean held the fate of the world economy within its grasp. The French and German titans of industry signed a letter warning that a collapse of the euro would be disastrous. These were the men and women who ran companies like BMW, Total, Renault, Siemens and EADS. They appealed for solidarity without revealing what that meant. The Greek prime minister, George Papandreou, was struggling to keep his country together. He tried to forge a government of national unity to build support for the package of spending cuts agreed in exchange for a second bail-out but opposition politicians shunned him. On 17 June 2011, Angela Merkel called and tried to stiffen his resolve. Papandreou told her he was ready to fight. The budget details had been prepared by George Papaconstantinou, the finance minister, but he and the prime minister doubted that he was the man to sell the new measures to a restive Parliament. 'I had been the poster boy for austerity,' he said. 'There was no way I could convince MPs to back the budget.' Papaconstantinou had become increasingly unpopular not just on the streets but even in the Parliament so he was replaced.

The Greeks were told by European leaders, 'There is no plan B.' If Parliament rejected the new round of cuts, there would be no fresh loans and Greece would default, opening up a possible exit from the euro-zone. The EU's economics commissioner, Olli Rehn, said: 'We're at a critical point in the most serious crisis since the Second World War.' In comment after comment, Europe's leaders applied the pressure: Greece would be cast out and left to face ruinous inflation, runs on its banks and violent upheaval. Some Greeks suspected Brussels was bluffing, but they could not be certain.

If Athens had called their bluff, they would have found Europe's leaders divided. The French were working on a plan

to roll over some Greek payments and so avoid default. The
weight of the European Commission would have come in
behind keeping Greece in the euro-zone. Other countries,
however, were ready to shut the door on Greece. It prompted
the British prime minister, David Cameron, to warn that it
was wise, particularly for banks, 'to prepare for all eventuali-
ties'. The governor of the Bank of England spoke of the need
for 'contingency plans' in the event of a Greek bankruptcy.
The German finance minister sounded a similar note. The
international financier George Soros warned: 'We're on the
edge of an economic collapse.'

As tens of thousands of protestors gathered outside the
Greek Parliament, the prime minister was warning that the
country's cash reserves would be exhausted by 15 July. Greece,
he told them, faced a historic choice, but the people were
increasingly numb to such appeals. Only a year before, they
had been promised there would be no more cuts. Many had
seen their wages drop by 15 per cent. In the past year, 400,000
jobs had been lost. Industrial production had slumped 11 per
cent. Now a further 6 billion euros in savings would have to
be found immediately, and another 28 billion of cuts would
have to be made by 2015. The middle class would pay a solidarity tax. 150,000 civil service jobs would disappear. The
threshold at which Greeks would start paying tax would drop
from 12,000 to 8,000 euros. The polls indicated that nearly 80
per cent of the people opposed making further sacrifices.

On the days of the crucial votes there were attempts to
encircle the Parliament to prevent MPs voting. There was a
two-day general strike. 'It was a difficult and dangerous
period,' said George Papaconstantinou. 'The streets were very
volatile. We had to leave with riot police protecting us.' There
were violent clashes. Protestors came with hammers and

chipped away at the marble in Syntagma Square. They smashed staircases and tore pieces off the facades of the buildings and threw slabs at the police. Others hurled petrol bombs. Some tried to burn buildings. A hotel was evacuated and people were rescued from a burning building. The police fired over 2,000 tear gas canisters and stun grenades. Tear gas was fired into the metro station where protestors had taken refuge. Some of the riot police threw the rocks back at the crowds. Over 300 protestors and police were injured. 'It was very fragile, very dangerous, with the social situation very difficult,' said the new finance minister, Evangelos Venizelos. 'There were great demonstrations and riots and in the centre there was a kind of occupation.'

Many of the crowd raked the Parliament with green laser pens, like fingers of accusation. As the names of those MPs who had voted in favour of the cuts were read out in the square, the crowd howled '*Kleftes!*' or 'Thieves!' but, in the event, the prime minister gained a narrow victory; on 21 June 2011 he won his vote of confidence and later the austerity measures were approved.

Europe's leaders betrayed their anxiety with the speed with which they dialled in their messages of congratulation. It was like watching a concert performance where the audience leaps to its feet before the last note has died away, engulfing the performers with a wave of applause. Berlin was quick with its 'bravo' – Chancellor Merkel showered praised on the Greek MPs for their 'brave' vote. The president of the European Council, Herman Van Rompuy, was on his feet applauding the country for having taken 'a vital step back – from the grave scenario of default.'

So this second bail-out deal meant the country was loaned a further 130 billion euros. It was a policy that had failed once but that did not deter Europe's leaders. They had placed their faith in austerity. They did not explain how Greece, mired in recession, would reduce its debt burden, which was only increasing. Indeed, the bail-outs themselves were adding to Greece's debts. What was important to the leaders of France and Germany, in particular, was to buy time for their banks to improve their balance sheets and to reduce their exposure to Greece. As to the country itself, it had become a laboratory, an experiment in austerity. No one knew or understood what further cuts would do to a country facing its worst recession in thirty-seven years. Later, an investigation would conclude that the EU and the IMF had consistently underestimated the impact of austerity on growth. Not since the thirties had a Western economy shrunk so fast.

George Papandreou declared, 'We have rendered our debt problem manageable,' but he had doubts. Within weeks he was berating Europe's leaders. 'It was time for Europe to wake up,' he said. Greece as a country had made an unprecedented effort, but without 'strong and visionary European leadership', a contagion of doubt 'could engulf our common union'. The Prime Minister understood that Greece would be able to finance its basic needs; what the bail-out did not do was to answer the fundamental question of what, in the final degree, stood behind the euro.

Those who openly questioned what Europe was doing were often dismissed as populists but the critics charged that untold damage was being done in an attempt to save the single currency. The Finnish politician, Timo Soini, declared that Greece, Ireland and Portugal had been ruined. They would never be able to save and grow fast enough to pay back the debts 'which Brussels had saddled them with'.

Once again all eyes turned to Berlin. Angela Merkel heralded the Greek vote as 'a significant step' and declared Berlin's 'historical duty' was to support the euro. But Europe had grown wary of the German Chancellor and uncertain of her commitment to its dream.

Chapter 10
The Turning of Frau Nein

A soft haze fell across the Bavarian lake at Waging am See. In the autumn sun, the crowd sat at long tables enjoying beer and *currywurst* served by young women in dirndl dresses. It was more like a giant cook-out than a political rally. When Angela Merkel arrived the applause was polite, even though these were her supporters; some even seemed reluctant to look up from their food. A few posters with the word 'Angie' printed on them were waved and they played the Rolling Stones song, 'Oh, Angie, don't you weep, all your kisses still taste sweet. I hate that sadness in your eyes.' It had become the unofficial soundtrack of her campaign although nobody, it seemed, had listened to the lyrics. She was just Angie on the stump, a few weeks before Europe's crisis broke.

Merkel did not know how to work a crowd, certainly not in the American style. She moved through the tables with a few perfunctory waves. Her smile was almost shy and self-effacing. She stood on the stage impassively, in her trademark trouser suit, waiting for the introductions to pass. At one point she received a text message and put her hand in her left pocket to examine her phone. So many politicians would have tried to conceal the move, wary of being seen as distracted or uninterested. Merkel just read the text, as if alone, away from the crowd. She was not a needy politician who sought an audience's approval, neither did she come to inspire or to pump up. This was a lakeside conversation on a still-warm Sunday afternoon in Bavaria.

Thomas de Maizière, her chief of staff, said, 'Her charisma is a special one . . . it is quiet, persuasive, full of conscience . . . a dialogue with the people, not shouting to the people.' She rarely spoke about herself or her political journey. She offered to continue as Germany's office manager. There was little ideology in her politics; she was a pragmatist shaped by solid, old-fashioned virtues. The recession had been caused, she told her audience, 'because the world did not behave like we did in Germany'. She got the biggest applause when she turned on the bankers and said, 'Greed won.' Her explanation for the recession was that 'the crisis did not take place because we were spending too little but because we were spending too much'. Her speeches were imbued with a strong sense of right and wrong. Angela Merkel would apply the same German virtues to fighting the crisis in the euro-zone but, over time, what made her popular at home would draw hostility abroad, and some would even question her loyalty to the European project.

The euro-zone crisis made Angela Merkel the most powerful woman in the world. Her impassive face stared out from countless magazine covers. There were others like Hillary Clinton, who vied for the honour, but indisputably the German Chancellor was the more influential. In her hands lay the future of Europe and the global economy. *Forbes* magazine liked to classify powerful women but there was no contest. They crowned Angela Merkel year after year. She was not just the 'Iron Lady' of the EU but the 'undisputed' leader of Europe and the head of its only 'real global economy'. She did not mind that in German political circles she was known as '*Mutti*' or 'Mom'. The more she was underestimated, the more space it gave her. She often eschewed the symbols of power: in mid-evening, she could be spotted being driven in an unmarked Audi along Friedrichstrasse; there were no sirens – she was just another professional returning to her modest Berlin apartment to join her husband.

She had not sought the role of *Macht frau*, a woman of power. Neither had her country. Economic strength made Germany the dominant player in Europe. In 2010, just as Europe was struggling with its debt crisis, the value of German exports rose by nearly 20 per cent in a year. It was the strongest performance in more than twenty years. After China, Germany was the world's largest exporter. The gap between Germany and most of the southern European countries was widening. For sixty years Germany had recoiled from a leadership role. The very word 'leader' came with flashbacks to the past. Now the country had leadership thrust upon it and that led to soul-searching. 'Scarcely a people is less suited to this task than the contrite Germans,' opined the paper *Die Welt*. This was a country that would have much preferred to have been left as a bigger version of Switzerland.

The longer the crisis continued the more it confirmed Germany's role as the indispensable nation. It alone had the economic and financial power to convince markets. Before any vital meeting the question was always posed: 'What is Germany's position?' From the outset, Angela Merkel would not be hustled into quick decisions. That was not her way. Appeals to act the good European did not move her. Those close to her say that in the midst of a crisis she liked to slow events down to buy her time to think, to weigh the arguments. She approached her politics with the mind of a trained scientist who valued calm analysis. She sounded out economists and business leaders. Often her closest aides would not know which side of the argument she would come down on.

It frustrated other leaders. They saw a German Chancellor hobbled by her instinctive caution and her core beliefs. Initially, she believed that Greece needed some energetic housekeeping. When it was apparent that Greece was broke and lacked the means to raise money she said 'no' to a rescue. She resisted until the last moment, until her aides explained that if Greece was allowed to go bankrupt, the crisis would spread across Europe: other countries would be drawn in and it would trigger a crisis in the financial system. She was shown the figures: German and French banks had lent nearly a trillion euros to Greece, Ireland, Portugal, Spain and Italy.

So during 2011 a pattern began to be established. By now Europe's politicians knew that Merkel's initial instinct was to say 'no'. She said 'no' to the European Central Bank buying the bonds of troubled countries in order to lower their borrowing costs. She said 'no' to the idea of setting up a permanent bail-out fund. She said 'no, to increasing its size. At the last moment, however, she would bend and compromise, particularly if the alternative was the risk of chaos. It led to her being called 'Frau Nein'. President Sarkozy believed that her dithering over Greece ended up costing Europe billions; swift action might also have prevented the markets questioning the will of Europe's politicians to defend their currency. Others railed against Germany's caution. The financier George Soros said that, 'Germany would only do the minimum necessary, so every opportunity was missed.' The Polish foreign minister, Radoslaw Sikorski, went to Berlin and demanded that Germany help the euro-zone survive and prosper. 'No one else can do it,' he said. 'I will probably be the first Polish foreign minister in history,' he said, 'to say so, but here it is: I fear German power less than I am beginning to fear German inactivity.' The lessons from the past were being turned on their head.

Angela Merkel was under relentless pressure in 2011. The Europeans questioned why she did not explain to the Germans that they had done well from the euro and that it was in the country's interest to save it. President Obama called frequently. He, like others, wanted her to show leadership but, when she did, she was often vilified for insisting on reforms and austerity. Greece needed to atone for its extravagance, and bail-outs would come with harsh conditions attached. 'It was not an economic or strategic issue,' said the French finance minister, François Baroin, 'but moral . . . The German position,' he continued, 'is a heritage of World War Two . . . they have never forgotten that. So they learn to fight against inflation as they learn spelling and grammar in schools.'

Angela Merkel's insistence that indebted countries must cut costs and reform their work ethic led to accusations that she was trying to redesign Europe in Germany's image. Soros pointed an accusatory finger and said, 'Germany dictates policies which lead to a spiralling debt.' For sixty years there had been peace in Europe and Germany had been a model democracy, but just beneath the surface suspicions remained. The French foreign minister, Alain Juppé, warned against a 'reawakening of the old demons of Germanophobia' but they resurfaced all the same, and old stereotypes returned. One Italian TV station portrayed the Chancellor wearing the spiked helmet of the Kaiser. A British columnist warned of 'the rise of the Fourth Reich' in which Germany was 'using the financial crisis to conquer Europe'. One of Greece's best-known journalists said his country had become 'a German protectorate of the Fourth Reich in southern

Europe'. Another British columnist wrote that it 'was a massive irony that old Europe's last gasp should be to seek ... German supremacy'. When the European Commission sent a technical task force to Greece to help with reforms it was led by a German, Horst Reichenbach. It did not take long for him to be called the 'Third Reichenbach'. A Spanish paper discussed the 'Germanisation' of Europe. When Mariano Rajoy was elected Spanish prime minister, Angela Merkel sent him a letter. It began 'Dear Mr Rajoy' and the formal tone continued with what was seen in Madrid as a virtual order: now that he had won a clear mandate from the people, the letter read, he should 'rapidly' take action to reduce the deficit. Some saw this as an example of Germany laying down the law to Spain.

A prominent French politician, Arnaud Montebourg, and a man who would later become industry minister under President Hollande, said, 'The issue of German nationalism is returning through Bismarckian policies championed by Mrs Merkel.'

It led the French prime minister, François Fillon, to intervene. He denounced it as 'irresponsible and indecent' to play with nationalistic ideas that belonged to the past. Merkel was reluctant to be drawn into such a sensitive arena but she, too, appealed for the old stereotypes to be buried. 'There are lazy Germans and hard-working Germans, left-wing Germans and conservative ones,' she said. 'Germany is just as varied as the rest of Europe.'

President Sarkozy was acutely aware of the dangers of opening up a rift between Germany and France, and awakening what an aide called 'the spirits of history'. He was frustrated by Merkel, but the Elysée Palace was determined to understand her thinking. 'She is something very calm, very cool, very professional,' said Xavier Musca, Sarkozy's chief of staff. 'She is an excellent chess player. She always has a lot of options on the table and she keeps secret what she will do until the last moment, and that's also because she has to strike two deals at the same time, with the Europeans and with her Parliament.' Certainly Sarkozy had understood this since early in 2010 that Merkel was always manoeuvring between two audiences: her tax-payers and her European partners.

At home she was accused of making too many concessions, that gradually Germany was becoming the pay-master of Europe, bankrolling countries that had mismanaged their finances. Her critics detected little or no passion for the European project. She was not from the war generation, which had over-seen the rebuilding of Europe and dreamed of an ever-closer union. The former Chancellor, Helmut Kohl, who had been her mentor, was reported to have said, 'She is ruining my Europe.' He reminded her that Germany's future lay with its neighbours. He wanted her to show solidarity and urged her to stick with the Greeks, 'even if it costs us something'.

In June 2011, Angela Merkel went to Washington. Barack Obama had awarded her the Presidential Medal of Freedom. It is the highest civilian honour that a US president can bestow. He saw both of them as political pioneers: she the first female Chancellor of Germany and he the first African-American president of the United States. She arrived in a black evening gown and the President gushed, 'You look wonderful tonight.' The White House had identified the euro-zone crisis as 'one of the headwinds' affecting the US economy. The Americans were impatient for action and, on this night, they showered the German leader with affection. They were careful that the Maryland crab ravioli was followed by a more German offering of apple strudel and *schlag*. The musician, James Taylor, was summoned to sing 'You've Got a Friend.'

Angela Merkel told the audience in the Rose Garden about the moment when Berlin was split. By a wall. 'I was seven years old at the time,' she said. 'Seeing grown ups, even my parents, so stunned that they broke out in tears. It shook me to the core. My mother's family, for example, was divided by the building of the wall.' It was a reminder that she had lived history, that freedom for her was still new and precious. But, back home, it was noted that in her thank-you speech she did not mention the European dream. So to many, Merkel was the reluctant European who was more attentive to the fears of German tax-payers than the survival of the euro.

And then her language began to change. She started describing the crisis as an existential threat not just to the euro, but to the entire European project. 'If the Euro fails, then Europe fails,' became her much-repeated refrain. It was not necessarily true, but it was aimed at German voters who would be asked to contribute more; to risk more of their funds in propping up Europe's weaker economies. They were told it was less about the Greeks or the Spanish and more about the future of Europe itself.

What influenced Angela Merkel was not just practical politics but her own sense of history. She was visited in her glass and steel office – which Berliners say reminds them of a washing machine – by former German Chancellors. Since World War Two, European unity had been Germany's guiding light. For the political class it was an article of faith. Their message to her, however coded, was unmistakeable. She did not want to be remembered as the Chancellor who allowed the European project to fail. 'I think,' said a close ally of the Chancellor, 'that she came to the conviction that a solution of the euro-zone crisis will be her legacy in history.'

So, gradually, she changed. She came to believe that in order to survive, Europe needed to integrate much more closely. The flaws of the currency would have to be remedied. There would have to be much tighter control over budgets and over the economies of those countries that used the euro. She dared other leaders to become 'more European'. Large areas of national sovereignty would have to be given up, she said. The hesitant leader of early 2010 was declaring in Leipzig, eighteen months later, that: 'The task of our generation is to complete economic and monetary union, and to build political union in Europe, step by step.' She told her party congress that that would mean 'not less Europe but more Europe'. She said it was the toughest hour since World War Two. It was almost as if she was born again, with a mission to save Europe.

Ralph Brinkhaus, who was a member of Merkel's party and sat on the finance committee in Parliament, said that the Chancellor's message was that 'either we get more Europe now or the project will die'. That would mean, he said, that Germany would have to give up some sovereign rights but there was no alternative.

Other leaders detected the change. During this period, an influential figure emerged. Herman Van Rompuy was president of the European Council, presiding over the work and the meetings of Europe's heads of government. He was the ring-master at the summits. He had been a surprising choice for the job. Outside Belgium, where he had been prime minister, he was scarcely known. And he liked it that way. He was known as 'the sphinx' or the 'grey ghost'; an official who shied away from the spotlight but was a skilful mediator.

He preferred to look down rather than make eye contact. One of his past-times was writing haiku verse like:

> 'A lost fly
> Flies wonderingly in a plane
> Thus she is flying twice.'

Van Rompuy observed that, 'Germany and Angela Merkel changed dramatically in 2011.' Speeches were studded with phrases like, 'We are pro-European' and 'We want the euro to stay.'

'In the rhetorical language that the Chancellor used,' said Van Rompuy, 'certainly in that time there was a dramatic change.'

Europe's leaders joked that she was Frau Nein until the last moment. When the single currency appeared close to collapse, she was most open to compromise.

Even though her language had changed, she still had her red lines. She was not prepared for Germany to become the pay-master of Europe. As she had indicated time and again, she would not allow the European Union to morph into a transfer union, where German treasure bankrolled the weaker economies. She would not countenance a sharing of debt. In her view, that would only encourage countries to back off reforms. She was guided by one over-riding principle: that the crisis could never be allowed to re-occur. Speaking in Davos, she said that, 'It does not make sense to promise more money, but not tackle the cause of the problem.' Tony Blair said that 'her constant fear, her constant desire, will be to make sure that any help that's given (to Greece) is given on a basis that cures the problem rather than merely postpones it'.

So Europe began to debate a quantum leap in European integration. It was ill defined at first, but the flaws in the single currency would have to be fixed. Budgets and economic policies would have to be properly policed and that would mean more power flowing to Brussels. As Jean Monnet, one of Europe's founding fathers, had once predicted, 'Europe would be born out of crisis.'

The French president became less a critic and more an ally. There were still major differences between them and fierce arguments lay ahead, but they would try and co-ordinate their speeches and mask their differences. It was not just that both leaders understood the importance of Franco–German unity to the markets; Sarkozy and Merkel also, over time, grew to like each other. It was a relationship that could even survive teasing. Angela Merkel realised that Sarkozy only knew one German word and that was '*genau*' which means 'correct'. Sometimes she would repeatedly interrupt and gently mock him by saying, '*Genau*'.

Once when they were in Brussels, they were both staying at the Hotel Amigo. Merkel said to Sarkozy, 'Come and have breakfast with me.'

Sarkozy replied, 'Yes, but not at the buffet. In your suite or my suite.'

'No,' said Merkel, 'I want to go to the buffet.'

'Why?' asked a by-now-intrigued Sarkozy.

'Because there is more choice,' said the German Chancellor. Sarkozy laughed. He realised she was still an Eastern European at heart, anxious about shortages.

Merkel was changing, and signalling that over the next five to ten years, Europe would have to change, too. There would be greater solidarity, but the German Chancellor insisted it would come with a price: greater control.

In a short period, Germany had assumed great power and responsibility, which left many uneasy. Most controversially, Germany would be accused of using its muscle to remove those leaders that it believed threatened the survival of the single currency.

Chapter 11
The Downfall of
Il Cavaliere

Over the summer and autumn of 2011, Berlin and Paris realised that the future of Europe lay in the grasp of the man they trusted least: the Italian leader, Silvio Berlusconi. He had entertained, charmed, offended and insulted. A wiretap had overheard him calling Angela Merkel 'an unfuckable lard-arse'. Yet, in the great drama to defend Europe's currency, he now held centre stage. He was the prime minister of the third largest country in the euro-zone with debts of 1.9 trillion euros. Italy's borrowing costs were rising to the point where it would struggle to service its debts. If Rome defaulted it could destroy the euro. Berlusconi's credibility, however, was long shot. *The Economist* magazine had put his face on its front cover with the headline: 'The man who screwed an entire country.' Chancellor Merkel and President Sarkozy faced a dilemma; what to do about an elected leader of a major European country who they had come to believe was endangering the European project.

During that summer, convoys of Europe's leaders had rolled into Brussels with increasing frequency. Summit followed summit. The heads of government disappeared into the Justus Lipsius building, a vast warren of bureaucracy in the heart of the European quarter with corridors that stretch for twenty-four kilometers. In the building's atrium, hundreds of journalists would set up camp, waiting for decisions to be passed down to them. Flacks, like publicity agents, from one government delegation or another would appear in the atrium to brief a huddle of their own national reporters on how their leader was fighting the cause upstairs. At times it resembled the American 'spin alley', where on the campaign trail, staff would scurry to talk up the performance of their candidate after a debate.

Rarely had a summit had a billing like that of 21 July 2011. The president of the European Commission, José Manuel Barroso, had said ominously that history would judge those leaders taking part if they failed. President Obama worked the phones, chiding Europe's leaders at their inability to fix the crisis. Indecision or failure, he said, risked plunging the world economy back into recession. On the eve of the summit, Chancellor Merkel and President Sarkozy had spoken for seven hours.

The focus was still Greece. Its Parliament, under great international pressure, had the previous month agreed to another dose of austerity and further painful reforms. Now, at the summit, a deal emerged that the leaders hoped would settle the Greek crisis once and for all. The leaders signed off on the loan of 109 billion euros as part of the second bail-out. There would also be a move to slice off a layer from Greece's mountain of debt. Angela Merkel insisted that private investors – the banks and the pension funds – share in the burden of rescuing Greece, alongside Europe's tax-payers. She proposed that investors take losses to reduce Greece's debt.

The banks would be 'encouraged' to take a 'hair-cut' of 21 per cent on the Greek bonds they held. It meant that Greece's debt pile would be reduced by almost 40 billion euros.

Investors would be told to accept the deal or risk much greater losses later. It was essential that the banks agreed to this voluntarily, otherwise the markets would declare it a default. That would be hugely damaging to Europe's reputation. Investors might take fright from other fragile European economies fearing they would have to accept losses there.

After the summit, the leaders rushed to declare this a one-off offer, which would never be repeated. The French President called it 'an exception'. The president of the European Commission said it was a solution that 'we exclude for other countries'.

The summit also agreed to give the euro-zone's bail-out fund sweeping new powers so it could act more aggressively to help banks and countries in difficulty. Afterwards, a four-page document was issued but much of the detail, particularly on the deal being offered to private investors, was impenetrable. Officials were bombarded with questions but they did not have answers. At one press conference they had to retreat, surrounded by angry and frustrated journalists. One of them said, 'It is probably the most opaque set of financial figures I have come across.' Four days after the meeting, the head of one of the world's most powerful hedge funds was still phoning reporters, trying to unravel what had been agreed.

Some time later, the president of the European Commission criticised officials for 'undisciplined communication'. It was not just skills in explanation that were lacking, however; one EU ambassador said it was clear that many of the leaders sitting around the table did not understand what they were agreeing to. A senior official from the ECB found himself trying to explain to baffled leaders how markets worked and that a deal, which imposed losses, would produce winners, too. Some prime ministers did not understand the difference between taking 'long' and 'short' positions. The official explained to them that 'a loss for those who are long is a profit for those who are short'. The Greek prime minister, George Papandreou, said that at one stage, investors stood to make a quick buck out of Greece: all they had to do was to buy Greek bonds cheaply and then exchange them later. 'It would have meant,' said Papandreou, 'European hedge funds making a windfall out of tax-payers.'

Europe's leaders, however, had left town with high hopes. Angela Merkel declared, 'We have shown we are up to the challenge. We are capable of acting.' The French president gasped, 'We have done something historic.' He seemed to believe a European Monetary Fund was on the way. The head of the IMF called the meeting 'game changing'. Luxembourg's prime minister said it would prove 'the last rescue package'. It was all hopelessly optimistic.

Europe's leaders were out of their depth. They were reacting to financial markets they only dimly understood. They believed that the murky compromises, the hallmark of so much of their business, would satisfy global markets. The opposite was true. It deepened suspicions that Europe was incapable of defending its currency. So once again a summit concluded with a power surge of wishful thinking only for the euphoria to evaporate days later. On this occasion they even disputed what had been agreed.

With the summit behind them, officials planned their ways of escape. Europe takes vacation seriously: the great migrations to the coast; the clogged motorways; politicians snapping up remote villas; leaders seeking refuge in mountain hideaways.

And then the euro-zone crisis returned like a violent summer storm. The relief had lasted under two weeks.

The markets were less concerned with Greece; they were focusing on two much bigger countries, Spain and Italy, where borrowing costs had soared to their highest level for fourteen years. There was intense irritation with the markets for intruding into the summer break. The Spanish prime minister begrudgingly delayed his vacation. The president of the European Commission said the market pressure was 'clearly unwarranted'.

Others knew that for all the high claims, the summit had failed to convince. 'I have to say sadly,' said Jean-Claude Trichet, the head of the ECB, 'that it was absolutely clear that the speculative side of the market had decided what had been agreed by the heads of government was not sufficient.' So the markets decided to attack, demanding higher rates for the risk of holding Italian and Spanish debt. 'We were in a situation,' said Trichet,' to decide what to do knowing that again, it was the start of a large scale destabilisation with attacks on both Italy and Spain.' The Finnish prime minister, Jyrki Katainen, said what was happening was 'very alarming. A scary thing.' The whole of Europe was in 'a very dangerous situation'.

Europe's leaders had failed to address the fundamental questions: how would debt be reduced, where would growth come from and what finally stood behind the euro. They had also failed to explain how Italy and Spain would be rescued if they needed help. At the summit, there had been a commitment to beef up the powers of the bail-out fund, but no extra money had been put in the pot. When investors cast their eyes over Spain and Italy they saw high debt, high unemployment, low growth and, in the case of Spain, fragile banks.

The focus of attention was Italy. Rome had already announced some savings and Brussels had applauded, but the markets were not persuaded. For a few weeks Berlusconi had been uncharacteristically silent. In Rome there was comment and speculation that he had gone missing. There were calls for him to reappear and to make a statement. When he did his comments were riddled with complacency. He reeled off a list of Italy's strengths. The banks were solvent and personal debt was low, he insisted. All the time the country's borrowing costs edged higher.

The European Central Bank decided to act, embarking on one of the most dramatic interventions in its history. Drawing on all its power and influence it attempted to muscle Berlusconi into implementing real and far-reaching changes. On 5 August 2011 the president of the ECB, Jean-Claude Trichet, sent Berlusconi a 'secret' letter which was highly sensitive. 'It was not a quid pro quo. It was not a negotiation,' said Trichet. He summed up his message to Berlusconi as: 'You have to make a u-turn if you want to surmount the crisis and these are the steps you should take . . . urgent action by the Italian authorities was essential to restoring confidence of investors.'

The letter was soon leaked to government circles in Rome. It contained a list of demands; that Italy take measures to support growth, to open up the labour market, to make it easier to hire and fire workers, to take tough steps to reduce the deficit and to balance the budget by 2013.

The tone of the message rankled with some of Berlusconi's advisers. The Central Bank had set a deadline of 30 September for legislation to be adopted. The advisers did not like the way the letter ended. Trichet signed off with the words 'we trust that the government will take all the appropriate actions.' Some senior officials in Rome bristled at an unelected bank official dictating Italian government policy, or that was how it was seen. Others saw it as a trap. One of his coalition partners believed it was an attempt to unseat the prime minister. Agreeing to the European Central Bank's terms risked provoking opposition, particularly from the unions. On the other hand, it was impossible to ignore the bank: the ECB could just stop buying Italian bonds and catapult the country into crisis. Rumours spread through Rome's political circles. One opposition leader demanded, 'We want the truth.' Another opposition MP, Antonio Di Pietro, said that, 'At the moment, Italy is under the tutelage of the EU, and a country under tutelage is not a free and democratic one.'

Berlusconi had no choice but to agree to the ECB's demands and he committed Italy to further savings and reforms. Five days later, the ECB announced that it would buy Italian debt, so easing pressure on the country. Statements of support had been co-ordinated with Paris and Berlin with both capitals also insisting that the measures start to be implemented in September.

However it was presented this was a case of Europe's Central Bank laying down the law to an elected government – with the implicit threat that if actions were not taken then the bank would stop buying bonds and force up borrowing costs. Even though the bank was independent it was also clear the actions had been agreed before hand with the Elysée Palace and the Chancellery in Berlin.

Berlusconi was in a bind. Without the support of the European Central Bank, Italy would struggle to raise the funds it needed, but neither could Berlusconi guarantee that he could deliver what the bank was demanding. After seventeen years in power, he was surrounded by enemies. Even within his own government some were plotting against him. He himself had advocated pension reform and lifting the retirement age from sixty-three to sixty-seven, but he had little chance of getting the reforms through Parliament. The politicians sniffed his vulnerability and there were days of horse-trading. The foreign minister, Franco Frattini, said there were MPs 'threatening to leave (Berlusconi) if they were not promoted or gained political recognition. It was a very uncomfortable position.'

Berlusconi was in coalition with the Northern League, a party that had ridden to power by exploiting resentment towards Rome. Its slogan was '*Roma Ladrona*', 'Thieving Romans'. The *Lega*, as the party was known, did not believe it was necessary to increase the retirement age, and neither would they accept Europe imposing its own agenda. The Italian prime minister understood his dilemma: if he could not deliver on the reforms demanded, then the other European leaders would turn against him. He told some of his ministers, 'They (the ECB, Sarkozy and Merkel) have decided to intervene in favour of our bonds to save themselves, not Italy.'

Even so, Berlusconi decided that he had no option than to do what the ECB was asking. He painted Italy as a victim at the mercy of great global squalls and storms. 'Our hearts are bleeding,' he told the Italian people, 'we're facing one of the greatest challenges on the planet. The whole system of relationships between states is changing.' With those dramatic words, which absolved Italy of responsibility, he announced an emergency budget with new savings of 45 billion euros. The retirement age would be raised. Taxes on the wealthy would be increased. Italy's culture of closed professions – where it was almost impossible for outsiders to get jobs as taxi drivers or pharmacists – would be ended. 'They (the bank) made us look like an occupied government,' he said bitterly. The opposition supported the proposals and inside Berlusconi's Cabinet there was relief. 'We succeeded in getting help from Frankfurt,' said Franco Frattini, referring to the European Central Bank. 'It was in the interest of Italy.'

Whilst agreeing to the reforms, the Italians were pushing another plan. Rome believed the answer to the crisis lay in Eurobonds, in common European debt. The Italian finance minister, Giulio Tremonti, described it as the 'master solution'. The attraction to countries like Italy was obvious: they could refinance their debts on the same terms as Germany. Tremonti tried to frighten the Germans into agreeing. 'Just as on the Titanic,' he said, 'not even first-class passengers can save themselves.' His message was that the euro ship was going down and the Germans, partying on the upper decks, would not be spared.

The Germans were instinctively opposed to Eurobonds and, in late August, their opposition deepened: Berlin had noticed that once the ECB had started buying Italian bonds, the government in Rome had eased off on delivering the promised changes: the plan to reduce pension costs was suddenly dropped; over 7 billion euros in ear-marked savings mysteriously went 'missing'; and black holes began appearing in the budget, with vague undertakings that they would be filled by yet another campaign against tax evasion. It had a huge impact on Angela Merkel. 'See what happens?' she told her advisers with real exasperation. 'You help them and they back off reforms.' It hardened her attitude against any sharing of debt in the euro-zone and deepened her mistrust of Berlusconi. 'The way the Italians handled it was an absolute catastrophe,' said a senior French official in the Elysée Palace. They characterised Berlusconi's position as being 'Let's be serious – I will never apply that awful programme because I am at risk at the next election.'

Berlusconi was locked in a feud with his finance minister, Giulio Tremonti. The arguments were bitter and public.

Tremonti believed that he and he alone stood in the way of Italy being savaged by the markets. The way he saw it was that his word, unlike that of the prime minister, counted. He could be trusted with reforms; the prime minister could not. 'If I fall, Italy will fall and the euro will fall,' he declared rather grandly. Berlusconi believed that behind his back he was bad-mouthing him to other European leaders. 'He wants to drag me through the mud,' he said, and 'the sooner he leaves the better'. Tremonti, however, was untouchable. He had credibility and if he was forced out it would further roil the markets and Berlusconi knew that. The prime minister came to fear that his finance minister, with other European leaders, was trying to oust him from power. 'Tremonti is going around Europe,' he complained, 'saying it is my fault that Italy's credibility has been tarnished because of the modifications I included in the budget. This is not on.'

In the autumn of 2011 Europe's leaders emerged from their interrupted summer in pessimistic mood. One of the architects of the euro, Jacques Delors, declared the single currency 'on the edge of an abyss'. The president of the European Commission, José Manuel Barroso, said, 'We are confronted with the most serious challenge of a generation.' The threat was existential. It was, in his view, 'a fight for European integration itself'. The depth of the leaders' fear could be detected in their warnings that conflict could return to the continent. 'The dissolution of the euro-zone is not acceptable,' said Alain Juppé, the French foreign minister, 'because it would also be the dissolution of Europe. If that happens, then everything is possible. Young people seem to believe that peace is guaranteed for all time.' At times, Europe's leaders seemed to be trying to frighten themselves into action. They were rolling out plan after plan. In the meantime, they were saddled with Berlusconi.

At home, Berlusconi was being circled by prosecutors. He faced charges of corruption, abuse of power and having under-age sex with a prostitute. The magistrates were also investigating whether he was being blackmailed over his sex life. In a phone conversation, Berlusconi's anger bubbled over. 'They can say about me that I screw,' he raged, 'it's the only thing they can say about me. Is that clear? They can put listening devices where they like. They can tap my telephone calls. I don't give a fuck. In a few months, I'm getting out, to mind my own fucking business, from somewhere else, and so I'm leaving this shitty country of which I'm sickened.'

He was also caught on tape talking to a twenty-eight-year-old Dominican woman, Marysthell Polanco. The prime minister complained to her about his work schedule: the meetings with the Pope, the summits with France and Germany, and then he sighed, 'Oh, to pass the day with my babes. I'm just the PM in my spare time.' Polanco was now on the circuit of fame. One afternoon she went for an interview in a Milan park. She was tall, wearing impossibly high heels, with a bodyguard introduced as a publicity agent. She was loyal to Berlusconi and insisted there had been no sex at the parties. She said that she had put on a toga – imitating one of the female magistrates who was prosecuting the prime minister – in order to make him laugh. On another occasion she had dressed up as President Obama. Sitting on the park bench, she took a call from Ruby, the girl who Berlusconi was accused of having under-age sex with. Ruby, she announced, was getting married. Many of the girls who had attended the parties had come from abroad. They now embraced fame's chance as they were pursued by magazines and magistrates. At this dangerous time for Berlusconi, thousands of pages of transcripts of intercepted phone calls were released. In another conversation with Polanco he said, 'I'm in a very tough fight but when I win the war, then I will see you and I will make the most of your lips.'

Berlusconi's friends did not believe any of this was accidental. One of them, Carlo Rossella, said Berlusconi's enemies were 'pushing public opinion, starting with the judges, the leaks and the press'. Almost every day some papers had three or four pages devoted to scandals or revelations. It was a 'bad cocktail', said Rossella.

By October 2011 there was a chorus of concern over Italy. The credit-ratings agency, Moody's, downgraded the country. Mario Draghi, who was waiting to take over as president of the European Central Bank, said the austerity measures promised were 'not enough'. In a briefing note, one of the world's largest brokers, BGC Partners, was blunt: 'The leader and his country are in danger of taking the rest of Europe, if not the world, into economic hell.'

Europe's leaders had lost faith in Berlusconi. They doubted he had the will or the support in Parliament to deliver what he had promised. They had already given him a deadline for adopting legislation to implement reforms. They now went further, issuing him with what amounted to an ultimatum. They insisted that he send a letter to Brussels listing 'concrete actions' that would be taken. It had to include a timetable when the reforms would be carried out. His coalition was fraying, however. The Northern League would not support pension reform. Its leader, Umberto Bossi, declared, 'We cannot make the retirement age sixty-seven years – people will kill us.' He thought the situation in the country had become 'very dangerous' with Italy being dictated to. 'It is not possible to move the pensionable age to please the Germans,' he said.

Berlusconi met with Angela Merkel and Nicolas Sarkozy. The meeting was tense. The French president and the German Chancellor all but told him they did not believe him. They said he no longer commanded a majority in his Parliament and his promises were worthless. Berlusconi was offended. 'Nobody in the EU,' he said afterwards, 'can appoint themselves administrators . . . no one is in a position to be giving lessons to their partners.' The two leaders wanted to see a signed letter outlining the reforms. The Italian leader snapped, 'I've never flunked an exam in my life.'

Two days before, on 23 October, President Sarkozy and Chancellor Merkel held a press conference in Strasbourg. They were asked whether Berlusconi had made any promises to them over his reform programme and whether they were reassured by them. Even before the reporter had finished, Sarkozy had begun smiling. When the question finished he did not respond immediately but rolled his eyes and looked towards Angela Merkel with a broad grin. She broke into a giggle. There was no doubting it: the leaders of France and Germany were smirking at the Italian prime minister. 'It was taken very badly in Italy,' said Italy's foreign minister Franco Frattini, 'for not respecting the Italian prime minister. Two leaders insulting Silvio Berlusconi.' The Italian president became involved, denouncing the smirk as 'inappropriate'. Even politicians, like Pier Ferdinando Casini, who were not Berlusconi's allies, complained that, 'No one is authorised to ridicule Italy . . . I didn't like Mr Sarkozy's sarcastic smile.'

Berlusconi's inner circle blamed Sarkozy. Carlo Rossella said that Berlusconi was 'very sombre when he saw the smirk . . . he did not forget the laughter of Sarkozy, nor the sleight'. Franco Frattini said that, 'Sarkozy had never liked Berlusconi.' In his interpretation, Merkel had been drawn into the smirk. Merkel's face, said the foreign minister 'was like a stone. It was Sarkozy's smile, inciting Merkel'. One of the papers owned by Berlusconi compared Sarkozy's 'grin' to the head butt delivered to an Italian player by France's Zinedine Zidane in the soccer World Cup Final 2006. His supporters organised a 'laugh in' outside the French embassy in Rome, where they mocked French diplomats.

The Italians fired off notes of complaint to Paris and Berlin. 'I got a diplomatic answer from the Elysée Palace,' said Franco Frattini. He mockingly recited the letter: 'The French president never intended to insult . . .' with his voice trailing off in disbelief. Berlusconi claimed to have received an apology from the German Chancellor. 'Mrs Merkel came to me to offer her apologies and to assure me that it was not her intention to insult our country,' he said. It was not long after that the Chancellor's spokesman tweeted: 'No apology because there was nothing to apologise for.' The spat was over but it was clear to Italy and the rest of Europe that its two most powerful leaders had no faith in Berlusconi.

A few days later, the Italian prime minister was in Brussels brandishing a fifteen-page letter outlining his reforms. The letter was surprisingly detailed and ambitious. The Italian government would adopt legislation to balance the budget. State assets would be sold. Hundreds of tax breaks would be abolished. The number of MPs would be reduced. The retirement age would be raised. Some European officials were impressed, but doubted Berlusconi's assurances that he could get the reforms adopted. 'Many leaders asked the prime minister directly,' said Frattini, ' "Do you have a majority which is strong enough for a full implementation?" At a certain moment, Silvio Berlusconi had to admit, "I do not." '

That time had not yet arrived. Berlusconi believed there was no credible alternative to his government. Calls for his resignation only encouraged him to resist. So much of his life had been involved in titanic battles; it was part of his personal narrative that, time and again when he had been counted out, he had survived. Even so, he understood that he would be finished if he could not get his proposals through the Parliament. On 1 November, he held what those present described as a 'very dramatic meeting'. His closest advisers were present and so were his coalition partners. Berlusconi asked them a simple question. 'We have,' he told them, 'to implement (these measures) in full and quickly, with a clear and strong majority. Can we succeed in that?' The head of the Northern League was doubtful. In that moment, Berlusconi realised he could not count on his allies.

As the days passed, Italy's borrowing costs edged inexorably higher. By the beginning of November 2011 they were at 6.2 per cent. Berlusconi could not understand why the ECB was not acting more robustly to hold the rates down. As the costs went up, so Italian employers and bankers vented their frustration, telling the prime minister to 'stop the haemorrhage' or 'resign'. Berlusconi's circle believed that, increasingly, their fate lay in the hands of the European Central Bank: in effect, it had the power to force him from office.

In early November there was a G20 summit in Cannes. Berlusconi knew that, once again, he would be under pressure to demonstrate he could implement reforms. Before he left for the French resort, he held an emergency Cabinet meeting and had a furious row with his finance minister, Giulio Tremonti, who was accompanying him to the summit. There had been months of bickering between the two men but now Tremonti, almost brutally, told the prime minister he was finished. 'In the eyes of both Europe and the markets, like it or not, the problem is you,' he told Berlusconi.

Even before he arrived in Cannes, Berlusconi learnt that two more MPs had defected from his side. He was a prime minister without a majority. On the surface he was the old Berlusconi, brimming with *braggadocio*. 'The restaurants (in Italy) are full,' he said. 'The planes are fully booked and the hotel resorts are fully booked as well.' But for all his confidence, he could not miss the signs that he was being frozen out and cold shouldered. Obama was 'not kind as usual', he told a friend: the American president would not speak to him for more than a few minutes. Berlusconi felt brushed aside. The world's most powerful leaders were shunning him. 'When he came back,' said Frattini, 'he was very sad. The atmosphere in France, he said, was "Not so friendly."'

The leaders in Cannes no longer accepted Berlusconi's word. France and Germany suggested that the International Monetary Fund become involved and 'exercise some control' over Italy's finances. Everyone sitting around the table knew that the involvement of the IMF would be a humiliation for Berlusconi. 'We knew,' said François Baroin, the French finance minister, 'that if he accepted – and he had no choice – that it would be the beginning of his political death . . . Slowly, he was being pushed into a corner.' Baroin denied that Merkel and Sarkozy had discussed the removal of Berlusconi but, he said, 'The conclusion was that as long as Berlusconi headed the Italian government, Italy was an easy target for the markets.' Another senior French official said, 'We put the Italians under pressure, not because we wanted a change of government in Italy but for the fact that they would not move.' However, he conceded that 'at the end of the meeting, it was clear there was no confidence at all between the Italian prime minister, the Chancellor and the president'.

Whilst Berlusconi was away, it had been reported that twice he had had to be woken up during meetings. One very senior French official said, 'He appeared very old, very tired, sleeping at some moments.' Some of these stories appeared in Italian papers, and Berlusconi saw this as part of the campaign to oust him. He suspected that the stories came from one of his own officials, but there were others only too happy to circulate these accounts.

On his return to Rome, it was confirmed to him that he had lost his majority. 'You can survive,' said one former ally, 'but you can't govern.' On the markets the borrowing costs were edging up towards 7 per cent, a level that was unsustainable. The ECB, he suspected, was allowing the costs to rise to increase the pressure on him. The relationship with his finance minister had broken down. Officials in Brussels were twisting the knife. Financial stability in Italy was 'very worrying', declared the economics commissioner, Olli Rehn.

On Tuesday 8 November, Berlusconi faced a crucial vote on the public finances. If he lost it he would be forced to resign. In a city built on blood and power, the people sensed the Berlusconi era was drawing to a close. Demonstrators arrived outside the Parliament, in Piazza di Monte Citorio, carrying bowls of fruit, symbolising the end of a long dinner party. The prime minister was caught between defiance and capitulation. He went on Facebook to deny he had already resigned. 'I want to look in the face those who are trying to betray me,' he said. On a piece a paper he had written '*i traditori*', 'the traitors', with the figure eight alongside: the number of his MPs who had turned against him. He lost the vote and went to see the Italian president. Later that day, he said he would resign once the legislation, demanded by Europe's leaders, had been passed. 'Paradoxically,' said Frattini, 'he felt liberated from the heavy weight of going ahead without having a solid majority.' Berlusconi told him, 'I feel like a person who says I did what I should have done . . . I am putting my country first.'

The announcement did not appease the markets; Italy's borrowing costs actually went up. Investors feared that the Italian leader might still engineer a way of clinging to power. Four days later, the Chamber of Deputies approved the package of economic reforms. Berlusconi was given a standing ovation by MPs from his own party. They chanted, 'Silvio! Silvio!' Outside Parliament, thousands of people had gathered. They had come to savour the moment of downfall, to relish the spectacle of humiliation, of the leader brought down. They jeered and shouted, 'Thief, go home.'

Berlusconi went briefly to his official residence, Palazzo Grazioli, where Bacchanalian nights had opened with him singing Neapolitan love songs. His resignation, he said, was a declaration of love for Italy. Even so, he could not disguise his bitterness. He recalled a letter that Mussolini had written to his mistress, Clara Petacci, in which he said, 'Don't you understand? I don't count for anything any more.' Berlusconi said, 'I have felt in the same situation.' He then drove to the Presidential Palace on the Quirinal Hill to hand in his resignation to President Napolitano. About 5,000 people gathered in the cobbled square outside. It was a festival of celebration. Some musicians played the 'Hallelujah' chorus, while others drank from the necks of champagne bottles. Others threw coins in the air, as had been done at the fall of a previous leader. They had come to mock, to scorn, to wound; to hurl words like 'thief' and 'buffoon' and '*mafioso*' at his car. Some women derisively threw their underwear towards him. They wanted to ensure he left without grace.

Berlusconi had to depart the Quirinal Palace by a side entrance. His friends say that in that moment, 'he felt very alone'. One of them said, 'He still believed the majority of the population was with him.' Outside the palace he was surrounded. This was the Roman mob, bent on his final humiliation.

When he returned to his palazzo he reassured himself. The crowd were 'leftists', he said. 'They have always been against me. They should be thinking of me,' he said bitterly. 'He was furious,' said Franco Frattini. 'He was thinking that, in a moment when I leave . . . only for creating a larger majority to implement what I signed . . . in that moment you say something against me so I am furious.' The Italian leader explained away his betrayal by saying 'it happened to Jesus'.

In his final years, Silvio Berlusconi had come to resemble a Roman emperor. He left office under a hail of coins with the strains of Handel's *Messiah* ringing in his ears. He did not stand for a political idea. His message was the narrative of his own life and his wealth. Some were drawn to his self-made story; some admired him as a rule-breaker; some envied him his women and his parties. He offered the dream that others, too, could make a similar journey from a cruise ship crooner to one of Italy's richest men. The philosopher Paolo Flores d'Arcais wrote that 'he legitimised and made normal a kind of behaviour, a style of illegality, that in other countries would not even be tolerated in small doses.' With his TV empire he had shaped Italy, its culture, its TV shows and its attitude towards women. Over time he had become mired in sex scandals, surrounded by plots and, in his view, hostile magistrates. In the end, it had not been his relationship with Ruby the heart-stealer that had sealed his fate, but the economy and fear. The knives were drawn against him not because he had shamed Italy but because he was leading the country to the point where it would need an international rescue.

Angela Merkel was at a reception in Berlin when she learnt of Berlusconi's departure. She did not comment but sent the Italian prime minister a formal letter. There was no message from Sarkozy, and that deepened Berlusconi's dislike of the French leader. When, the following year, Sarkozy was himself defeated, Berlusconi deliberately snubbed him by not sending a note. Sarkozy, he later said, lost power through arrogance.

Berlusconi was convinced he had been toppled. He later directly accused Merkel and Sarkozy of 'trying to assassinate my international political credibility'. Even some of those who despised Berlusconi were uneasy at the manner of his departure. They believed that an elected prime minister had been removed with the help of the leaders of France and Germany and the European Central Bank. One of Berlusconi's friends said that, 'Sarkozy and Merkel were the new masters of Europe. The ECB could break governments.' *The Times* of London said the price of membership of the euro was 'having your finances, and your future, decided by people you have not chosen'.

Berlusconi's successor had been groomed for high office even before his resignation. Mario Monti, a former EU commissioner, had been made a Senator for Life and the president swiftly invited him to form a government of academics and unelected bankers. The rule of the technocrats had begun. The Germans were delighted: Monti was a man in their mould. 'I have always been considered to be the most German among Italian economists,' he said, 'which I always received as a compliment, but which was rarely meant to be a compliment.'

President Putin, an old friend of Berlusconi, said, 'He was the last of the Mohicans' – a leader whose flamboyance and decadence could no longer be tolerated in the midst of crisis.

Europe was fighting to save its currency and, in its determination to protect its dream, was prepared to compromise democracy.

Chapter 12
The 'Madman' from Athens

Greece commemorates a moment in time when the country said 'no'. It is called '*Ohi*' or 'No' day – it remembers 1940 when the Italian dictator Benito Mussolini issued an ultimatum to surrender. Athens refused and reaped a whirlwind of occupation and famine. It is one of history's dates cherished by the Greek people, who resisted at great cost. The day of the stubborn 'No' is marked by an annual military parade attended by the president of the Republic.

On 28 October 2011, the president and senior military officers mounted a stand in the northern city of Thessaloniki. The large crowd was restive. Some raised banners and chanted 'Thieves' and 'Traitors'. Others declared that Greece had become a German colony and held high placards that mimicked the Nazi slogan, '*Ein Volk, Ein Reich, Ein Fuhrer*' – in place of '*Ein Fuhrer*' they had written '*Ein Euro*'. German and EU flags were burned. There were 'Wanted' posters carrying the faces of the prime minister and his finance minister.

As soldiers, right arms swinging high, marched behind the Greek flag, there was applause but also jeers and catcalls. Protestors invaded the parade, forcing the soldiers to side-step them. Even the flag bearer was jostled. Arguments broke out and punches were thrown. The parade route was blocked with hundreds of people.

When President Karolos Papoulias began to speak he was interrupted with boos. It had never happened before. On that day something snapped. It was as if the crowd had grown weary of respect and vented their frustration on the symbols of the state. On the president's face was incomprehension; he could not understand what was happening and tried to continue. Behind him were grim-faced officers with their swords and medals. The head of the air force, standing to the left of the president, had his mouth clenched shut in silent fury. The president felt insulted and abandoned his speech. As he was leaving the stage, he picked out the word 'traitor' among the cries of the crowd. It stung him and he paused. As a fifteen-year-old boy he had fought the Germans. 'So who is a traitor?' he demanded to know. 'They should be ashamed,' he said. 'I came here to honour this city,' he continued. 'There are some who want to prevent the celebrations. I am very sorry,' and he stalked away. Later some retired officers were spat at.

The government in Athens was fearful of this new mood that so casually trampled on respect and memory. Two days earlier, on Greek Independence Day, the defence minister had been heckled. 'It was beyond normal,' said George Papandreou, the prime minister, to disrupt a national day and shout down the president. He heard other disturbing reports. 'During the parade,' he said, 'some of the military personnel made some kind of action.' The prime minister would not elaborate but, four days later, on 1 November, the military high command was dismissed. The government insisted the changes were long planned but the move was never fully explained. It was not forgotten that the rule of the Colonels had only ended in 1974. The prime minister feared that the country was splintering and turning against itself.

A week earlier, Europe's leaders had celebrated what they regarded as a successful summit. At four in the morning, the French finance minister had emerged to declare, 'The euro has been saved.' The German Chancellor Angela Merkel was less effusive but said, 'We have done what needed to be done.' Greece once again had dominated the meeting in Brussels. The details of the second bail-out, so long discussed, had finally been approved and private investors had agreed to take much greater losses than in July. This time they accepted a hair-cut of 50 per cent on their investments. It meant that Greece's debts would be significantly reduced, by around 100 billion euros. Afterwards, Papandreou declared, 'We have escaped the trap of default.' He believed that the Greek debt crisis was now sustainable. There had been a 'bare-knuckle' meeting with the bankers who were holding out; Merkel and Sarkozy had taken them into a small meeting room in Brussels and faced them down. 'This is the last offer,' Sarkozy told them. 'Take 50 per cent or risk getting back nothing if Greece defaults.' The deal, which the French president described as 'ambitious', exceeded expectations.

It was not seen that way in Greece. The debt write-down, said Papandreou, was 'historical. It hadn't been done anywhere else in the world.' However, 'When I came back,' he said, 'I was considered a traitor.' The people were not impressed that bankers had been persuaded to accept steep losses. Their focus was on what Greece had offered in return: a reduction in wages and a further culling of public sector jobs. Property owners would have to pay a solidarity tax. One austerity measure followed another with no end in sight, or that was how it appeared. Years of hardship stretched out ahead. When EU officials were despatched to Athens to help administer the reforms, a local paper printed their photos with the caption: 'The prison guards have arrived.' The Greek banks, in particular, were angry with the deal in Brussels. They, too, would have to endure losses and some of them would only survive by being nationalised. They turned to their friends in the media and helped shift opinion against this second rescue.

The unions were vowing to paralyse and break the government. They called on members to occupy government buildings. It was chaotic. In the finance ministry, normal business was disrupted. TV teams would walk the corridors filming the arguments between the staff and their managers. For a time, important meetings about the nation's finances had to be held elsewhere, in secret. The finance minister, Evangelos Venizelos, said, 'the image created over the last few weeks is one of lawlessness . . . but there is a limit. The state must continue to function.' The crowds were defiant. Almost every night they gathered in Syntagma Square. 'Burn, burn, burn down the bordello Parliament,' they cried. The head of the Greek national bank said, 'There is no doubt we are living in wartime conditions.'

Some believed that the Greeks were being asked to make sacrifices as harsh as those demanded of the Germans after World War One. The Versailles Treaty of 1919 had punished Germany through reparations, and the terms had been onerous. Greece was paying a similar amount of its income to pay off its loans as the Germans were in the twenties. The former British Chancellor of the Exchequer, Alistair Darling, said to impose on a country 'something that would have been worthy of the Treaty of Versailles is absolutely ludicrous. It just isn't going to work.'

Papandreou realised he needed national consensus. The bail-out agreement would not work in the face of determined resistance. He had approached the leader of the opposition, Antonis Samaras, and offered to share power with him but was rebuffed. 'I had a wide front of opposition,' said the prime minister. 'I did not have the possibility of coalition government but I did have the possibility of a referendum.'

It had been an idea he had been toying with since June. The protesters, he believed, had to be denied their moral authority. The will of the majority of the Greek people had to be established. That is what Papandreou thought. So he crafted legislation for a nationwide referendum. It took months of negotiation. The MPs had to work out what percentage of votes would make it valid, how the poll would be funded, how long the debate would be. By September, Papandreou had his new law.

On the evening of 31 October 2011, he surprised MPs by telling Parliament that the second bail-out deal with its new austerity measures would be put to the people in a referendum. 'The command of the people will bind us,' he said. 'If the Greek people do not want it, it will not be adopted.' The prime minister believed he would win. The polls suggested that a majority of Greeks wanted to stay inside the euro. He calculated it would wrong-foot the opposition, for if they voted 'no' they would be putting at risk Greece's place in the euro-zone.

The news of the referendum took time to reach Europe's leaders. Papandreou's comments were leaked from the Parliament. It left Europe's leaders frantically phoning the Greek government to confirm the rumours. Europe was stunned. In one move, the agreements hammered out in a long Brussels night the previous week had been cast into limbo. Xavier Musca, the chief of staff at the Elysée Palace said, 'Sarkozy and Merkel had negotiated directly with the bankers to reduce the Greek debt and Papandreou had thanked them very warmly for all their efforts. A few days later, they learnt via the radio that Papandreou was going for a referendum . . . they felt completely betrayed and at that moment it destroyed their confidence.' They realised that the Greek leader was not in a position to deliver the commitments he had made. Now what lay ahead was dangerous delay and uncertainty.

The following day the German Chancellor cancelled her appointments. Her office made abrupt calls informing those with meetings at the Chancellery that they had been called off. Papandreou said the reaction was quite explosive. 'It surprised me,' he said, but on reflection he understood. 'They (Europe's leaders) had seen the summit as a great success and all of a sudden I call a referendum.' He phoned Europe's leaders and tried to explain but he encountered hostility. One asked him whether he was trying to bargain for a better deal. Another leader demanded to know whether he was deliberately trying to put the Brussels agreement in jeopardy. Papandreou replied, 'This is the best way not to put it in jeopardy,' but it was a thankless task. 'They didn't have a picture of what was going on in Greece,' he said. Even persuading his Cabinet was difficult. His finance minister, Evangelos Venizelos, later said the decision had been taken 'without my knowledge and without my personal involvement and agreement as finance minister'. It took seven hours to get Cabinet support for holding a poll. Venizelos, at the time, was at a medical clinic.

The referendum should not have come as a complete surprise. In September, Papandreou had spoken to Merkel about it in Berlin. She had not been against the idea but said it should be done after the rescue programme had been agreed. According to Papandreou, she revealed she might also hold a referendum herself if the crisis required changes to the German Constitution.

Key officials in Brussels also knew that a referendum was being considered. 'I had been on a flight to Cannes,' said Xavier Musca, President Sarkozy's chief of staff. 'I opened my mobile and saw five missed calls. People were telling me it was a catastrophe and the markets were completely in trouble so I called Nicolas Sarkozy and told him.' The president was enraged. 'The announcement,' he said, 'took the whole of Europe by surprise.' Papandreou's tone offended him. The Greek prime minister believed he had seized the democratic high ground. He had told his Parliament, 'We will not implement any programme by force, but only with the consent of the Greek people. This is our democratic tradition and we demand that it is also respected abroad.' Sarkozy did not accept that. There was, in his view, a higher calling beyond the will of the Greek people. 'Giving people a voice,' he retorted, 'is always legitimate, but the solidarity of all euro-zone countries is not possible unless each one agrees to measures deemed necessary.' One Greek official said that defending the euro clearly trumped democracy.

President Sarkozy had another reason to be angry. He was about to host the G20 summit in Cannes on the French Riviera; the same meeting where Berlusconi had been cornered. All the world's most important leaders would be there. This would be a show-case for Sarkozy, reminding the French people that he was a statesman with powerful connections. It was the kind of occasion he excelled at and it was intended to be a curtain raiser for his election campaign. Now it was overshadowed by the Greeks. Papandreou, who had not been due to attend the G20 meeting, was summoned to Cannes.

Sarkozy met most of the leaders in person. For the Chinese president he was prepared to stand on his own for several minutes so as to ensure he was waiting when the Chinese cavalcade drew up. There was no one to meet Papandreou. The snub was deliberate. 'Sarkozy was livid,' said Papandreou. 'I had spoiled his party in Cannes but that was not my problem.' A dinner was hastily arranged and the Greek prime minister faced Europe's most powerful officials and leaders. They were determined to shape the question that the Greek people would be asked. Sarkozy and Merkel said the vote should be on membership of the euro. Angela Merkel said the question should be, 'Do you want to be in the euro or not?'

The French prime minister, François Fillon, was among those with blunt advice to Papandreou. 'The Greeks,' he said, 'must decide fast whether to stay in the euro-zone or not.' Papandreou had envisaged a question on the austerity package so recently agreed in Brussels. Over a two-hour meeting, 'All the Europeans told the Greeks, "We can't accept that,"' said Musca. It was the German nightmare where Greece took the money but argued over the reforms. 'This was not acceptable to the Germans,' said Musca. 'Here was a member state not accepting the discipline of the euro-zone. Sarkozy said, "We can't play it this way."'

Papandreou tried to argue, to justify himself, but finally agreed that the poll would not just be on austerity but on membership of the euro. The other leaders told him that the vote should be held no later than mid-December.

Even during the evening, some doubted Papandreou's will to go ahead. The Spanish finance minister, Elena Salgado, turned to the German finance minister Wolfgang Schäuble and suggested a bet. On a bottle of wine, she wagered that Papandreou would never hold a referendum.

Afterwards, and publically, Sarkozy raised the possibility of Greece leaving the euro. It had been hinted at before but never had it been so openly raised as an option. 'It is up to the Greeks to decide whether they want to continue down the road with us,' said the French president. 'The real question is whether Greece remains within Europe or not,' he continued. 'We will never let the euro be destroyed, nor will we allow Europe to be destroyed or torn apart.' The message was intended for the Greek people. Their membership hung in the balance. Sarkozy had calculated that the Greeks believed that they would never be excluded. He wanted to raise that as a distinct possibility. 'Papandreou understood,' said the French finance minister, François Baroin. 'It was about staying or going. He had to ask the stay or go question. Merkel and Sarkozy's position was identical. They were ready to say to Greece take it or leave it.' Baroin said the room was full of poker faces.

Papandreou realised that the stakes had been raised. 'The way Sarkozy handled it,' he said, 'undermined me in Greece. He came out with a very sour face.' The French leader did not want to disguise his anger or his contempt. Papandreou thought that he had the support of Angela Merkel but, in the end, that did not matter. This was Sarkozy's parade and in the press conferences he took the lead and set the tone. Sarkozy's true feelings were only revealed later. A microphone picked up a three-minute conversation with President Obama. Sarkozy referred to Papandreou as a 'madman'. His acts were those of a depressed man, he said. It was not worth laying into a man who was already down. 'He's already on his knees,' he said, 'knocked out'.

Papandreou tried to find a recording of the remarks but could never track them down. Even so, he replied to the

French leader that it is, 'Greece that is depressed and in Greece, being a little bit crazy is what people feel.' Sarkozy's intervention left a scar and not just in Greece. The idea of a poll had been derided if it stood in the way of defending the single currency.

On the way back to Athens, Papandreou was exhausted and fell asleep. The man next to him was his finance minister, a rival and a political bruiser. Evangelos Venizelos was not afraid to take on his opponents. He had recently thundered during a Parliamentary debate, 'We are in a state of war.' Now, with Papandreou resting beside him, he took out a piece of paper and crafted a statement. On arrival in Athens, at four in the morning, he issued a press release without telling his prime minister. 'Greece's position within the euro is a historic conquest,' the statement read, 'it cannot be put in doubt.'

Venizelos had picked up on the Sarkozy threat and denounced the referendum. 'My duty,' he said, 'was to protect the credibility and equilibrium of the banking sector before the opening of the markets.' The statement fatally damaged and undermined the prime minister, who arrived home to a full-blown political crisis. Four other ministers immediately said that they, too, opposed holding a vote.

Papandreou was a mild-mannered politician but a wily operator. If he backed down he knew he would have to resign immediately. His authority would have gone. The leader of the opposition, Antonis Samaras, gave him a way to exit gracefully. He said that the opposition was now ready to join a coalition government. The bail-out deal signed in Brussels, he said, had to be safeguarded. There was a condition, however. Papandreou would have to stand down. It enabled the prime minister to say that he had the consensus that he had been seeking and that a referendum was now not necessary. Within days he had resigned and was replaced by a technocrat, an unelected banker, Lucas Papademos.

Papandreou was seen as the leader who had put at risk Greece's place in Europe: President Sarkozy had made sure of that. The Greek people wanted to remain European. They did not trust themselves. What they opposed was the slow strangulation of their country in the name of defending the single currency. They wanted to be heard, but they did not want to return to the drachma. As in Italy and Spain, Europe and its institutions were seen as having saved the country from itself and the demons of its past.

Papandreou accepted his defeat as part of the vicissitudes of politics. He was a leader who could easily let go the reins of power. He remained convinced he had been right. Greece needed a referendum. Indeed, he believes that in 2013 it might still be necessary, although he concedes that over time it becomes more difficult to win. What the politicians needed in order to implement the reforms and the austerity measures was the clear backing of the people. The prime minister had noticed the 'sense of disempowerment' in the country. Decisions were seen as being imposed from outside: the reforms were not owned by the Greek people; they were decided elsewhere. It seeped into the nation's consciousness that they were being punished. That, in Papandreou's view, was dangerous for any country and allowed extremist, even neo-Nazi, parties to gain a foothold in Parliament. If a vote had been held, he said, 'We wouldn't have had the extremes.' No party would have been able to claim it was the champion of the Greek people.

In a matter of weeks the long knives had flashed and Berlusconi and Papandreou had fallen. The rule of the technocrats had begun. In the place of elected leaders were an economics professor and a banker nourished by the world of Europe and its institutions. In parts of Europe, democracy was being discarded like unwanted clothing. It had not passed unnoticed that a democratically elected leader had been denounced as a 'madman' for offering to consult his people. The French professor of economics, Jean-Paul Fitoussi, said that what was at issue was democracy itself. 'In Greece and even in Italy, you cannot expect to rule without the support and consent of the people,' he said. 'You can't impose an austerity programme for a decade on a country, and even chose for them the austerity measures that countries must implement.' Decisions that affected people's lives were being taken during walks on the beach, at informal summits, in phone calls. 'The European ruling classes,' said one observer, 'once had their power checked through daily contact with the tumble of national politics.' Not any longer. It was hard to know who was accountable for the decisions that were reshaping Europe.

Europe's leaders mounted a fierce defence. They believed they were fighting not just to save a currency but the European project. The threat was existential. The great dream of uniting the continent was in jeopardy. It rankled that some portrayed the European Union as a victim of its own hubris.

For the first time since its creation, the European élite had to listen to predictions that the euro-zone would break up or collapse. The high priests of the project rounded on their critics. The president of the European Council, Herman Van Rompuy, said, 'We have together to fight the danger of a new Euro-scepticism.' For him, these critics risked taking Europe back to the barbarities of the past. 'The biggest enemy of Europe today is fear,' he said. 'Fear leads to egoism, egoism leads to nationalism, and nationalism leads to war.' President Sarkozy, too, summoned up the spectre of a return to the past.

'Those who destroy the euro,' he said, 'will take responsibility for the resurgence of conflict on our continent.' The critics of the euro, of its design, of its ambition, were condemned as threatening the peace.

None of this could disguise the fact that in attempting to save the currency, 'the consent of the governed' was in danger of going missing. It had been the definition of democracy in the American Declaration of Independence in 1776 that 'governments are instituted among men, deriving their just powers from the consent of the governed'. The opposite was true in Europe. Leaders had ceded control over tax and spending to unelected officials in Brussels who would get first sight of national budgets.

At the heart of the European project lay a suspicion of the people. The European Union had been built by stealth, often without the support of the voters. 'Don't ask me too much about the ultimate goal,' says President Van Rompuy. 'We are more used to working in a gradual way.' Countries were committed to 'ever-closer union'. Few were willing to define that as a United States of Europe. The problem with the step by step approach was that Europe was changing, without the explicit consent of the people.

Those who criticised the project were dismissed as 'populists'. It became the easy Brussels put-down, the way of curtailing an argument. Even when a reporter challenged the perks of the commissioners, his question was dismissed as 'populist'. When politicians in Britain argued for a reform of the EU treaties, the deputy prime minister, Nick Clegg, declared that only 'populists, chauvinists and demagogues' would benefit from such an exercise. Samuel Brittan, writing in the *Financial Times*, said that 'words such as unthinkable, unmentionable and un-discussable are hurled at anyone who dares question EU orthodoxy'. At a time of deep-seated fear, little tolerance was shown the dissenter.

By the end of November 2011, the unreliable Berlusconi had gone, along with the unpredictable Papandreou. Yet Europe was still divided. Angela Merkel and Nicolas Sarkozy had improved their personal relationship but they still disagreed. President Sarkozy had lost patience with Merkel's incremental approach. In particular, he believed that the markets would only relent when they knew what stood behind Italy and Spain. The question was left hanging. The French president wanted to increase the fire-power of the bail-out fund by turning it into a bank, allowing it to access funding from the ECB. Angela Merkel said no. She felt it would encourage countries to back away from reforms, knowing the bail-out fund could always tap the bank. It was exactly the kind of loose arrangement that made the German Chancellor uneasy. The only answer, she believed, was for weak countries to embrace bold reforms that fundamentally restructured their economies. It was 'not possible' in her view, 'to erase the mistakes of the past in just one stroke.'

The answer provoked Sarkozy. He warned that Europe faced disaster if Merkel continued blocking plans to increase the role of the ECB and the bail-out fund. 'Europe,' he warned, 'had a rendezvous with history.' The argument continued to threaten their relationship. Later they would call a truce and they agreed not to argue any more in public about the roll of the European Central Bank.

The disagreement between Europe's two most powerful leaders over-shadowed the farewell of the president of the European Central Bank, Jean-Claude Trichet. It was held in Frankfurt at an ornate concert hall called the Alte Oper. It was a glittering turnout of Europe's leaders and the Brussels élite.

There was a film celebrating Trichet's eight years in office set
to the strains of Beethoven's Ninth. The farewell evolved into
a crisis meeting. The markets were on edge, sensing that the
leaders could not agree how to defend the currency. President
Sarkozy flew in from Paris, even though his wife, Carla Bruni,
was in a Paris maternity clinic awaiting the birth of their
daughter. The president was willing to miss the birth in order
to talk to Merkel.

The French president was impatient as he wanted a decision on his plans for beefing up the bail-out fund. Merkel
complained that the document was not even in German. She
tried to turn Sarkozy's attention back to his wife. 'She was
saying, "Phone Carla",' said one of Sarkozy's friends. '"You
take care of your baby instead of discussing this with me." She
was saying that every ten minutes. She was fierce one moment
and warm the next. "Phone! Phone! Take care of your family.
The euro can wait!"'

Sarkozy was persistent. He accused Merkel of delay and of
endangering the euro. Even though he was bowing out, Trichet
was drawn into the argument. The French leader insisted that
the European Central Bank needed to do more. He wanted it
to act like the Federal Reserve in the United States and be the
lender of last resort. 'It was more than heated between the
three of us,' said Trichet, 'but I refused to put the Central
Bank alone on the front line when Sarkozy was pushing. I said
it was up to governments to demonstrate their real will and to
implement what had been decided earlier.'

Merkel would not be stampeded into action, either. She
reminded Sarkozy that, 'We live in democracies and have to
operate according to the fundamental rules.' The argument
flowed back and forth with the German Chancellor repeatedly saying, 'Go and see your wife.' Eventually Sarkozy strode

out of the room, the door slamming. He asked his finance minister to finish the talks. French officials insist it never got personal, but it was a major argument.

Merkel was torn between competing obligations. She wanted to protect the German tax-payers from unlimited liabilities, whilst defending the currency. At the concert hall in Frankfurt, the former German Chancellor, Helmut Schmidt, was pushed onto the stage in a wheelchair and said that 'anyone who considers his own nation more important than common Europe damages the fundamental interests of his country'. Some saw it as a veiled criticism of Merkel and her caution. 'Of course,' said Schmidt, 'the strong should help the weak.' For Merkel, with her fine political instincts, it was not that easy.

It was what irritated the French. They put great store by solidarity. It was, for them, the core value underpinning the union. They were not certain Merkel saw it that way. One French minister said, 'This is the first time Europe has faced a crisis as serious as this because it is a crisis that puts in doubt European solidarity.'

Papandreou's sudden call for a referendum had left a deep impression on Angela Merkel. She realised that any leader could throw the euro-zone into crisis. The currency was vulnerable to a political squall or the actions of a national politician fighting for survival. That could not continue. Leaders had to be bound to their commitments. The euro-zone would not survive if it kept breaking its rules. There needed to be new structures that all but excluded the rash move or the temptation to overspend. Words were not enough. The rest of the world needed that reassurance. The Chancellor believed that 'Europe's plight' was now so 'unpleasant' that fundamental reforms were needed. That would 'mean more Europe, not less', with countries giving up more of their sovereignty.

On 15 November there was a dinner at the German ambassador's house in Brussels. Angela Merkel's closest adviser on Europe, Nikolaus Meyer-Landrut, was among the guests. What he had to say shocked them. The Chancellor, he told those present, had decided to push for a pact to instil discipline over national budgets and she wanted that enshrined in a new treaty. This was anathema to Europe's officials and they began sending urgent messages on their phones. Treaty change was a long, uncertain process that, in some countries, would trigger referenda with an uncertain result. In 2005 French voters had rejected the advice of its political élite and had used a referendum to reject a European constitution.

Merkel knew that for some people treaty change was taboo but she wanted governments held to their word. When she was negotiating the second bail-out with the Greeks, she had insisted that not only the prime minister sign the agreement but also other party leaders. She was most insistent: otherwise, no more money would be paid out. It led the leader of the opposition to remark, 'There is such a thing as national dignity.' Merkel wanted to ensure that the euro-zone would face no further shocks in the future. That in itself, she believed, would calm the markets.

Merkel and Sarkozy patched up their differences. The French leader was not prepared to have a lasting row with the German Chancellor. Merkel believed it would 'take years to find a lasting solution' to the crisis. She saw changing the treaties as a way of avoiding splits in Europe.

The opposite was to happen. It opened up new divisions and condemned Europe to being a union with an inner and outer core.

Chapter 13
The British Outsiders

In the black and white photo are three men sitting at a table. The meal is over, the carafe of red wine almost finished. The man in the middle has a cigarette hanging loosely from the side of his mouth. He is at once recognisable. Imperious, haughty and unbending. It is General Charles de Gaulle dining at the French House pub in Dean Street, Soho. War-time London had provided a refuge for the two-star general, and a headquarters for his Free French Forces.

On 18 June 1940 Winston Churchill had agreed to de Gaulle addressing the French people via the BBC. Sitting stiffly in front of the microphone, the General said, 'The flame of the French resistance must not and will not be extinguished.' With its call to resist and not to capitulate, '*l'appel du 18 Juin*' entered French history.

In June 2010, President Sarkozy and his wife Carla Bruni had gone to London to remember Britain's support for de Gaulle. Standing beside 200 war veterans in the grounds of the Royal Hospital in Chelsea, the French president had expressed the 'eternal gratitude of the French people, who remember what Britain had accomplished for our freedom'. David Cameron replied that the event was a 'reminder that Britain and France were not just neighbours in the geographical sense but also in the emotional sense'.

The occasion seemed to mark the stirrings of a new relationship between Britain and France. Cameron effusively
described Sarkozy as 'a devoted friend of Britain' and Sarkozy
called him 'my dear David'. The two wives received much
attention. Carla Bruni had helpfully removed a fly from
Samantha Cameron's dress during the main ceremony. That
evening, the two couples dined together in Downing Street.
Photographs were issued showing a relaxed, informal evening
meal. The *entente cordiale*, so it seemed, was in good health.

Over a year later in October 2011, and in the heat of another
European summit, President Sarkozy rounded on David
Cameron. 'You've lost a good opportunity to shut up,' he said,
jabbing his finger towards the British prime minister. 'We're
sick of you criticising us and telling us what to do. You say you
hate the euro and now you want to interfere in our meetings.'

During the previous twelve months, the French had grown
increasingly irritated by the comments coming from London.
'We didn't appreciate at all,' said an Elysée Palace official,
'that repeatedly the UK was saying that the euro-zone was a
very dangerous place to be.' In particular, they resented
remarks about the health of French banks. 'When a friend has
a problem,' said the official, 'and you say it is very bad and
even worse than you expected, it is not very helpful.' The
Elysée feared that British comments about French banks
might turn market sentiment against France. In September
the French had raised the issue with London. 'We repeatedly
said to the British,' said the official, '"Do like the Americans."
They shared the same views as the British but they did not air
them publically.'

The relationship between Sarkozy and Cameron, however,
was strong. 'Sarkozy on a personal basis loves Cameron,' said
a friend of the president. 'He always found him a little

childish. He considers him as a young guy beginning in the business but it was a very good relationship.' The prime minister never forgot that the president provided him with a helicopter so he could be at the bedside of his dying father on the French Riviera.

The two leaders had become close allies during the bombing campaign in Libya although Cameron found Sarkozy, at times, unpredictable. When, in March, it had been decided at a meeting at the Elysée Palace to launch the military operation, the prime minister was more than a little surprised to be told by the French president that his planes were already over Benghazi. One adviser to the president said that, 'Sarkozy felt he could rebuke Cameron because of the Libyan war.' He knew their bond would survive a public row over the euro-zone.

Outwardly, Cameron was unruffled by the French president's outburst. Sarkozy's flare-ups, his *coups de théâtre*, were a feature of European meetings, but the euro-zone crisis, so stubbornly resistant to solution, was straining relationships.

When the euro was launched, the British were the doubters. From the sidelines they had questioned its design. They did not believe that one size, one interest rate, would suit such different economies. When, eventually, the currency's flaws were exposed, the government in London resisted the temptation of *schadenfreude*. Britain was not immune from the crisis. David Cameron said it was having a 'chilling effect' on the UK economy. His own political survival, in part, came to depend on the euro-zone returning to health. The British, like the Americans, were infuriated by what they saw as indecision and delay and half-measures. Cameron became more strident in his pleadings. He told Europe's leaders 'to get a grip', to get out the 'big bazooka'. If anything, the statements from London irritated Angela Merkel more than Nicolas Sarkozy, but she was happy for the French president to stage his row with the British.

One of the ironies of the crisis is that it turned British ministers into champions of further European integration. The Chancellor of the Exchequer, George Osborne, said the 'remorseless logic' of monetary union was to co-ordinate taxes and spending in a fiscal union. The British were in the curious position of opposing Brussels gaining further powers whilst telling other Europeans they needed a closer union if that is what it took to restore confidence in the currency. The party that had once fought to save the pound was now campaigning to save the euro. The ailing British economy needed Europe to succeed.

It was not just President Sarkozy who bridled at British advice. Others resented the cacophony of complaint. They recalled that Britain had refused to contribute to the bailout fund. It had been deaf to the pleas for solidarity. Now, when the European project was in jeopardy, they did not want a British lecture. In November 2011, at the Lord Mayor's banquet, Cameron spoke of 'we sceptics' being right to question 'grand plans and utopian visions'. In Paris and Berlin, they did not like being told they had dreamed dangerously.

In December, another summit loomed – each was billed as more critical than the last. This was one of two moments when the European Council's President Van Rompuy 'felt very uneasy' about the crisis. The French finance minister, François Baroin, said that, 'Sarkozy was convinced it was a last-chance summit to save the situation and so did I.' The markets still did not believe there was a plan to support countries like Spain and Italy.

With each meeting the rhetoric and the pleadings became more strident. The Polish foreign minister warned that any break-up of the euro-zone would be apocalyptic. The French foreign minister Alain Juppé said it was an 'existential crisis for Europe' and warned that failure would threaten the peace. The president of the European Commission, José Manuel Barroso, said: 'The entire world is watching. We must do everything to save the euro.'

Privately, some of Europe's leaders believed the euro-zone was in danger of breaking up. Their comments, made out of desperation, were aimed at goading their colleagues into action. It was, at times, like watching a team low on morale before a big game pumping itself up in the vague hope it might break a bad run and put in a winning performance.

Angela Merkel and Nicolas Sarkozy agreed that the flaws in the euro-zone were systemic. The French leader spoke of rebuilding the European Union. The German Chancellor had her own radical plan to restore confidence in the euro. She wanted much greater discipline over national budgets. Over-spending and debt were supposed to have been controlled by the Stability and Growth Pact which had been created in 1997 setting limits for deficits and debt. The rules, however, had been broken more than sixty times. Germany had been among the countries that flouted the regulations. What Merkel now sought was for governments to be bound by their commitments. She wanted countries to introduce a 'debt brake' into their constitutions, binding them to reduce borrowing and balance their budgets. The hands of future administrations would be tied: if countries failed to implement the new rules properly, they would face sanctions. Privately, President Sarkozy was uncertain what difference this would make to the current crisis but he was persuaded to back the German plan.

'What we want,' he said, 'is to tell the world that in Europe . . . we pay back our debts and reduce our deficits.' The French hoped that by agreeing to greater discipline over budgets it would encourage the European Central Bank to intervene more aggressively in support of countries like Italy and Spain.

Merkel wanted these changes to be written into a new treaty. Only that way, she calculated, would the markets believe Europe was serious about never again allowing a repeat of the debt crisis. It was, for her, about restoring trust in Europe. A new treaty would require the signatures of all twenty-seven members of the European Union, including Britain.

As much as London was supportive of moves to calm the crisis it was nervous about treaty change; David Cameron knew that it would stir his own backbench MPs to demand something in return. It also put Britain in a bind. The more closely the euro-zone integrated, the greater was the risk that the group would take decisions that might threaten key British interests.

In November, Cameron had gone to see the German Chancellor in Berlin. Two days before his visit, one of Angela Merkel's closest allies had, almost casually, re-ignited old fears about German power. Volker Kauder, who led Merkel's parliamentary group, spoke of how the rest of Europe was falling into line behind the German economic model. 'All of a sudden,' he said, 'Europe is speaking German.' Some British papers were quick to say that it smacked of German arrogance. It prompted some German TV stations to question the British journalists covering the Cameron visit as to whether they spoke the new language of Europe.

During this crisis, history's ghosts were never absent. Mr Kauder was sharply critical of Britain. He depicted a country looking to its own advantage and unwilling to contribute to the success of the wider project. 'That cannot be the message we accept from the British,' he said. It reflected a wider irritation. The headline in the German tabloid *Bild* was: 'Why are the English still in the EU?' The paper depicted the UK as pampered with special treatment and opt-outs.

On a personal level, Angela Merkel liked Cameron. She found him easier to talk to than almost any other European leader. She liked his old-fashioned courtesy. He had invited her to Chequers, the prime minister's country residence, and they had gone walking together in the Chiltern Hills. On most economic questions they agreed, but Europe put their relationship under strain.

At the November 2011 meeting they spoke together in English, although there were translators present. Over a lunch of roast duck, Angela Merkel explained that in order to instil discipline over the budgets of countries in the euro-zone, she needed either a new treaty or a change to the existing treaties. She could have negotiated a pact with just the seventeen countries that used the euro, but Cameron assumed that she wanted a treaty change because that would include all twenty-seven members of the EU, and would avoid dividing the Union between insiders and outsiders. 'We were absolutely clear,' said one German official, 'that we prefer it to happen by treaty change. There would be no new obligations for Britain. We also said this was of paramount importance to stabilise the monetary union.'

Treaty change needed a British signature and Cameron said that he would want something in return. He wanted to ensure that this more tightly knit group that used the euro would not be able to take decisions that threatened key British interests like the City of London. He was after specific safeguards written into any new treaty. Merkel replied that she would look at it. She did not say 'no'. Cameron asked about France and Merkel said that, 'Nicolas (Sarkozy) would agree.' Some in the British camp thought they had the Chancellor's support.

Others were not convinced. The agreement, in their view, was only to have a negotiation. Crucially, some of Cameron's advisers believed that Merkel was determined to get a deal involving the whole of the EU. If that was the case, then it increased Britain's bargaining power and it could strengthen its demands.

As the December summit approached, so did the tension. Across Europe there was a countdown of the days remaining to save the euro. Angela Merkel spoke of a 'new phase in European integration'. The expectation was that the summit would be 'challenging'. Some officials warned that it might take up to Christmas to reach a deal. David Cameron was under pressure at home to play his hand well and to return with concessions. The day before the summit, he said, 'Our colleagues in the EU need to know that we will not agree to a treaty change that fails to protect our interests . . . Our requirements will be practical and focused,' he continued, 'but euro-zone countries should not mistake this for any lack of steel.'

German officials warned of a 'violent dispute' if Britain insisted on an opt-out from the regulation of financial markets. 'Then proper regulation in Europe would no longer be possible,' said one official. Jean-Claude Juncker, who chaired the meetings of euro-zone finance ministers, said that he would not accept that when it came to financial services, 'Britain reserves rights and freedoms of actions for itself that others will not have'. The French paper *Le Monde* complained of 'Britain's eternal ambiguity' towards Europe. 'Make a choice or shut up,' it demanded.

Cameron seemed to relish the fight. On arrival in Brussels he promised 'bulldog spirit'. Angela Merkel still hoped for compromise and asked for 'understanding from those who do not have the euro'.

What the British wanted was a protocol to be attached to the treaty to protect the single market from decisions taken by those countries that used the euro. They also wanted to defend the City of London against excessive regulation. On measures that affected its financial centre, Britain wanted the EU to switch from majority voting to unanimous decision-making. Asking for a veto was a high-stakes gamble, and London chose to conceal these demands until the very last moment: it had not presented the protocol to the European Council's legal department until the day before the summit.

The Germans were the only country to be given early sight of what the British were seeking. In Berlin's view, of the four or five British demands only one of them was acceptable. 'What we could not accept,' said one of those familiar with the negotiations, 'was a deal to go back to qualified majority voting for the financial sector where lack of regulation was part of the problem.'

At 7.30 p.m. on the first day of the meeting, Cameron met with Merkel and Sarkozy in one of the French delegation's rooms. Merkel waited for Sarkozy to read the British document. He was clearly irritated that he had not been briefed. 'David,' he said, 'I've never seen this before and my answer is very clearly "No".' He thought the British demands unacceptable. Merkel sided with Sarkozy. The British had thought they might be able to play Germany off against France but when it came to defending the euro, France and Germany would not be divided. It was one of a number of miscalculations.

'The fact that Cameron didn't show the text before,' said a senior French official, 'was implicitly saying the contrary to what he was telling us. He was saying, "It's just a few changes, the text is quite innocuous, it is not big stuff, it will just make my life easier in London." Sarkozy said to him, "If that was the case, you would have shown it to me from the start. The fact that you tried to negotiate it bilaterally with the Germans and not show it to me is clearly a sign that you want to claim victory over France."'

Cameron was undeterred. He believed that Merkel was wedded to a treaty change, which would require British assent. Rather than face a British veto, he still thought he could win support from the other leaders around the table. It was not until the early hours of the morning that he was able to make his case for British safeguards. Sarkozy treated Cameron as if he were an extortionist. 'David,' he said, 'we will not pay you to save the euro.' Cameron thought that some of the other countries outside the euro might support him but almost no one did: they had not seen the British document and there had been little attempt to build alliances beforehand.

The newly elected Danish prime minister, Helle Thorning-Schmidt, said it was important to get a deal that involved all twenty-seven countries. She did not want to see a two-tier union, with an inner core that used the euro and those, like Denmark, that did not. Sarkozy turned on her. She was not only new, he told her, but her country was outside the euro. 'We don't want to hear from you,' he said dismissively.

The Italian prime minister, Mario Monti, went on the attack. Britain, he said, was wanting to turn back the clock. Decisions affecting the single market were made by majority voting. What the UK was seeking was a veto over financial regulation. That, said Monti, could end up unravelling the single market, ironically so important to the British.

Monti was a believer in the European cause and the British, in his view, were tampering with the sacred 'acquis', the body of agreements that could not be unpicked. One French official said that, 'David Cameron could have obtained some concessions but a financial services veto would have given the UK a competitive advantage and undermined the single market.'

The British had over-bid. They had misread Angela Merkel. She was committed to treaty change but not at any price. She could also achieve what she wanted by a pact between governments. In the end, every other European country signed up to an agreement between governments. Cameron could not return home empty-handed and had no alternative than to use his veto. He became the first British prime minister to veto a European treaty.

Merkel had got her binding rules, albeit without a treaty change which would have required the signature of all twenty seven member states. Afterwards, and at her most withering, she highlighted David Cameron's isolation. 'I don't really believe that David Cameron was even with us at the table,' she said. One German official said, 'It turned sour for Britain. They didn't veto anything. The core content of what we wanted to write into the treaties we obtained.' The French portrayed Cameron as an isolated leader, 'a man who goes to a wife-swapping party without a wife'.

The use of the veto enabled President Sarkozy to make a more damaging charge against Britain. 'We were not able to accept (the British demands),' he said, 'because we consider . . . that a very large and substantial amount of the problems we are facing around the world are a result of lack

of regulation of financial services and therefore we can't
have a waiver for the United Kingdom.' The French made it
look as if the UK was seeking an exemption for the Anglo-
Saxon casino capitalists, the City wideboys so despised in
France. One commentator said, 'He cares more about the
spivs in the City than he cares about us.' The British had
handed Sarkozy an opportunity. The Foreign Office in
London was wary of the French leader and his motives as
they had heard accounts of a comment the French president
had made to a meeting of French ambassadors in which he
was reported to have said the crisis was 'a great opportunity
to do down the City of London'.

The European press tore into Britain. It was as if they had
been waiting for such a moment to vent all their pent-up frustration with British demands to be treated as a special case.
'Bye Bye Britain' was the headline in the German magazine
Der Spiegel. The French paper *Le Monde* said 'the Europeans
have booted the English out of Europe', a deliberate reference
to Joan of Arc who, before beating the English at Orleans in
1429, is reported to have said, 'I am sent here by God, the
King of Heaven, each and all, to put you out of all France.'
There were lots of reference to 'perfide *Albion*,' and '*Les
Angliche*'. Another French paper said, 'there is nothing to be
sorry for in what happened in Brussels. An ambiguity has
been removed.' The British, it said, have only ever been interested in the single market and the rest of the European project
leaves them indifferent. The president elect of the European
Parliament, Martin Schulz expressed doubts whether in the
long-term the UK would remain in the EU. President Sarkozy
said, 'There are clearly now two Europes.'

Britain was cast as the spoiler, the renegade, the outsider: the
island nation incapable of understanding the European idea. At

home, Cameron received a very different response. There was 'veto-bounce', a spike in his poll ratings. The mayor of London, Boris Johnson, showered praise on the prime minister. 'He'd played a blinder,' he said. Others said it had put down a marker that the UK would not allow euro-zone countries to dictate policies that affected countries that did not use the single currency. Some papers drew on the reference points of British identity. They quoted Enoch Powell after the Falklands invasion, who said of Margaret Thatcher: 'In the coming months . . . we will learn of what metal she is made.' Cameron, they predicted, would have to fight this battle time and time again.

The dispute raised fundamental questions about Britain's future relationship with Europe. The veto ushered in a period of uncertainty. The political consensus in Britain in favour of continued membership of the European Union was breaking up. The crisis in the euro-zone had delivered a Europe of tiers, with Britain on the outside. The UK could no longer be certain its voice would be heard, that it would have a seat at the table when its vital interests were at stake. The abiding images of the crisis, the violent protests against austerity imposed from Brussels, had only served to weaken Britain's faith in the European project.

In Britain, standing alone is not feared. In the past, it has served the country well. It is part of the national psyche and the Europeans have long known it. General de Gaulle said that history divided Britain from Europe. 'England is an island, maritime, and linked through its trade, markets and food supplies to very diverse and often distant countries,' he said. 'In short,' he continued, 'the nature and structure and economic context of England differ profoundly from those of the other states of Europe.' Before the D-Day landings in 1944, Sir Winston Churchill had turned to de Gaulle and said,

'Every time Britain has to decide between Europe and the open sea, it is always the open sea that we shall choose.' Earlier Churchill had said, 'We are with Europe, but not of it. We are linked but not compromised. We are interested and associated but not absorbed.'

In the great argument over Britain's relationship with Europe, Sir Winston is claimed as an ally by all sides. In a speech to the University of Zurich in the aftermath of World War Two, he had told his audience, 'We must recreate the European family in a regional structure called, it may be, the United States of Europe . . .' His words were sufficient for a building at the European Parliament in Strasbourg to be named after him, but it remains unclear how he envisaged Britain's place in his vision for Europe.

When European integration was still just a germ of an idea, Britain had been sceptical. The British had been invited to the talks to form a Common Market. They sent along Russell Bretherton, a former Oxford don and under-secretary at the Board of Trade. He took the floor and, according to accounts, dismissed the whole enterprise. 'The future treaty which you are discussing has no chance of being agreed. If it was agreed, it would have no chance of being ratified; and if it were rati- fied, it would have no chance of being applied. And if it was applied, it would be totally unacceptable to Britain. You speak of agriculture, which we don't like, of power over customs, which we take exception to, and institutions which frighten us. Monsieur le President, Messieurs, *au revoir et bonne chance*.' There can scarcely in British history have been such a disdain- ful dismissal, made more sneering with the French phrases tagged on at the end.

A short while later, the prime minister, Harold Macmillan, recognised, with much prescience, Britain's dilemma. 'Shall we be caught,' he said, 'between a hostile (or at least less and less friendly) America and a boastful, but powerful "Empire of Charlemagne" now under French but later bound to come under German control.' For all of that, Britain applied for membership of the Common Market and was rebuffed by de Gaulle. Only in 1973 did Britain become a fully fledged member of the European Economic Community. It was never an easy partnership. In 2012, the French finance minister, Pierre Moscovici, said, 'In essence, it is rather a strange membership with a renegotiation and then a rebate. The UK has always been a bit of a special case.'

Turbulent times would follow. Margaret Thatcher would bang the table, fighting for a British rebate, and insist, 'We are simply asking to have our own money back.' Jacques Chirac, the French president at the time, asked, 'What more does this housewife want from me? My balls on a plate?' Thatcher, who sought to roll back the frontiers of the state in Britain, was not prepared to see intrusive regulation re-imposed via Brussels. Yet for all the arguments over budgets and opt-outs, Britain played a significant role in pioneering the single market, one of the European Union's greatest achievements.

Britain has never committed to the idea of Europe. It is indifferent to the dream of ever-closer union. It fears the weakening of its own power as more and more decisions are taken at a European level in Brussels. The euro-zone crisis has changed the club it joined. In order for the currency to survive, Europe's leaders have embarked on an uncertain road, but the direction is towards a political union as yet undefined. Britain wants no part of that and so has to accept it will play the outsider.

This changing Europe persuaded prime minister David Cameron to address Britain's future relationship with

Europe in a speech in January 2013. It was partly made to try and heal the divisions within his own party. It was also recognition that a much closer union had profound implications for Britain.

Cameron accepted that history had left Britain with a different attitude towards the European project. 'We have the character of an island nation,' he said, 'independent, forthright, passionate in defence of our sovereignty. We can no more change this British sensibility than we can drain the English Channel.' He dismissed the notion that he was a British isolationist. Instead he argued that Europe had to reform. There was a crisis of competitiveness and a growing democratic gap between the EU and its citizens. 'If we don't address these challenges,' he argued, 'the danger is that Europe will fail and the British people will drift towards the exit.' So he promised to re-negotiate a new settlement with Europe. At the end of that process, in 2018, the British people would be given a choice in a referendum to stay in the European Union or to leave.

So Britain's future destiny in Europe is unknown. Although the British prime minister has allies in wanting to reform Europe he has little support for allowing the UK to take back powers from Brussels. Other European leaders were quick to say they would not allow Britain to 'cherry pick' what it liked or disliked. So it is not clear what concessions the UK will be given and whether they will be sufficient for the prime minister – if he wins the next election – to campaign to stay in the EU.

The German Chancellor Angela Merkel said she was 'prepared to talk about British wishes'. The French were less willing to negotiate a new deal with Britain. A long and difficult negotiation lies ahead. Amidst all the criticism of Britain there were words of warmth. *Bild,* the German tabloid, wrote that some 'want the friends of mint sauce and those who drive on the left completely out of the EU.' 'But dear Britons, please stay!,' appealed the paper. 'You are so crazy. We need your opposition, your obstinacy rather than a united Europe. And above all, we love your quirky Royals! Your punk! Your sense of humour.'

The tongue-in-cheek article reflected how divided Europe itself is over Britain. Whilst some have lost patience with the UK others recognise that the European project would be severely undermined if the UK economy was outside the EU.

Britain was also compared to Statler and Waldorf, the two irascible old men staring down from their theatre box in *The Muppet Show.* From their seats, over-looking the stage, they heckle the rest of the cast. For them, every performance is 'horrible' or 'terrible'. With the show just under way, one turns to the other and says, 'OK, I've seen enough. Let's go.'

The Germans, in particular, want the British to stay at the heart of Europe. The two countries share an instinct for an open and competitive economy. What Berlin will not accept is Britain standing in the way and obstructing the new Europe. After the iciness of the summit in December 2011, Angela Merkel went out of her way to hold the door open for Britain. She does not want the euro-zone crisis to lead to the departure of Germany's largest trading partner in Europe, but elsewhere there is growing weariness and intolerance towards what is called 'British exceptionalism', the island nation as special case. Radoslaw Sikorski, a friend of Britain and the Polish foreign minister, told a British audience, 'Please don't expect us to help you wreck or paralyse the EU.'

It is an unintended consequence of Europe's crisis that it has triggered a new debate in Britain about its involvement

with Europe. Some in the UK want to strip back its relationship to a free-trade agreement. It will be a titanic battle.
Europe, battered and weary from its struggle for survival, is
not in the mood to offer Britain an *á la carte* menu. Britain's
deputy prime minister, Nick Clegg, believes that repatriating
powers is a 'false promise, wrapped in a union jack'. Almost
no one, however, believes the current situation is sustainable.
The former EU commissioner, Peter Mandelson, says that
the 'European mandate that the (Edward) Heath government
secured in the 1970s belongs to another time and another
generation'. He has called for a national referendum as a way
of 're-establishing a consensus'.

Roy Jenkins was the British politician who knew Europe best.
He served as president of the Commission. In 1999 he said,
'There are only two coherent British attitudes to Europe. One
is to participate fully, and to endeavour to exercise as much
influence and gain as much benefit as possible from the inside.
The other is to recognise that Britain's history, national psychol-
ogy and political culture may be such that we can never be
anything but a foot-dragging and constantly complaining
member and that it would be better, and would certainly
produce less friction, to accept this and to move towards an
orderly, and if possible, reasonably amicable separation.'

Britain is caught in a dilemma. It fears being excluded,
becoming the permanent outsider, and yet it is unwilling to
commit to further integration. It wants a looser arrangement
but may not get it. The instinct of many is to separate, but
standing against them will be the titans of big business who
will say that Britain outside Europe will deter companies from
locating and investing in the UK.

At the highest levels of the British government there is unease
about Britain's place in the Europe that is emerging from the

crisis. In 2012, David Cameron met the new French president, François Hollande. At their first meeting, according to senior French officials, Cameron asked the new president, 'Do you believe a member state should continue in the EU without being in the euro-zone?' Hollande replied, without hesitation, 'Yes, we need you in the EU.' Cameron responded, 'Well, I am grateful. Sarkozy was saying the contrary.'

Much as Britain is divided over Europe, so Europe is divided over how to handle Britain. President Van Rompuy insists that countries must not 'seek to undermine the EU by seeking special privileges . . . If every member state,' he says, 'was able to cherry-pick those parts of existing policies that they most like . . . the union, in general, and the single market, would soon unravel.' Yet Jacques Delors, the French politician often regarded as the father of the euro, says, 'If the British do not follow the tendency towards more integration in Europe, we can anyway stay friends.' Delors even suggests offering Britain another kind of partnership. That is the challenge for Europe: whether it can live with a club with different types of membership.

For all the passion and intensity and false drama that accompanied Europe's meetings, after two years they had not addressed the fundamental problems facing the continent. A pact to enforce discipline over budgets would have little influence on the current crisis. One EU diplomat said, 'No one else but the Germans wanted it.'

So, as 2011 ended, there was no respite. President Van Rompuy said, 'Although we agreed on a fiscal compact, no one believed us' – investors still doubted the will to stand behind the weaker countries. Some of these countries were trapped in a spiral of decline, cutting expenditure while in recession.

In the twenty-first century, parts of Europe faced the spectre of a Great Depression. Prime Minister Mario Monti of Italy warned that too much austerity could split Europe, with conflict between a 'virtuous North' and an allegedly 'vicious South'.

Chapter 14
A Great Depression

Patission Street in Athens has a past. Another life. Forgotten and obscured. The traces are still there: the National Archaeological Museum with its Agamemnon mask; the Athens Polytechnic that defied the Colonels; the apartment of the singer Maria Callas; the glimpses of the Acropolis. It is as if they have been uprooted and set down in some decaying urban landscape, an after-hours dystopia.

The daytime traffic gives an illusion of vitality. By nightfall, the public space has been abandoned, left to the broken, the desperate, the scavengers and the scrap-metal collectors with their supermarket trolleys. The drug dealers make their trades in the shadows of one of the world's greatest museums. A prostitute offers her tricks in front of the derelict apartment block where Callas lived with her mother and sister. The building is covered with scaffolding and banners. Inside is an anarchist squat. On the stairs are wooden poles, chunks of marble and helmets: a base camp for protesters. The homeless lie in the doorways or stretch out on the air vents; in the summer heat, the air reeks of stale urine. The bakery on the corner hands out yesterday's bread to the hungry. Those shops still in business are shuttered at night, their grills down. Each one is marked with graffiti; perhaps a signature, a mark of territory, or just the angry slash of a spray can. Even the mayor describes the centre of his city as a hotbed of 'crime, drugs and prostitution'.

*   *   *

Dimitris Christoulas knew these streets. He knew what they were and what they had become. He was aged seventy-seven, a retired pharmacist and divorced, existing on a pension that had been cut. He would pass the soup kitchens and the lines outside and watch who had succumbed. There were men and women there, like him, and they were now standing in food queues. He knew the mark of shame when familiar faces would turn away from him. It gnawed away at him, the decay, the failure, the defeat in their eyes and he could not accept that.

One morning he headed for Syntagma Square, the forum for the people's rage. The commuters leaving the nearby metro station heard a sharp crack, a single shot. Dimitris Christoulas had killed himself, his body slumped beside a cypress tree. It was planned: a sad, deliberate act of defiance. He had left a handwritten note nearby. In it he said that he could not face the prospect of 'scavenging through garbage bins for food and becoming a burden to my child'. He blamed the government for 'annihilating the means for my survival' by cutting a pension that he had contributed towards for thirty-five years. He died, bursting with anger, calling on the young to hang the traitors, to confront what he called the government of occupation.

At 8.30 that morning his daughter, Emy Christoulas, received a text from her father with the words, 'The end.'

'I tried reaching him on his mobile,' she said, 'but it was switched off. At his home no one answered. I immediately took the car to go to his house. On the way I heard on the radio about a man who had committed suicide in Syntagma Square.' A short while later the hospital called her and told her it was her father. 'He was always a very loving and sensitive man,' she said. 'It was not a simple parental relationship. It was characterised by deep companionship.'

Her father had left two notes. One was in the square. 'The second note he had left on his desk at home,' said Emy, 'exactly because he knew that the first person who would go there would be myself.' He had written two notes in case the police hid the one in the square.

Emy is a slight, dark haired, educated woman, full of intensity, with a small sculpture of a clenched fist in her apartment. She knew, at once, that the death was intended as a political act. 'It happened,' she said, 'in order for silence to be broken. He prepared a proud death, an act of deep political content. He decided he had something more to offer. His life. And he did so.'

Notes of sympathy were pinned to the square's trees. 'This is not suicide,' declared one, 'it is political murder.' Another note said simply: 'Austerity Kills.' One note stood out for her. It read: 'Today the name of the dead is Democracy and we are eleven million people alive and our name is resistance.'

'Those first three or four days were days of grief, loss and of great political reflection,' said Emy. Sitting on a green plastic chair at home, she reflected on what had driven her father to take his life. 'What is happening,' she said, 'invades our daily routine. In Greece it is not just the soup kitchens; it's the two million unemployed, the seventy thousand padlocks on the businesses, the people with diseased kidneys or cancer that cannot follow their treatment, the children that faint in the soup kitchens.'

The death made the government nervous. They feared it might become totemic, a rallying point against hardship. The new and unelected prime minister, Lucas Papademos, said, 'In these difficult times for our country we must all . . . support those next to us who are in despair.' Hundreds of people attended the funeral and there were protests, some violent, but they subsided. Suicides were rare in Greece, but they had risen by 25 per cent.

In the middle of the day Dimitris Manikas walked into the plastics factory where he used to work, in Komotini. He had been laid off seven months before. He was carrying a hunting rifle and he opened fire on his former boss and another worker. His life and his identity had been bound up with the factory; he had even had its name tattooed on his arm. The man he shot had been the best man at his wedding. They had known each other for decades. Manikas was aged fifty-two and knew there was no hope of further work in a country where a quarter of the people were jobless. He had been hoping to get married again but his chance had gone with his job. One of the factory workers said that Manikas had not eaten anything for four days. Later, speaking from custody, he said, 'I was nothing without a job. I was like a dead man walking.'

At times Greece no longer seemed like a modern Western society. One morning, farmers from Crete brought 25 tonnes of vegetables to hand out to the Athenians. Word spread and several thousand people turned up. They nudged and jostled each other, knocking a barrier to the ground, desperate not to miss out on the aubergines, the peppers and tomatoes. Among them was a woman in her Dolce & Gabbana sunglasses, a vestige from a different life. 'Can't you see what I have sunk to,' she blurted out, her shame mingling with bitterness. No one had a precise figure but, each day, thousands of people in the capital were dependent on handouts for food or medical care.

A country in conflict or in decay is always a place of rumours. They absorb conversation. Everyone has their stories as they watch the familiar world recede. The hospitals were bankrupt. They had not been paid and they could not pay their suppliers. Doctors were scavenging essential supplies like gloves and gauzes from other medical facilities. Charities reported that they were running out of antibiotics. Pharmacists would only accept cash, after the public insurance scheme that funded prescription drugs announced it was so short of funding that it could no longer reimburse the chemists. It was said that HIV infections were rising sharply, with people suspected of deliberately infecting themselves to qualify for a special monthly benefit. Children fainted in the classrooms because they had not enough to eat.

In the centre of Athens, only the pawnshops and the gold dealers prospered. There were scores of them. They were walk-in places, a step off the street to slide a piece of jewellery under a grill for an immediate valuation. Most stores reported that between twenty or thirty people a day would come in to part with an item that had been in their families for years. Few of them spoke; they nodded at the price, their faces set firm and expressionless. One store advertised that it would accept gold teeth. Teeth for cash. Each day, the dealers would sweep up the broaches, the rings, the bracelets, the crosses, the pendants, and take them to the cottage-industry smelters with their small electrical furnaces.

Homer is a musician, a man who in his time has held the attention of crowds. It is not his real name. He says he prefers it that way, as he twists a sachet of sugar over coffee. 'I used to have thirty students,' he says sadly, 'I was turning people down. Now I have two and they pay me less than in the past.' He earns a fifth of what he used to. There are, he says, universities without professors: they cannot afford them any more. 'Our cultural life,' he says, 'is disappearing.'

Young people he meets have become radicalised. 'Most of them want to leave Greece. They come to me and I encourage them to go . . . We will become a society without a middle class,' he says thoughtfully.

He is an educated man. He speaks quietly and earnestly, as if it is important that the truth be told precisely. 'I know people,' he said, 'who don't have anything.' At the hospitals, the doctors ask people to bring whatever medicines they have at home, to empty their cupboards. They tell them not to throw away expired prescriptions. They give them to patients ignoring the sell-by dates. 'I gave medicines,' Homer said, 'and they took them.'

Each day he says he passes ten or fifteen people scavenging for metal. They remove metal doors, gates, locks and chains. Some of the metal boxes from the power companies have been stripped out. Even cables from the train lines have gone missing. 'My parents,' he said, 'see things that remind them of the occupation during the war.' He is modest, courteous and grateful to be given the chance to describe life in a European capital.

There are streets in central Athens where between thirty and fifty shops lie empty. Solonos is one of the city's main shopping areas and yet its fashion stores have become isolated outposts amongst the vacant stores for rent. In 2009 there had been a million companies and small businesses in Greece. Three years later, a quarter of a million had closed. One of the anchors of society – the middle class and small-business owners – were slowly disappearing. By the beginning of 2012, the Greek banking system had lost a quarter of the deposits it had two years earlier: two to three billion euros a month were being withdrawn; most of the money was at home, in safety deposit boxes, or parked in foreign bank accounts.

Some gave up on the cities for the islands and the villages. Young families, the unemployed, the pensioners, were returning to the land. Ancient deeds were dusted down and half-abandoned properties reclaimed. Others moved in with extended families. They cleared plots, hillsides, gardens; any space where they could grow crops. The villages were suffering, too. The staple crop of many rural communities is olives, but prices had slumped by 50 per cent in less than ten years. The economist, Luis Garicano, observed that 'the euro has converted developed countries into developing ones'.

The Greek prime minister told former president Bill Clinton, 'You had the Great Depression in the United States. This is exactly what we're going through in Greece – it is our version of the Great Depression.'

Early in 2012, the Germans and other European leaders were boiling with frustration. They had negotiated two bailouts for Greece and had congratulated themselves, but there was scant evidence of reform. Promises made had not been kept. Athens had agreed to reduce the bloated public sector: up until the middle of 2011, they were still hiring. The government said it would raise 50 billion euros from privatisations. One official described the pledges as a 'work of fiction'. At best, a billion might be raised from a telecoms sale. There was an undertaking to root out tax evasion. Little had changed. An estimated 60 billion euros in taxes lay uncollected. The German finance minister, Wolfgang Schäuble, said that 'unless Greece implements the necessary decisions and doesn't just announce them – there's no amount of money that can solve the problem'.

In desperation, in early 2012, Germany called for Brussels to take control of the Greek budget, to despatch a budget commissioner to Athens. The official would, in effect, control the country's tax and spending. The German economics minister, Philipp Rösler, said, 'If the Greeks can't do it themselves, there must be strong leadership and supervision from the outside.' Chancellor Merkel said that 'strict controls were needed if a country doesn't comply with requirements'.

The Greeks were enraged and insulted. The education minister, Anna Diamontopoulou – and a former EU commissioner – said the idea was a 'product of a sick imagination'.

'It was like another occupation,' she said, 'there is no way we, as Greeks, can accept this.' One Greek paper said Merkel had called for the 'unconditional surrender of the Greek finances'. The Greek finance minister, Evangelos Venizelos, said, 'This was a permanent German ambition – to organise a commissioner or to site our accounts in Frankfurt . . . We have a limit,' he said. 'We have a red line. It is absolutely impossible to accept, to abandon symbols of sovereignty of this country.' The leader of one of Greece's smaller left-wing parties said that 'reform cannot happen at gunpoint' and warned of social unrest. Even President Sarkozy weighed in on the side of the Greeks. 'There cannot be any talk of putting any nation under wardenship,' he said.

Europe was in a dilemma. It had agreed to a second bailout for Greece but had set conditions that had to be met before any further money could be paid out. Greece had to deliver on its side of the bargain. The EU and the IMF had given Greece a ten-page list, outlining actions that had to be taken quickly. They included losing 150,000 jobs in the public sector in three years.

The Germans, in particular, were out of patience. Some of their papers called Greece a failed state. The finance minister Wolfgang Schäuble called the country a 'bottomless pit'. He said, 'The promises from Greece are not enough for us any more.' This caused further offence. The word of a Greek no longer counted in Berlin. The Greek president demanded to know, 'Who is Mr Schäuble to insult Greece? Who are the Dutch? Who are the Finnish? We always had the pride to defend not just our freedom, not just our own country, but the freedom of all Europe.' (The Dutch and the Finns had also favoured stationing a budget controller in the country.)

There was a dangerous stand-off. Many Germans were washing their hands of Greece and many Greeks were resentful at what they saw as German diktats. Greece, however, had the weaker hand. Without further funding, the country faced bankruptcy. Its finance minister, Evangelos Venizelos, warned, 'There are several euro-zone countries who no longer want us and we must convince them to continue supporting us.' The prime minister, Lucas Papademos, said, 'We are a breath away from ground zero.' The country faced a disorderly default which, he said, would 'create conditions of uncontrollable economic chaos and a social explosion'.

In Athens, the government believed it had no choice but to do the bidding of Europe's leaders, even though the terms were harsh. Europe's finance ministers dismissed an austerity package that amounted to 7 per cent of GDP as insufficient. They wanted job cuts in the public sector. They wanted steep cuts to the minimum wage. Salaries and pensions had to be reduced and they wanted a timeline for implementation.

Once the measures had been agreed, they had to be put to the Greek Parliament for approval by MPs. Weighing on the minds of the Greek politicians was a date in the diary. Without more funding, the country would be bankrupt by 20 March. Many Greeks, however, believed they were being bullied into submission. The leader of the radical left party Syriza, Alexis

Tsipras, said, 'Soon they will tell us to abolish democracy in return for loans.'

The prime minister Lucas Papademos, had only been in office since November when George Papandreou had resigned. He was a quietly spoken banker who had been plucked from obscurity to lead his troubled country. 'I was in Boston at the time and was contacted by phone,' he said. The mission of his government was to negotiate the implementation of the second bail-out before elections were held. 'There were divisions between the parties,' he said. 'Some wanted the government to stay for a year or more. Others only wanted it to last a few months. We needed at least six months and that is what the party leaders agreed.' He was an interim prime minister who said the vote on the rescue package was a vote about Greece's place in modern Europe. 'It would be a huge historic injustice,' he said, 'if the country from which European culture sprang . . . reached bankruptcy and ended up, due to one mistake, with national isolation and national despair.' When asked whether there was a risk of Greece being pushed out of the euro-zone if parliament rejected the austerity measures that were a condition of the bail-out, he answered with one word: 'Absolutely.'

On the day that parliament came to vote, in mid-February 2012, a group of communists invaded the site of the Acropolis. They stood there waving red flags; they unfurled a huge banner that carried the rather obscure slogan: 'Down with the dictatorship of the Monopolies EU.' Later, an immense number of protestors took to the streets: 100,000, maybe more. They surged towards the Parliament, taunting the lines of riot police. Violence hung in the air. Many of the crowd were wearing masks against the tear gas they knew would be fired. There was a bang. It might have been a flash grenade; it might have been tear gas, but the crowd cheered ironically. It served as a starting gun for the worst rioting the city had seen since the shooting of a schoolboy in 2008. Masked youths, who had come with picks and hammers, began tearing up the marble in Syntagma Square and throwing it at the police. Others lobbed petrol bombs.

While this almost ritual confrontation continued in front of Parliament, groups of hooded anarchists moved to other parts of the city, which lay unpatrolled and unprotected. They attacked cinemas, cafés, shops and banks. Over a hundred shops were looted and over forty buildings set on fire. At least ten of the buildings that were torched were neo-Classical: reminders of a different past. One of them was the Attikon Cinema, a movie palace with plush red seats that dated back to 1870. It had survived the Nazi occupation but it was burnt to the ground, a smoking pile of blackened beams and twisted metal. It was almost as if the anarchists wanted to sever memory. Nikos Konstandaras, the editor of the paper *Kathimerini*, questioned whether in some way the burning was a fitting sacrifice: 'A symbol of our need to destroy because we cannot create, an expression of our need to abandon memories and pass into a future, blackened with ashes and rage.'

The following day, crowds gathered to stare at what had been lost. Many feared for the country. They shook their heads before walking away. On the metal hoarding erected around the ruins of the cinema, someone had scrawled in red paint: 'Can a revolution be selfish?' But it was not a revolution, at least not yet. It was just rage, blind, resentful and inarticulate. There was no great cause, no regime to be over-thrown. This was a lashing out at distant leaders and officials that insisted their country change.

In the event, and by a small majority, the Greek Parliament agreed to a long list of further savings and tax rises. It opened the way for the second bail-out package to be finally signed off.

After months of negotiations, private investors finally agreed to accept losses of up to 50 per cent on their Greek investments. It meant that Greece's debts would be reduced by 100 billion euros and it would save the country 4 billion euros a year in interest payments. The losses were described as voluntary, although the *Wall Street Journal* opined that it was voluntary 'in the Spanish Inquisition sense of the word'. Banks and hedge funds had been given a stark choice: take a loss, or risk losing everything if Greece leaves the euro. It was the largest restructuring of sovereign debt in history – and it happened in Europe.

In Germany, the second Greek bail-out prompted the tabloid *Bild* to print a large headline with the single word: 'Stop!' Underneath it ran the words: 'It's payday again in the Bundestag (the German Parliament). 130 billion is meant to save Greece from ruin. *Bild* appeals to all MPs. Do not proceed with this folly.' Angela Merkel took on the doubters in her own party and in Germany. 'Some people,' she said, 'ask whether Greece isn't a bottomless pit, a hopeless case, and ask whether it wouldn't be better for all if Greece just reintroduced the drachma . . . that the opportunities outweigh the risks of turning away from Greece. I believe those risks are incalculable and therefore irresponsible.' The German Chancellor, risk-averse and instinctively cautious, was not prepared to gamble on the unknown consequences of Greece being forced from the euro-zone.

Many of Europe's leaders believed the Greek crisis had finally been laid to rest. 'I want to tell the French people,' said

President Sarkozy, 'that the page of the financial crisis is turning . . . and today the problem is solved.' The president of the European Council, Herman Van Rompuy, chimed in: 'The turning point in the crisis has been reached.' The head of the IMF, Christine Lagarde, said, 'Economic spring is in the air.' The Greek government, too, heralded it as a 'historic chance to stabilise Greece'.

They envisaged a country with less debt, its finances under control and committed to reforms that would rebuild the economy in the future. What they had miscalculated was the effect of the medicine they were prescribing. In the case of Greece, one austerity measure was being piled on another, even while the country was in the fifth year of recession. No other country in recent times had endured such an experiment and no other modern country had seen its economy collapse so fast. The cuts were deeper and swifter than had ever been tried elsewhere.

Germany had got its way. Greece had been saved but the conditions were harsh and deliberately so. 'The Greek deal very much plays to the public in the northern European countries,' said Christian Schulz, the senior economist at Berenberg Bank. 'Conditions for Greece are tough so that no other country will ever want to get into that position.'

Many economists did not share the politicians' euphoria. They did not see Greece unbound and saved. They saw a country caught in a trap. The only way it could regain its competiveness, in a monetary union, was by cutting living standards, but the more cuts it made the more businesses closed and the smaller the tax revenues it collected. Falling revenues only increased the pressure for further reductions in spending or new taxes. The government announced a solidarity tax that would be attached to electricity bills, but people were unwilling to co-operate. The truth was that much of Greek society was determined to resist what its creditors were demanding.

Economists queued up to say that the strategy would not work. Joseph Stiglitz, the Nobel Prize-winning economist, said, 'It is clear that austerity alone is a recipe for stagnation and decline.' The international financier George Soros said, 'Germany is acting as the task-master imposing tough discipline. This will generate both economic and political tension that could destroy the EU.' The accusation levelled at the Germans and European officials was that austerity was killing the Greek economy. 'I am afraid,' said Paul De Grauwe, an economist who has advised the European Commission, 'that we have chosen, in a very masochistic way, the most painful path, where everybody bleeds.'

Germany was seen as the author of austerity. It had taken the lessons of its own history and applied them to the rest of Europe. It demanded that countries in southern Europe rein in their spending and balance their budgets. Living standards would have to be sacrificed if those countries were to become competitive once again.

Many European leaders had been reluctant to challenge Germany, such was its economic power. In 2012, that gradually changed. The Italian prime minister, Mario Monti, had no reason to be reticent. Having replaced Berlusconi, this sixty-nine year old economist and academic was fêted wherever he went. He said that squeezing countries into shape could lead to political upheaval and sent a warning to Berlin. He envisaged that 'a protest against Europe will develop . . . and against Germany, which is viewed as the ringleader of intolerance . . . Economic discontent,' in his view, 'could force Italy to flee into the arms of the populists.'

The ring-master was the German finance minister, Wolfgang Schäuble. He had been a rising star in Germany, the politician destined to replace Helmut Kohl as Chancellor. A week after German reunification, he had been leaving a restaurant in the town of Oppenau when a deranged man pulled out a gun and fired three shots, hitting him in the face and the spine. 'I can't feel my legs any more,' he had said, before losing consciousness. Schäuble was confined to a wheelchair and has struggled with poor health ever since, but has retained enormous influence: his words move markets. He has the licence to speak out. 'The Chancellor,' he said, 'can count on my loyalty but that doesn't mean I'm going to keep quiet, that I'm going to be easy. I have the freedom to do what I think is right.' Schäuble, almost as much as Angela Merkel, is the architect of Germany's strategy for the crisis in Europe.

He remains a passionate believer in European unity but there is nothing sentimental about him. He believes the euro will only survive if countries embrace far-reaching reforms. Deficits had to be reduced, wages cut and labour markets opened up to more competition. There was, in his view, no other way. For some countries it would mean changing their economic cultures. To his critics he replied that, 'All the rescue funds in the world won't help if the causes of the crisis aren't tackled directly.' For a long period, he doubted whether Greece had the will to reform itself. 'The crisis can only be solved through reforms,' he said. 'You get assistance, but only if you agree to go for reforms.' He stressed the word 'only', wagging his finger. Solidarity in his view has to come with conditions. 'Increasing public indebtedness is damaging growth and not enhancing growth,' he insisted.

Powerful voices, however, began arguing that too much austerity risked breaking some countries. Christine Lagarde is the head of the IMF and, along with the German Chancellor, one of the most influential women in the world. The tall, elegant, tanned, effortlessly chic, former synchronised swimmer had become an influential figure on the world stage. She was at ease with herself and power. Early in 2012, she came to see Angela Merkel at the Chancellery in Berlin. It was a custom that the two women gave each other small gifts: a few months earlier, Lagarde had given Merkel a trinket from Hermès and had received a Beethoven recording in return. On this day she arrived with an orange-scented candle from Fragonard that represented 'Hope'. They sat down to dinner on the eighth floor of the Chancellery building. Lagarde was in Berlin to make a speech to the German Council on foreign relations. Out of friendship and political calculation, she wanted to share her speech with Merkel. The leader of the IMF was going to make a pitch for 'growth'. It was not that she was discarding the need for budgets to be controlled; it was more a rebalancing, a recognition that Europe needed growth as much as austerity; and that could be interpreted as criticism of Germany.

Lagarde's speech, however, had an apocalyptic tone. She warned her mainly German audience that the world could slide into a '1930s moment of isolationism', which led to the Great Depression and World War Two. She spoke of the risk of trust and cooperation breaking down and countries turning inward. 'A moment, ultimately,' she said 'leading to a downward spiral that could engulf the whole world.' Nations had to embrace policies that restored growth, she said, and she finished with a quote from Goethe: 'It is not enough to know, we must apply. It is not enough to will, we must do.'

It was a clarion call echoed by others. The Nobel Prize-winning economist Paul Krugman said, 'By introducing a single currency without the institutions needed to make the currency work, Europe reinvented the defects of the gold standard – defects that played a major role in causing and perpetuating the Great Depression.' Without countries in a currency union being able to devalue, he foresaw a long period of mass unemployment and 'slow, grinding deflation'. Europe was caught in a trap of its own making.

The German Chancellor listened but was unmoved. She insisted that Greece could rebuild its economy despite austerity. She was influenced by what had happened in Germany after reunification: it took time, but the former East Germany was forced to become more competitive. The key was opening up the economy, making it more flexible, making it easier to hire and fire workers.

For a brief period Greece faded from attention, but not for long. It still had an unelected prime minister. Elections were planned for May 2012. As they approached, Europe's leaders fretted. They feared that the winners might be parties that had not supported the latest bail-out agreement and who believed austerity was a failed policy. One leader threatened to tear up the deal. If that were to happen, it would reignite the Greek crisis. Europe's leaders once again would have to decide whether to re-open negotiations or risk Greece leaving the euro, with all the unpredictable consequences. Wolfgang Schäuble wanted to know who would guarantee Greece's commitments after the elections. 'I find this very alarming,' he said. He even suggested that Greece postpone the poll. That produced a withering response from a Greek economist, who publicly told him, 'you don't control our destiny'.

As polling day neared, the warnings and threats increased. The Greeks were told that a vote against austerity could lead to their having to leave the euro. It made no difference.

They were told that being outside the euro would usher in a period of 'mass poverty'. It did not deter them. In large numbers they voted for parties that rejected the terms of the bail-out deal.

No party, however, could form a government and a second election was scheduled for June. There was the prospect that these anti-austerity parties could do even better and, if successful, would demand a wholesale renegotiation of the bail-out deal. Europe's leaders rushed to define the choice for Greece: a vote for candidates that rejected the bail-out deal was a vote to leave the euro.

Just in case that seemed the lesser of evils, European officials lined up to describe the world outside the single currency. The Greeks were told they would face mass poverty, civil war, a coup, and hunger. Safe corridors would have to be set up to bring in humanitarian aid. Charles Dallara, the man who had negotiated with private investors to accept losses on their Greek holdings, said the consequences of leaving the single currency were 'somewhere between catastrophic and Armageddon'. The Jeremiads were in full cry. A return to the drachma would lead to a run on the banks, exchange controls, bankruptcy and hyperinflation.

The out-going prime minister, Lucas Papademos, sent a letter to the Greek president, which was shown to the party leaders. 'He did not give it to them,' said Papademos, 'because he felt it would leak. They read it during the meeting.' Greece, he said, would run out of money in weeks if there was no stable government. He said that a few days after the elections, the government would have no funds of its own. It would be completely reliant on the EU and the IMF to pay salaries and pensions. He wanted the country to understand what was at stake in the election. He also delivered a warning. 'If there were further substantial outflows of deposits from the country, the strains on the banking system and the economy would entail very substantial risks,' he said. He had witnessed, after the first election, significant funds leaving the country. What he feared was a run on the high-street banks.

Just before the second election there was an informal poll indicating strong support for parties opposed to the bail-out deal. Billions of euros immediately left the country. 'The game would have been lost a week later after the election if no government had been formed,' said Papademos. 'In that case,' he continued, 'I think we would have seen a run on the banks by a large number of people.'

The warnings were directed at one young Greek politician in particular. Alexis Tsipras was hailed as the man who held the fate of the euro in his hands. He was thirty-seven, open, engaging, good-looking and the leader of a radical leftist party that had been the big winner in the first elections in May. He was untainted by links with the mainstream parties. His message was beguilingly simple: the austerity measures were barbaric and he promised to tear up the bail-out deal. 'After two and half years of catastrophe, Greeks are on their knees,' he said. 'The social state has collapsed.' He did not want to leave the euro but he demanded a new deal.

He was denounced as a leftist fire-brand whose hero was the Venezuelan leader, Hugo Chavez, whose birthday he shared. He spoke of a war between workers and ordinary people on one side, and global capitalists and bankers on the other. The Germans feared him and his popular appeal. One German paper even ran a headline in Greek which read: 'Resist the Demagogue'. Beside it was a picture of Tsipras with his arms upraised. Greeks resented the interference. One of their papers retaliated by saying that 'Greeks are a proud people who know how to vote. Take your suggestions elsewhere.'

Some believed the election was a defining moment for the country. The editor of the Greek paper *Kathimerini*, Nikos Konstandaras, said 'my country is hurtling towards an election that will decide its fate: whether Greeks will fight on to remain part of Europe's core or succumb to their own weaknesses and turn inwards, choosing isolation, anger and uncertainty greater than that from which they wish to flee.'

On polling day, Tsipras came second and Europe sighed with relief, but the parties that supported the bail-out deal only commanded 40 per cent of the vote. The new leader was the Conservative, Antonis Samaras. He immediately spoke by phone to Angela Merkel who was on a plane to Mexico. She gave no reassurances but said that 'she would work on the basis Greece would meet its European commitments'.

The European Union was hugely relieved. President Van Rompuy said, 'The Greek people made their choice. The first election was on the past, who was responsible. The second election was on the future. They made a choice knowing all the elements and, democratically speaking, you cannot be clearer than that.'

Fear had also determined the outcome of the election. Many voters agreed with Tsipras that austerity had ruined Greece. They wanted to rebel, to defy, to resist, but they shied away from the unknown. Some regarded themselves as prisoners of the monetary union: inside it, they were stuck with grinding poverty; outside it, they risked a run on the banks and chaos.

Before the year was out there would be more austerity. There were further cuts to pensions and salaries. Doctors, police and fire-fighters saw their wages cut. All of this was intended to reduce Greece's deficit to 3 per cent by 2016. It was, however, as if Europe had learnt nothing from its past, from its history. For out of this broken society emerged the 'Golden Dawn'.

They are enforcers, vigilantes, street thugs, who parade under a flag whose symbol is inspired by the Nazis. Their enemy are the migrants who flock to Greece as the gateway to Europe. 'We want all foreigners out of the country' is their creed. Their slogan is: 'Greece for the Greeks. Blood. Honour. Golden Dawn.' They course through local markets, over-turning the tables of migrant store holders. They are the self-proclaimed protectors of neighbourhoods from crime and foreign criminals. They are frequently called instead of the police. At the last election, they won eighteen seats.

Their flag, their salutes, their parades, their street violence, are drawn from the fascist playbook. Against the night sky, men, muscled, in black T-shirts, stand holding up flares. Their music of choice is from the band Pogrom. Immigrants are regularly beaten up by Golden Dawn thugs, and the police rarely intervene. Indeed, the party boasts that half the police force are Golden Dawn members. One of its MPs threatened to 'drag migrant children from the kindergartens'. When they demanded a list of kindergartens with high numbers of immi-grants, the education ministry obliged.

It is mid-morning at Attikis Platia. The square is sealed off with red and white tape. At each corner stand men in black shirts with white writing of the words 'Golden Dawn'. They carry heavy poles with the Greek flag wrapped around them. In the centre of the square are piles of vegetables, potatoes, oranges, carrots, oil and milk. There is also pasta with the words on the box: 'Made in Greece.' There are hundreds of Greeks queuing to receive free food courtesy of the Golden

Dawn. They shuffle forward to a table where they have to show their I.D. to prove that they are Greeks.

Many of the Golden Dawn guards wear army boots and combat fatigues. Some wear fingerless leather gloves and carry motorcycle helmets over their arms. It is as if bouncers had set up an aid agency – charity mixing with menace. The men relish the paramilitary style, the militia symbols, the sunglasses, the padded black jackets, the army boots. It is a public square, but there are no police. Part of a neighbourhood has been sealed off by enforcers from a party that many regard as neo-Nazi.

One third of voters now say they support the party and its brand of law and order and efficiency. They escort vulnerable elderly people to ATM machines. They hand out food but it is 'food for Greeks only'. They give blood but it is 'blood for Greeks only'. They lean on companies to offer 'jobs for Greeks only.' They closed down a performance of a play they disapproved of: Corpus Christi portrayed Christ and his disciples as gay men. Golden Dawn members surrounded the theatre with the actors trapped inside. Rocks landed in the auditorium. The play's director Laertis Vassilou said, 'What happened that night was like *Kristallnacht*.'

At an event in Crete, one of Golden Dawn's MPs unfurled the flag of the former junta. Another of its prominent members, and an MP, has spoken of Greek society being ready 'to have a fight, a new form of civil war'. On the streets there are clashes between extreme right-wing gangs and anarchists. Mihalis, the motorbike-riding anarchist, says that an anti-fascist movement has developed. 'I expect to see people dead,' he said, without any emotion. 'Already there is a small civil war and we will take up arms.' Antonis Samaras, the Greek prime minister elected in 2012, warned that social cohesion was 'endangered by rising unemployment, just as it was towards the end of the Weimar Republic in Germany'.

History is laced with irony. The EU was set up to prevent conflict returning but has presided over the very conditions that offer fertile ground for the rise of far-right extremists: the Germans, who know how humiliation and hardship was the breeding ground for the Nazis, have imposed terms on Greece that have been compared to the Treaty of Versailles after World War One.

History never repeats itself exactly and the Golden Dawn may disappear when growth returns, but modern Europe once again has caught a glimpse of neo-Nazis on its streets.

Those who argued that the policy of austerity was too severe and introduced too quickly were about to get a leader for their cause.

Chapter 15
The Rebellion of Mr Normal

It was a pseudo event, or that was how it seemed: an unknown man walking through the concourse at St Pancras station in London is surrounded by a posse of cameras. The lenses attracted the curious, who jostled and collided with each other. The chaos gave the impression of a news event. It was February 2012 and a campaign stop for François Hollande, the Socialist candidate for the French presidency. He was in London to seek the votes of the 300,000 French people who reside there.

Hollande and his closest aides arrived on the Eurostar from Paris. They travelled standard class. They were attentive to that kind of detail. With them had come fifty or so French journalists. At St Pancras they formed a pack around him, a swarm without direction. They meandered through the station, stumbling into bags and passengers. The British Railway police were baffled. They questioned journalists as to who this small, smiling man was and when he might leave their station. They seemed unprepared for the visit and tried to corral the candidate towards the exit.

Hollande did not mind the confusion; he revelled in it. He shook hands with random people. When they turned out to be from Amsterdam or Angola, he just smiled. He was informal, relaxed in himself. He did not have the candidate's cursory handshake; he engaged, he stopped, he posed for pictures. He was a rare politician: a candidate with time. The chaos of St Pancras was not to be feared as an indication of poor planning. It was all part of building the brand, of creating Mr Normal, an ordinary, likeable Frenchman who reminded voters of themselves. Above all, Hollande wanted to be the opposite of the super-kinetic Sarkozy.

Outside his own country, François Hollande was largely unknown, but he had caught the attention of the British when he said, 'My true adversary does not have a name, a face or a party. He never puts forward his candidacy, but nevertheless he governs. My true adversary is the world of finance.' As he moved through the British railway station he was asked whether he had any message for the City of London. He threw his head back and laughed, with just a trace of embarrassment, before replying in English, 'We must have more regulation.' The French journalists phoned, texted and tweeted. They had a story. A French candidate was in the lion's den, in Europe's financial capital, telling the Anglo-Saxon chancers they could expect to be reined in if he took up residence in the Elysée Palace. It was precisely such a moment that the Hollande team had hoped for, although the candidate thought it was necessary before he left to reassure the British that he was not 'dangerous'.

In his speeches he began describing himself as 'Mr Normal'; and therein lay part of his success. He presented himself as the French everyman. He did little to define himself. It was enough to be ordinary. After campaign rallies there was never any urgency to leave. He liked to hang around, to meet, to talk, and to laugh. He worked a rope line like a man seeking friends. If the voters knew anything about him, it was that he promised to squeeze the rich and that touched a chord; many French people still saw *égalité* as the essential partner to *liberté* and *fraternité*. Hollande believed that to dip into the soul of France was to find equality. The day before the visit to London, he had announced that he would slap a 75 per cent tax on people earning over a million euros a year in France: a piece of socialist red meat for far-left voters whose support he needed in the first round of the campaign.

His rival President Sarkozy despised him. 'Hollande is useless,' the French president had said. He described him as 'a sugar cube that looks solid but quickly dissolves'. Sarkozy's supporters called Hollande a 'Flanby': a brand of wobbly caramel pudding. Others labelled him 'Mr Marshmallow' or 'Mr Mayonnaise'. Even his former partner said that he had not had an idea in thirty years. Sarkozy thought him an unworthy opponent and so misjudged him.

President Sarkozy's weakness was himself: a political impresario in perpetual motion. This whirl of activity unsettled the French. His opponents called him 'Mr Zig Zag'. 'People behave according to their temper,' said one of the president's friends, Alain Minc. 'That's his character, always moving, always pushing; he's hyperactive.' Despite all that energy, Minc thought Sarkozy was sensitive. There were lots of outbursts of anger but at heart he was 'a gentle guy'.

That was not how Hollande saw him. In an unguarded moment he called him *un sal mec*, 'a nasty piece of work'. His private life, his rich friends, his flashy watches, earned him the title 'President Bling-Bling'. Ruefully – with the polls predicting his defeat – Sarkozy conceded that 'perhaps the mistake I made . . . was not being solemn enough in my acts'. Hollande and his advisers detected that the French people had grown weary of the Sarkozy show. In an age of uncertainty, they wanted reassurance. They might have forgiven Sarkozy if he had revived the economy. When he was elected he had promised the French *une rupture*, a break with the past. He had vowed to modernise the country but his reforms were tepid, ground down by the French antipathy to change.

Sarkozy's strength lay in his experience. He believed that the debt crisis shaking Europe was his strongest card. The continent was living through dangerous times and France needed a leader bloodied in battle in those late-night meetings convened to save the euro. It was not a moment to take a risk with the untried Hollande, a man who had never held ministerial office. So, during the election, Sarkozy decided he would parade his relationship with Angela Merkel.

They had become Europe's indispensable couple. They were meeting every ten days. 'You know,' said one of his friends, 'that there are only three women in Sarkozy's life: Carla Bruni, his daughter and Angela Merkel.' Sarkozy and Merkel had become the continent's crisis managers. They still, on occasions, had sharp differences but they would stand together at moments of high tension. Sarkozy had understood the reality of the French–German relationship and its importance to Europe. He would tell visitors in private, 'Germany without France frightens everyone. France without Germany frightens no one.' Over time, he and Merkel had morphed into 'Merkozy', and Sarkozy felt that was a vote winner. The German Chancellor was highly regarded in France. For her part, she feared Hollande would undermine her pact to instil discipline over national budgets. So she promised to campaign for Sarkozy on French soil. No German Chancellor had so openly taken sides in a French election.

It was not just his relationship with Merkel that Sarkozy wanted to put at the centre of his campaign. He wanted

Germany to be a model for France and to learn from its economic success. 'We need to be as competitive as the Germans,' he said, early in his campaign. If re-elected, he promised to shake up France, to reduce the social charges paid by employers and to make the labour market more flexible. He had even invited the author of those German reforms, the former Chancellor, Gerhard Schröder, to the Elysée Palace. Schröder told Sarkozy that despite introducing dramatic reforms, 'I nearly won. I was on the verge of being re-elected. You should do the same.' Sarkozy was impressed and was tempted to sell himself once again as the reformer.

'Sarkozy thought Merkel's support would be strong and meaningful,' said Alain Minc, 'but after one month we discovered that the impact on the polls was zero.' The French did not want to be like the Germans. They did not want a German Chancellor interfering in a French election. So Sarkozy changed direction with a suddenness that advisers in the Elysée had become accustomed to. A new Sarkozy emerged: a defender of *La Forte France*, a strong France, of French jobs and French identity. Almost immediately he went up 5 per cent in the polls. As one adviser said wryly, 'When he decided not to be serious, he recovered.'

Sarkozy believed the 'Parisian caviar left', as he called it, did not reflect the silent patriotic majority. 'The France you represent,' he told his audiences, 'is the France of Jeanne d'Arc, the France of Victory Hugo, the France of de Gaulle, the France of Robert Schuman, the France of Jean Monnet, the France of humanity.' He consciously sought the mantle of de Gaulle. Standing in front of a crowd at the Place de la Concorde, Sarkozy appealed to the French to help him: 'Françaises, Français! Aidez-moi!' It was the very same words used by de Gaulle when he faced a putsch by French officers in Algeria.

Sarkozy vented his anger on those who had migrated to France and then challenged its values. 'All of those who make remarks contrary to the values of the Republic will immediately be put outside the territory of the French Republic,' he said. 'There will be no exception. No leniency.' He turned on Europe, accusing it of 'weakening the concept of the Nation'. He attacked globalisation for diluting France. 'I say no,' he said, 'to a Europe that opens its markets when others don't.' He questioned the benefits of free trade and proposed a 'Buy European' Act. He attacked Europe's open borders enshrined in the Schengen agreement. 'We cannot accept,' he said, 'being subjected to the shortcomings of Europe's external borders. Reform is the only way to avoid an implosion of Europe.' Schengen, and the freedom to travel without passport controls, was regarded as one of Europe's great achievements. When he campaigned against it, Angela Merkel cooled; there would be no barnstorming for Sarkozy. She was privately dismayed by his campaign.

His dilemma was that the political space on the right was congested. Marine Le Pen had managed to rebrand and reinvigorate the far-right National Front. It was still fiercely anti-immigrant but it had sidelined the overt racists and extremists. She saw that more votes were to be had in addressing economic insecurity. She had also become a powerful, almost operatic, campaigner.

At the Zenith convention centre in Paris, Le Pen bounced onto the stage, blonde hair, black trouser suit, waving and smiling. She looked out onto a flag-swaying, foot-stamping audience of 6,000 people. She understood they wanted passion; they wanted certainty; they wanted for one brief political moment to believe in the glory of France, to believe that the past could be rekindled and revived. She spread her arms wide and shouted, 'Yes, France – shout your rage and scream your hope.' She threw her arms out wide once more and concluded with a simple cry, 'Yes, France!' and stood there, enjoying the rapture.

Like Eva Peron, she presented herself as a champion of neglected working people. She railed against *les aristocrats*, the élites. Sarkozy and Hollande represented the interests of the rich and powerful. France's identity was being destroyed by immigration and the fantasies of a European élite. 'You want to feel at home in your own country,' she told her supporters, and they knew what she meant. Globalisation, she said, had taken their jobs from them. The European dream, she said, had become a nightmare.

In the first round of the French elections, 6 million people voted for her. It was immediately apparent that Sarkozy would not be re-elected as president unless he could persuade some of those voters to back him in the second round. It was a difficult task. However much they disliked the socialist François Hollande, the Le Pen voters felt betrayed by Sarkozy. They booed every time his name was mentioned. They accused him of now trying to steal their clothes while having ignored their fears and concerns when in office. Sarkozy was trapped, pursuing votes from a section of society that mistrusted him.

In the second round of voting, Marine Le Pen made it clear she would abstain. 'Sarkozy lost because Ms Le Pen decided he would lose,' said one of the president's allies. She thought it was in her party's long-term interest to let the socialists into government.

In the final days of the campaign, Sarkozy wrapped himself in the tricolour. On May Day, the traditional date for workers' marches, he staged *un grand spectacle* at the Trocadero. It was a piece of Hollywood theatre, with the Eiffel Tower as backdrop. Giant jibs swung cameras across the flag-waving crowds, capturing a blur of red, white and blue. Some of his supporters wore T-shirts that carried pictures of de Gaulle and the words: 'He saved France, so did Nicolas Sarkozy.'

The president had lost none of his fight. He challenged the left to 'lay down the red flag and serve France'. On what was traditionally an international day for workers Sarkozy promised to showcase 'real work'. That offended and enraged his opponents: the phrase '*vrai travail*' was coined by the pro-Nazi Vichy regime in 1940. It prompted some opposition rallies to sing the '*Chant des Partisans*', the song of the Resistance. Sarkozy was leaving power in a hail of controversy. He depicted Hollande as dangerous, but the problem was that the mild-mannered candidate did not appear that way. Hollande, they said, would give France 'a one-way ticket to Greece', but few believed it. The president said his opponent would embark on a 'festival of spending' but his case was weakened by the fact that it had been on his watch that France had lost its much-valued triple-A credit rating.

The mood in France was resentful and nostalgic. Many disliked the president personally: they were offended by him, and no grand rallies would change that. They also blamed him for France's fading economic power. Hollande promised that the French way of life and its social welfare benefits could be preserved. It was a debatable promise, but the French people wanted to believe it. The reality was different. France's labour costs were among the highest in Europe. The post-war model of high social spending was not sustainable, an inconvenient truth that Hollande did not share with the voters.

On the night of his defeat, President Sarkozy bowed out gracefully. A few months before polling day he had said that if he lost he would change his life completely. 'You won't hear from me again,' he said. The French playwright, Yasmina Reza, saw in his great restlessness the urge to 'combat the slippage of time'. The day before the election he had sat down with his wife and friends and told them he had three wishes: not to be humiliated, not to destroy his political family and not to leave the Elysée a bad loser, as one of his predecessors had done. Valéry Giscard d'Estaing could not disguise his bitterness at losing the French Presidency with a curt, perfunctory farewell speech. Sarkozy achieved his three wishes.

In the event, he was surprised to run so close to Hollande. Back at the Elysée, he spoke to his closest aides. 'Sarkozy is a man who is extremely transparent,' said Xavier Musca, his chief of staff. 'There is no difference between what he says privately and publically. He said that firstly I am responsible for this . . . he was surprisingly calm . . . Some said he had feared a more severe defeat.'

Later Sarkozy told Alain Minc, '"I left politics but there may be some circumstances which would oblige me to come back." He will not fight,' said Minc, 'but will do everything to leave the door open.'

As the election result was confirmed, crowds surged onto the boulevards; they sat on the rooftops of their cars waving flags; they hooted; they rode around Paris celebrating a socialist victory. They knew what they disliked; they knew far less about what they were getting. For many of them it was enough that Hollande was not Sarkozy. He had campaigned on one major theme with far-reaching implications for Europe. 'Austerity,' he said, 'is not the only option.' His priority was growth. He believed that the policy of austerity, of cutting deficits in Europe, was not working. He openly challenged the German narrative that had become the policy of the eurozone. He promised to renegotiate the treaty enforcing budgetary discipline in the euro-zone. 'Mrs Merkel knows that,' he said, 'my first trip will be to confirm to her that the French have voted for a different kind of Europe.' The German Chancellor said that the pact 'was not open to new negotiations'. The new French president replied that, 'It is not for Germany to decide for the rest of Europe.' France was not just challenging Germany's core policy for addressing the euro-zone crisis; it was challenging German leadership in Europe.

On 15 May 2012, François Hollande was sworn in as the seventh president of France's Fifth Republic. Sarkozy handed over to him the French nuclear codes. In a simple ceremony at the Elysée Palace, Hollande wore a gold collar, weighing nearly a kilogram, engraved with the names of his predecessors. He promised to exercise power with 'dignity, simplicity and soberness' – a last jab at Sarkozy. He used his first speech as president to say that Europe needed growth: a message for the German Chancellor. On that first day power clung to him uneasily. For the ritual trip up the Champs Elysées he stood in an open-topped Citroën DS5 hybrid in the pouring rain without an umbrella. He appeared bedraggled, an ordinary man in a modest car dwarfed by Republican Guardsmen on horseback. One commentator said it seemed like a scene from a film where, by a series of accidents, a man from the crowd had assumed power.

Within hours of becoming president, he was on his way to Berlin. The speed of the visit was testament to the importance of the French–German relationship. Soon after he had taken off from a military airfield close to Paris, there was a gigantic bang as the plane was hit by lightning. One of those on board said it seemed as if red and white lights were swirling around the plane. The captain came into the cabin and said to the new president he had to turn back. Hollande said they could not be late to see Angela Merkel but the captain insisted. When they landed, two holes were found in the plane. They changed to another executive jet.

When he eventually arrived in Berlin, he and Angela Merkel were awkward and formal with each other. They had not met before: she had refused to meet him during the French election campaign. Now they shook hands, without a kiss or an embrace. His first words to Angela Merkel were, 'Sorry. My plane had a problem.' Merkel, with a slight nudge, steered the new French president down the red carpet.

Even for a visit by an American president the Chancellery had never known such attention from the media. Every nuance, every gesture was scrutinised. Sarkozy and Merkel had liked to talk directly with each other in English. Even though Hollande's English was much better than his predecessor's, he and Merkel quickly reverted to French and German, with translators at their sides. One of those who travelled with Hollande said that, 'On a personal basis they understood each other. They were more compatible as characters (than with Sarkozy). They were firm but they didn't argue.' Hollande, however, was determined that he would not play the junior partner; he would be the champion of growth. He believed that austerity alone was leading to a dead end, socially and politically. He thought it a 'policy without hope and no hope was very dangerous'. His political allies back home stiffened his resolve. One politician, who later became a minister said, 'Chancellor Merkel's ideas had been beaten by French universal suffrage.'

At this first meeting, Angela Merkel made clear that her pact – enforcing greater discipline over budgets – could not be renegotiated or watered down. It was a red line for her. She was prepared to add a growth element to it and Hollande understood that that was the best he could expect. They spoke for an hour and later had dinner together on the eighth floor of the Chancellery, but there was an edge between them which could not be disguised.

In the weeks that followed, Hollande signalled that he wanted a different relationship to the one Merkel had had with Sarkozy. Often to the irritation of other European leaders, Sarkozy and Merkel would meet before a summit and essentially agree the agenda. Hollande wanted to end that ritual. 'The Franco–German relationship has been exclusive,' he said. 'European institutions have been neglected and some countries, notably the more fragile ones, have had the unpleasant feeling of facing an executive board.'

Without Sarkozy, Merkel was weakened. Mario Monti, the Italian leader, confided to a French official that summits and meetings had changed without Sarkozy. In Monti's view, Sarkozy had acted as Merkel's bodyguard. This had encouraged her to stick to her position, knowing she was protected by the French president. Without him, Monti observed, 'She didn't dare to establish her power. She was more isolated than before.'

:The French-German relationship was Europe's foundation stone. Hollande believed that but he wanted a partnership of equals. Some of his political friends had derided Sarkozy as 'Merkel's poodle'. Hollande did not underestimate the importance of his relationship with Berlin, but he allied himself more closely with Rome and Madrid. One of his advisers said that he 'did not want to present himself as a leader of the south or the poorer nations', but in time it came to seem that way.

Merkel and Hollande are two leaders uncertain with each other. They are polite but they have not bonded. They circle each other, cautiously. Some of the differences are fundamental. The French president remains critical of what he sees as Germany's obsession with cutting deficits. 'It is France's task,' he said, 'to tirelessly tell our partners that there are alternatives to austerity.' Merkel wants further integration in Europe. She envisages Brussels having greater power over national budgets and the euro-zone's economy. 'We should give Europe,' she said, 'a real right of intervention in national budgets.' Berlin even envisages Brussels having the power to override national parliaments. That is not Hollande's priority. He favours solidarity, helping the weaker countries with their debts. He favours common debt, something the German Chancellor will not countenance without much greater control of spending.

These differences were laid bare during a meeting in Rome. Standing beside the French leader, Angela Merkel said, 'Where solidarity is given, control must also be possible. Liability and control belong together.' Hollande replied, 'There can be no transfer of sovereignty if there is not an improvement in solidarity.' For the French, the union is all about mutual help. For the Germans, solidarity will only come once they have control, and that means giving Brussels more power over the member states.

At an early meeting, Angela Merkel had turned to François Hollande and said, 'I think we need a treaty change and a convention.' She believed that Europe needed rebuilding and redesigning. The French president replied, 'Are you sure people in Europe will be ready for such a negotiation? Will they ratify a treaty change?' The German Chancellor responded confidently, 'I will convince the people to ratify it and to hold a referendum.' Hollande disagreed. 'First we need growth and jobs,' he said, 'and then after comes the political project.' Hollande believed changing treaties was a distraction; he also feared holding a referendum in France. The people had said 'no' before to further European integration and might well do so again.

French and German leaders have not always bonded, particularly at the start. The early relationship between Hollande and Merkel has been marked by misunderstandings and sleights. Berlin did not like it when Hollande quipped, before a summit, that Merkel 'has her own deadline, September 2013', a way of saying that her decisions were driven by the German electoral calendar. The Germans also noticed that soon after he took office, Hollande sided with the leaders of Italy and Spain. The Chancellor felt muscled into agreeing that money from the euro-zone's bailout fund could be injected directly into troubled banks. Merkel increasingly spoke of political union but in Paris they were not clear what she meant. Once again Hollande could not resist jabbing at the German leader: 'Those who speak most passionately about political union,' he said, 'are often the ones who hesitate the most when it comes to making pressing decisions.'

During Europe's crisis, it has often seemed that the great days of the French–German embrace belong in the past. On 8 July 2012, the two leaders met at the cathedral in the French city of Reims. They were there to remember another moment fifty years earlier. Then, the German Chancellor, Konrad Adenaeur, and President Charles de Gaulle had celebrated a Te Deum, kneeling and praying together in the vastness of the Gothic cathedral. It was one of history's moments: two statesmen, sombre, worshipping together, sealing reconciliation between their countries. Much German and French blood had been spilled in the countryside of

Champagne but on that day, the two leaders watched French and German troops parade side by side on a training ground at Mourmelon. These were the leaders of a generation shaped by conflict.

It was a tribute to Europe's success that when Merkel and Hollande visited Reims the need for a defining gesture had passed but, as the weight of history shifted, it was less clear what bound these two countries together. Merkel said, 'Long live the friendship between France and Germany,' but it seemed more of an obligatory toast than the celebration of something dynamic and creative. Reconciliation was taken for granted; it had been woven into the fabric of Europe. Yet throughout the crisis in Europe the reminders of the past have never been absent: on the day Merkel and Hollande were in Reims, the headstones of forty German soldiers killed in World War One were uprooted and damaged in an incident unexplained.

France's power was political and diplomatic; German power was economic. Germany understood that its future lay in being European. The French saw themselves as the architects of the European project. Together, they were the engine room for European integration. 'Europe will not make progress without a functioning Franco–German axis,' said a senior member of Angela Merkel's party, yet the crisis in the euro-zone has exposed French weakness and confirmed German strength. The relationship between the two countries has shifted and has become unequal.

Before France adopted the euro, its labour costs were lower than those of Germany. It ran a current account surplus. In the past ten years, however, its competitiveness with Germany has declined by 25 per cent. The French state sector has expanded: 5 million French people – 22 per cent of the workforce – are now *fonctionnaires*, civil servants. There are ninety civil servants for every 1,000 people in France; in Germany, the number is fifty. In France, employers pay twice as much in social charges as their dynamic neighbour. Public spending accounts for 57 per cent of national output, the highest in Europe. Quite simply, France has been out-paced by Germany.

France still has major international companies with global brands: L'Oréal is the largest cosmetics and beauty company; the world leader in luxury is LVMH, with names in its stable like Louis Vuitton, Moét & Chandon and Christian Dior. Michelin, with its starred restaurants and guides, is one of the two great tyre manufacturers in the world. Danone has a global reputation for producing fresh dairy products. Areva is the largest nuclear power company. EDF is a giant electricity producer. Renault and Peugeot still manufacture cars. Axa is a major player in global insurance, and BNP Paribas in banking. Paris is the global headquarters for Sanofi-Aventis, one of the largest companies in pharmaceuticals. Many of the products for Europe's construction industry come from Saint Gobain. Accor is the world's leading hotel operator and Pernod Ricard, the drinks company, helps close many a day.

It is an impressive list but it disguises another reality. Debt has risen to over 90 per cent. Unemployment remains stubbornly above 10 per cent and is rising. Growth is spluttering and French society is resistant to change. The labour market is one of the least flexible in Europe: it is almost impossible to fire workers. That is why there are so few middle-sized companies compared to Germany. The restrictions on laying off workers become even more stringent for companies employing over fifty people. French business complains that it is being hampered by the high social security costs it has to pay. France needs reforming, but President Hollande's allies are the unions and the left. They are alert to any change that, in their view, weakens the French social safety net. When Sarkozy raised the retirement age to sixty-two they had taken to the streets and blocked the oil refineries.

The crisis is challenging the welfare states that helped define Europe. The former Dutch politician and former European commissioner Frits Bolkestein said, 'The party is over . . . we shall all have to work longer and harder, more hours in the week, more weeks in the year, and no state pension before the age of sixty-seven.' It is a message that no French leader has yet fully shared with the French people. One French economist, Christian Saint-Etienne, said, 'We are on the verge of an industrial and economic defeat as ignominious as the one suffered in 1940.'

The Germans fear France's weakness. A former French prime minister, Dominique de Villepin, said, 'Germany has lost faith in France.' Other countries like Greece and Spain and Italy are embracing painful reforms in the teeth of fierce opposition. Volker Kauder, a German MP from Merkel's coalition said, 'It would be good if the socialists there (in France) undertook real and courageous structural reforms. That would be good for the country and good for Europe.' In the myriad conversations between politicians and officials from the two countries, the Germans agitate for action. They mutter that Hollande wasted his first hundred days in office. The Germans warn that, sooner or later, investors will demand a higher price for buying French debt. And, if its borrowing costs become unsustainable, there is no bail-out fund that could protect France.

*   *   *

The view in the Chancellery in Berlin is of a country that is 'extremely inward-looking'. They want Hollande to convince his own supporters that 'competitiveness is not a crime'. They want him to shed his 'ideological preferences' and to start taking decisions that reflect the real world. The German view is that France 'must move fast'. It is the country that concerns Merkel's circle of advisers the most. Critics in France say that Hollande is behaving as he did when he was head of the socialist party. 'He negotiates with everyone, every second of the day. As head of the socialist party secretariat, you don't learn to decide but compromise.'

It is not just a question of leadership. It is a question of France itself, a country 'deeply nostalgic and narcissistic', as one German paper called it. Much of French energy is directed at protecting its way of life. It can be seen in its manicured cities. It is there in rural France, timeless and unchanging, a place to withdraw to, to reconnect with old certainties. It is why Paris fights so fiercely to protect subsidies for its farmers. Many of the towns in the south west are shrines to the past. Places like Issigeac, a perfectly preserved medieval village with its houses of wood and stone, or Monpazier, a film set from the Middle Ages. The country roads, bounded by sunflowers, their heads lowered, or rows of vines or lines of poplars, is the landscape of memory and identity and must be protected. France's partners are questioning whether it can modernise as well as preserve, whether it can grow as well as defend its social programmes. In 2013 the French Labour minister Michel Sapin said of France 'there is a state but it is a totally bankrupt state.'

The crisis has weakened France and strengthened Germany. It is more powerful than at any time in the past sixty years. The German paper *Süddeutsche Zeitung* said,

'Germany stands where it never wanted to stand again after 1945, as the dominant power in the middle of Europe.' The former German Chancellor, Helmut Schmidt, is not alone in fearing Germany's ascendancy. 'The present German government,' he said, 'has not understood that Germany must be bound into a union, an entity greater than itself. This bond is in the German interest.'

France resents its loss of influence. It chafes at the German Chancellor being named 'Frau Europe' on successive magazine covers. It bristles when Berlin is called the capital of Europe. It questions why the German finance minister is the most quoted European on the crisis. It objects to Germany redesigning the future of Europe. It struggles to accept that no European idea can survive without Berlin's support. It was not supposed to be that way. The European Union was largely a French design, but the crisis has handed power to the continent's strongest economy, the country across the Rhine. France feels injured and vulnerable, and so the key relationship that has under-pinned Europe is unstable.

Despite a plethora of summits and meetings, Europe's crisis could not be contained. During the summer of 2012 it spread to the fourth largest country in the euro-zone – Spain.

Chapter 16

Spain: Resisting the Men in Black

Spain conceals itself. It is not like Greece. Central Athens can feel abandoned, the will to disguise the marks of a failed state exhausted. Not so Madrid. The *Madridlenos* mask their downfall. Their city carries fewer scars. It is less boarded up after hours. It is not defaced. It clings to its pride. The wide, tree-lined Paseo del Prado. The galleries nestled together with their Picassos, Velázquezes and Goyas. The flashy white-marbled City Hall. The Fountain of Cibeles glinting in the sun: the goddess of nature pulled by sinuous lions where Real Madrid fans celebrate. The time-passing squares like Santa Ana. The fashion shopping of Calle Serrano and the moneyed elegance of Calle Lagasca. The Spanish party on whilst spending less. It remains true, as Hemingway observed, that, 'Nobody goes to bed in Madrid until they have killed the night.'

Yet societies unravel in small ways. Spain vies with Greece for the worst unemployment in Europe. There are nearly 2 million households where no one holds an official job. For much of the early part of Europe's crisis, the priority was to prevent contagion, to stop it engulfing Spain. By 2012 that was no longer possible. The country was in its second recession in three years.

On the surface, Spain seems unchanging and then, a brief encounter, an incident, a newspaper story, reveals a society cornered, its energy turned to survival. In countless villages and small towns there is hardship.

Cenicientos is 80 kilometres south west of the capital. It is a long climb towards the foothills of the Sierra de Gredos. The flatlands are planted with olives and vines but higher up are oaks and junipers and moss-encrusted rocks. There is a lookout point, overseeing a red-tiled town below. Cenicientos appears tidy, peaceful and slow; but it is bankrupt.

In a corner of the main square is the town hall. Hunkered down behind a heavy door is the mayor. He is a young, earnest man with an impossible job. Just over 2,000 people live in Cenicientos, but its debts exceed 6 million euros. The mayor cannot pay the wages of his municipal workers. He has not taken a salary for two years but he is wary of walking the streets of his own town: he is hassled and abused by those demanding to be paid for work done.

In a small bar, with its fruit machines and faded photos of bullfights, sits a group of women. Some of them are in their early twenties, others older. They are teachers, school cleaners, administrators, and the recorder of births and deaths. They have banded together, a sisterhood of the unpaid. 'I haven't been paid since October 2011,' says one. The woman beside her nods her head. She has not received a pay cheque for almost a year. Not one of them has been paid in eight months. Their means of survival are the same. 'My parents and partner,' said one. 'Family,' said another woman crisply. 'My parents,' said one of the younger women, 'I live with them.' Even though they are not being paid, they continue working. They do not want to give the town hall the excuse not to settle with them eventually.

Here, even in the smallness of Cenicientos, they have to live with a past, defined by extravagance. On the outskirts of the town is a new bullring that seats more people than the entire community. Some of the fiercest bulls are bred on these lands, and the dream was that the town would stage great *corridas de toros*. Now they can scarcely afford the ring's upkeep. Central government has set up a fund to help local governments settle their bills but, in exchange, they have to commit to deep cuts in services. Many of the municipal workers have been told they will lose their jobs but they do not know when. Some of them doubt the town's survival. 'It will be a place for old people,' said one of the unpaid women.

Across the vast plains of Castilla-La Mancha lies the town of Pioz. It is one of the most indebted communities in Spain: 3,500 people live there and it has racked up debts of 16 million euros. It, too, dreamt big. It imagined a town of 25,000 people and started building rows of trim, red-roofed houses. Now, 600 of them lie empty and crumbling. Looters have stripped out the shutters, the electric wires and the fittings. The town spent 500,000 euros on a medical centre and 12 million euros on a sewage and water treatment plant, which now lies idle. There is no money to keep it running. At night they cannot afford the street lighting. Without outside help, it will take Pioz fifty-eight years to pay off its debts.

Alcalá de Henares lies just thirty-five kilometres to the north west of Madrid. It is a world heritage site. The city rises out of the valley of the Henares River, and is home to one of the oldest universities in the world. The author, Miguel de Cervantes, was born there. Thousands of people visit, to sit in the squares and to walk the mediaeval streets. On the edge of the town are the industrial parks. Many small businesses have their shutters down. Consumers are not spending and credit has dried up. The new mayor is Javier Bello, an open and modern official. He has started dismantling the perks of municipal workers: he could not understand why the city was paying for driving tests, but much deeper savings are needed so he has decided to cut the street lighting and to reduce waste collection. He could not do that in the centre where the tourists come, but has done it in the suburbs where most of the local people live. So, at night, residents leave darkened neighbourhoods to walk ancient streets, which still have lighting.

Out west, in Andalusia, Jerez de la Frontera sits between the sea and the mountains. It is the city of sherry making, of gypsy flamenco, of Formula One racing. It is also broke. A city of 212,000 people has debts of over a billion euros and is struggling to survive. It is unable to pay the bills for electricity and water. Half of its infant and junior schools are closed because the cleaning staff have not been paid and have gone on strike. The police can only go on patrol on foot because there is not the money to pay for fuel for their patrol cars. In late 2012, rubbish lay uncollected and local people began burning it in the neighbourhoods. There were fires across the city. Mayor Jesus Manuel Ampero says, 'My health is cracking, and I am ashamed.'

It has become the story of modern Spain. A third of city councils have stopped settling bills and making payments. Hundreds of thousands of public sector workers are not receiving their wages. It is a society that only survives through family networks. The crisis is changing the Spanish way of life: the working day is built around a break between two and five in the afternoon; in many cities, workers eat together at lunchtime. In Madrid, the tradition was to find a café or restaurant with a set menu for about 10 euros. It was the main meal of the day, with the expectation that the staff would stay at their desks until eight in the evening. Now, gradually, people are bringing lunch boxes to work. 'The crisis has hit citizens so hard,' said Rogelio Barahona, the chef at the restaurant, Urkiola Mendi, 'that people haven't had any choice but to get over the embarrassment of taking food to work. Once someone has lost the shame factor, it makes it easy for everyone else.'

In November 2011, Mariano Rajoy had become prime minister. He was a conservative who rode to power on the back of disillusionment with the socialists. They were blamed for the excess, for the intoxicated spending and the broken economy that followed. 'The socialists,' Rajoy boldly claimed, 'did not know how to manage Spain's economy.' He was a lucky politician who had bided his time, waiting for the political wheel of fortune to spin in his favour. In Europe it was the era of the usurper. Political incumbents were being discarded. Rajoy said he would win back the investors yet despite years in politics he is taciturn, closed and a poor communicator. He is a lanky man with rimless glasses who wears a beard to cover the scars from a traffic accident which prevents him from shaving. He wanted power but could not explain what he wanted it for. The opposition leader said to his face, 'If you said what you have in mind, not even your own supporters would vote for you.' One paper said he offered the 'discreet charm of austerity' but others accused him of running a 'valium campaign', aimed at lulling voters rather than levelling with them.

A month after taking office he revealed his hand: he announced 15 billion euros of spending cuts. There would be a freeze on civil servants' wages. Working hours would be extended from 35 to 35.7 a week. The minimum wage was frozen. Even so, the country missed the targets set by the European Union to reduce its deficit. In March 2012, Rajoy was told by Brussels he had to get the budget deficit down to 5.3 per cent. Europe's leaders were not in the mood to cut Spain any slack. They had just agreed to a pact to enforce tight discipline over national budgets. They could not be seen to be easing off on their targets. The Austrian finance minister was insistent: 'No,' she said, 'Spain has to make an effort . . . we've got to be tough.' The strategy, however, was as ever flawed. As the country reduced wages, pensions and government spending, the economy shrank as tax revenues fell and the debt pile grew. Spain was proving true what most economists knew: that deflation is the debtor's enemy.

The country was particularly vulnerable because of its banks. They held around 200 billion euros of bad loans from the collapse of the construction industry. That was the equivalent of 18 per cent of Spain's economic output. Many of these debts were hidden away in the *cajas*, the banks of the regional governments. Some of them had begun life as charities run by local Catholic churches; over time many of these savings institutions formed links with local politicians, who had built up stakes in property and construction companies. It was these local banks that provided the funds for the airports without planes, the ports without ships, the vanity projects without purpose: twelve of the forty-five *cajas* which existed when the crisis started were being investigated for corruption. At some of these savings banks, members of the board were being loaned money from the bank they were supervising.

One of them was the Caja de Ahorras del Mediterráneo. It flaunted its history, its seriousness. It dated back to the 1800s but it could not resist the lure of the housing boom. The governor of the Bank of Spain called it 'the worst of the worst'.

Places on the board were given to political friends and allies, so among those tasked with signing off on multi-million euro projects were a supermarket check-out assistant, a dancing teacher and a university psychologist. The ballet teacher Isabel Cambronero ended up on the bank's control committee. Later, before an inquiry, she conceded 'I can't audit an auditor because I don't know how to audit anyone.' A small businessman on the board José Enrique Garrigos, said 'Did I check through the accounts?' 'Look I'm an average businessman. I don't have the time or the training to do that.' An 8 billion hole was found in its balance sheet. Senior management have been accused of receiving millions in loans on easy terms. Some of these smaller *cajas* were riddled with greed and corruption and some were forced into 'shotgun marriages' with Spain's larger banks.

In May 2012 the Spanish government announced that the giant Bankia group needed rescuing: a state with almost no funds was promising to inject 19 billion euros into a bank. One of the international credit rating agencies immediately downgraded sixteen Spanish banks, fearing what it called 'undisclosed toxic debts'.

'The Spanish banks are in trouble because of real estate loans,' said Francis Lun of Lycean Holdings, 'and the hole is so big that the Spanish government will find it difficult to save the Spanish banks without blowing a big hole in its budget.'

Investors and savers were rattled. Significant sums began to be withdrawn from Bankia: in one month, foreign investors withdrew 31 billion euros. Rosio Lopez was a young woman who had done well in animation. She decided not to take a risk; she withdrew 30,000 euros and placed the money in a non-Spanish bank. Many of her friends did the same. There was no panic, no bank run, but people were afraid. On a

Madrid street, a distraught woman spotted the minister of finance and asked him about her life savings, which she had built up since she was thirteen years old. As the minister tried to reassure her, she demanded to know whether her money was safe. The fears could not be allayed easily. The people were losing faith in their own institutions. The former Spanish prime minister, Felipe González, said, 'We're in a state of total emergency, the worst crisis we have ever lived through.' The finance minister, Luis de Guindos, said that the 'battle for the euro is going to be waged in Spain'.

As had happened with Greece, Ireland and Portugal, the country's borrowing costs were edging closer to dangerous levels.

Once again, Europe faced a dilemma. One official in Brussels said it was as if the 'crisis was set on replay'. Spain was not Greece. It had functioning institutions and a government that delivered on its commitments, but Europe's leaders feared the fall-out from Spain. Investors were turning their backs on Europe. The Italians believed their economy was being undermined by the crisis in the Spanish banks. So the pressure built on Spain to settle the fears of others by asking for a rescue. Pride was at stake. The government was unyielding, adamantine; its face set against a general bail-out that would place the country in the hands of the IMF. The finance minister declared, 'The men in black will not be coming to Madrid.' In popular imagination, the IMF inspectors were black-suited financial undertakers who would put the country into administration and force it into a straight-jacket of austerity. Rajoy was defiant: the banking sector, he said, would not need a bail-out. On 28 May he declared, 'There will be no rescue of the Spanish banking sector.'

The German government and its press were unimpressed. They called on Spain to give up 'false pride'. They accused

Rajoy of indulging in 'kamikaze politics' and 'fatal hubris'. The prime minister, however, believed his credibility was on the line. He feared a bail-out would come with conditions attached, dictated by the so-called troika of the EU, the IMF and the European Central Bank. He was reportedly sending texts to his finance minister, urging him to resist. 'We are the fourth largest power in the EZ (euro-zone),' he told him. 'Spain is not Uganda.' The Ugandans were insulted. Its foreign minister retorted, 'Uganda does not want to be Spain.'

Rajoy believed Spain's economic size strengthened its hand. 'We are powerful,' he told his finance minister, 'and if they don't give in, the whole thing will go down. It will cost Europe 500 billion if Spain goes bust, and then another 700 billion if Italy goes bust.' What the prime minister wanted was for the EU to ease its targets for cutting the deficit.

In the end, Madrid could not resist the power of Brussels and the urging of Germany. One Friday afternoon in June, the rumours deepened that the country was on the verge of requesting aid. Denials followed. The following day, Spain sought a rescue for its banks and was promised 100 billion euros.

It was a curious day. It was the story of a bail-out that dare not speak its name. The government tried to pretend it was some technical adjustment. The prime minister went missing. Only the following day did he re-emerge at his official residence, Moncloa Palace. 'It was,' he said, 'a rescue without humiliation.' The impression was given that the much-feared IMF would play no part. It was untrue: the fund would have a monitoring role. Despite all the comments in the European press calling on him to act, Rajoy insisted no one had leant on him. 'I was the one who pressured to get the credit,' he said. With that, he headed to Poland to watch a game of football.

The government believed that if it downplayed the significance of the loans for the banks, the public would too.

The markets and the investors were not so easily distracted. It took two days to establish that the loans would be added to Spain's debt. Once again, the problems of the banks were jeopardising a country's finances: Europe had not yet broken the dangerous loop between banks and governments. The financial health of one depended on the other. The Spanish banks would have to pay back the loans but if they failed, it would be the government that would be on the hook. Increasingly, as foreign investors shunned Spain, it was local banks who were the only institutions buying Spanish government debt. These were some of the very same banks that were now queuing up for international help. Alejandro Varela from the brokerage company Renta 4 said that 'it was as if the government was buying its own debt . . . like a dog chasing its own tail.'

Internationally, the doubts deepened. The economist Paul Krugman commented, 'You get a picture of a European policy élite always ready to spring into action to defend the banks, but otherwise completely unwilling to admit that its policies are failing the people which the economy is supposed to serve.'

The government in Madrid knew the banking bail-out would not settle the markets. Investors still wanted to know what, in the last resort, stood behind the currency. Spain's deputy prime minister, Soraya Sáenz de Santamaría, called for the EU to enforce the euro-zone with some sort of mechanism. 'It's not about who leaves the euro,' she said. 'It is about the EU itself. What is Europe without the euro?' What Spain wanted was for the EU to stand behind its debt, to save it from humiliation and a further round of cuts.

During the summer of 2012, Spain was being buffeted by the markets. Its borrowing costs were moving inexorably higher. Investors could not see how the country could tackle its debt crisis with the economy in recession and falling revenues. The question lay unanswered as to what would happen if Spain needed a general bail-out. It was not clear that the euro-zone's bail-out funds could save Spain. Figures were bandied about. The country would need 300 billion euros or 700 billion or even more. Once again, eyes turned towards Germany. The economist Niall Ferguson penned an article saying that the news had to be broken to German voters that 'they are going to be handing over very large sums of money to Southern Europeans for the foreseeable future'. Merkel was not ready for that. She would stay the course; deficits would have to be cut and reforms implemented. The French minister for industry said, 'Certain leaders, led by Mrs Merkel, are fixated by blind ideology.' A German columnist, Jakob Augstein, said Merkel's 'abrasive pro-austerity policies threaten everything that previous German governments have accomplished since World War Two'. Spain, it seemed, was heading for the moment when it would need a general bail-out, and that would tip Europe into a deeper crisis.

And then came an unexpected moment, a line buried in a speech. On 26 July, Mario Draghi, the president of the European Central Bank, addressed an investment conference at Lancaster House in London. Towards the end of his remarks he said, 'There is another message I want to tell you. Within our mandate,' he continued, 'the ECB is ready to do whatever it takes to preserve the euro.' He then paused for dramatic effect before continuing 'and believe me it will be enough.' The president had never spoken in such terms before. One of those present said the comments seemed to be 'off the cuff'. A senior banking official wondered whether Draghi had gone further than he intended. He was certainly nervous by what he had unleashed. The markets, however, were buoyed; they believed that Draghi's words could only mean that the European Central Bank would intervene to buy up the bonds of troubled countries like Spain and Italy. That would force down their borrowing costs.

Draghi spent two days on the phone trying to coax the leaders of France and Germany to fall in behind him: he feared that the German Bundesbank, a critic of bond-buying, would undermine his position with a fatal reaction from the markets.

Only in September did Mario Draghi finally explain what he had meant in London. He swept aside German concerns and announced a new bold bond-buying programme that would help hold down interest rates for countries like Spain. The European Central Bank would act as backstop. It would be willing to buy up the debt of troubled countries on an unlimited basis. The countries would first have to request help and then accept conditions monitored by the IMF. Draghi had come to believe that part of the explanation for the high borrowing costs being demanded of countries like Spain was the fear that the euro would collapse. By promising 'unlimited' intervention, he wanted to remove that uncertainty. Almost immediately, Spain and Italy saw their borrowing rates fall. Stock markets recovered and the flight of capital stopped.

The German Bundesbank opposed the move by the ECB. It saw it as dangerous: a back-door way of financing governments. One German paper accused Draghi of writing 'a blank cheque' to debtor countries. The head of the German

Bundesbank, Jens Weidmann, saw a weakening of will by a political class grown weary from three years of fire-fighting. Policy makers had reached the limit of what they could do. This was a last throw of the dice made more attractive because it was not politicians that were footing the bill. Some close to the Bundesbank thought it 'a very dangerous political mood'.

Crucially, Chancellor Merkel said little about the European Central Bank's decision, but her silence indicated she had sided with Mario Draghi rather than the Bundesbank. Previously the German government, too, had been wary of the ECB buying bonds. By the time Draghi was running the ECB the mood was different. Bond-buying was the only way of transferring payments to the weaker nations without incurring the wrath of the German voters. Merkel attached great importance to countries having to accept conditions in order to qualify for the ECB's help but, faced with the threat of the euro-zone breaking up, she once again compromised.

Wolfgang Schäuble, the German finance minister, insisted that 'nothing had changed in Germany' but he could not disguise there were now rifts over the ECB's policy. 'Public disputes between board members of an independent central bank can be harmful to its independence,' he said. What the German government was watching carefully was whether Draghi's move allowed countries to back off from making painful reforms. One senior government official said, 'We need a certain amount of market pressure to keep reform on the table.'

Rajoy and his ministers faced a dilemma. They had accepted a bail-out for the Spanish banks. Now, after the Draghi announcement, a route was open to them to lower their general borrowing costs but that would involve placing Spain in a general bail-out programme. Rajoy still feared that, like other leaders before him, he would be punished by the voters for agreeing to a rescue. He was able, however, to postpone taking such a sensitive decision because, in the aftermath of the Draghi statement, market pressure eased. Investors were unwilling to bet against the ECB. They believed the European Central Bank would stand behind Spain and Italy.

The government in Madrid, however, still believed it might need help so it passed another tough budget in the hope that if it had to ask for a general bail-out, no further conditions would be demanded of it. Rajoy's view was that it was better to put the cuts in place himself rather than be seen to be acting under pressure from Brussels. In fact, all the new measures were discussed with officials at the European Commission. It reflected the new reality; that sovereign governments had to run their decisions on taxes and spending via Brussels first.

So Madrid held out against the stigma of applying for a rescue. The lower borrowing costs helped, but they could not ensure recovery in the real economy. With the economy in recession for the second time in three years, the tension in the country was growing.

La Línea is a small Spanish town that feeds off the nearby territory of Gibraltar. It is another town broken by debt. La Línea owes the equivalent of 3,000 euros for each of its 65,000 inhabitants. It is a scruffy, down-at-heel port that ekes out a living through smuggling into the British enclave nearby. Here, too, municipal workers have not been paid for almost a year. Mayor Gemma Araujo has had eggs thrown at her house, and her secretary's car has been set on fire. In March she saw an opportunity. She was attending a ceremony in Cadiz attended by King Juan Carlos. She handed him a letter describing the tragedy of a town, without funding, living on the margins. She never heard back.

The king went elephant hunting in Botswana. The safari cost an estimated 40,000 euros and would have gone unnoticed if he had not broken his hip. The monarch's high spending sat uncomfortably alongside the towns with no money. He was forced into making an abject apology: 'I'm sorry,' he said, 'I made a mistake and it won't happen again.' He and the crown prince cut their salaries by 7 per cent. However, not long after, as he left a funeral for an aristocratic friend, the crown prince was approached by a woman. She was homeless, and opened up her hand in the hope of receiving a few coins. The prince, however, grabbed her hand and shook it before strolling off. In a country where more than half of young people were without work, respect could no longer be taken for granted.

Slowly, as 2012 passed, resistance to spending cuts and austerity stiffened. The demonstrations became more frequent and more violent. There was not the rage of Greece but Spanish protests changed. The people became defiant. Parliament was ringed permanently by police vans and metal barriers. Even the police joined in the protests. At one point, a hundred plain-clothes officers had to be corralled by riot police when they tried to disrupt a police graduation ceremony.

On the streets, however, the police seemed unprepared for the sit-ins, for the occupation of squares, for the angry chants and the clenched fists. In September 2012, after a general strike, a police officer raised his stick and repeatedly beat a woman who had sat down and refused to move. On 14 November, an officer snapped on the Grand Via, after an argument with a protestor, and lashed out at those around him. Later in the evening, arrested protestors with blood streaming from their faces were lined up in the Calle de Cervantes and forced to wait for medical treatment. Two young girls were brought there. A police officer punched one of them in the face. A police officer then hit him. There were signs that the years of austerity were straining society.

In November, in the Basque town of Barakaldo, Amaia Egana jumped from her fourth-floor apartment to her death. She was fifty-three. The bailiffs were preparing to move in after she had failed to pay her mortgage. Her washing was still out on the balcony. She had worked at a local bus depot and could not bear the humiliation of eviction. Her friends do not believe the suicide was planned. It was as if something snapped in her.

A local judge, Juan Carlos Mediavilla, arrived at the apartment as the body, covered with a black sheet, was removed. 'This cannot be allowed to continue,' he said. Across the country, there had been 400,000 evictions since 2008. In the first six months of 2012 there were on average over 300 evictions each day. News of Amaia's death brought crowds onto the streets. They vented their anger on the bank that had demanded that Amaia leave her apartment. Stickers with the words 'Murderers' were stuck to cash machines. Red paint was thrown against the bank windows and the people shouted, 'Guilty! Guilty!'

Fifteen days earlier, fifty-three-year-old José Luis Domingo had hanged himself rather than allow the bailiffs to evict him from his home in the southern city of Grenada. The prime minister Mariano Rajoy sensed a dangerous and unpredictable mood in the country. 'We are living through things that no one likes to see,' he said, 'situations that are completely inhumane.' Parliament, fearful of the streets, hastily passed a two-year moratorium for the most vulnerable families.

The high-speed train eases out of Atocha station. Spain vies with France for the best rail network in Europe: it is a reminder that not all the money went on feeding the vanity of politicians. To the Spanish, the network is the product of another era: '*Cuando pensabamos que eramos ricos*', 'When we were rich', they say. In the carriages, the digital display flashes up the speed until it settles at 300 kilometres per hour, hurtling by olive groves and fields of solar panels. It is just two and a half hours to Barcelona, the capital of Catalonia.

On the balconies they hang their dreams, the yellow and red horizontal stripes of the *Senyera*, the Catalan flag. Many of the flags carry a white star emblazoned on a blue triangle. It is the flag of independence. There is not a Spanish flag to be seen. The European crisis has reawakened nationalism in Spain. In the period of choking austerity, the Catalans resent the funds they have to contribute to the coffers in Madrid. They blame the capital and its politicians for their hardship and want to be in charge of their own finances. Amidst the economic gloom, independence has become a cause: noisy, brash, exhilarating and, to the rest of Spain, threatening.

Barca is a name that requires little explanation: Barcelona is a global football brand. The Nou Camp football stadium is also a cock-pit of cultural identity, proud of its motto, 'More than just a club.' Inside the stadium, supporters and their sons and daughters come draped in a flag, not just of the club but of an independent Catalonia. It flutters from the shoulders of the drummer who stands behind the goal setting the beat of the chants from the most impassioned supporters. They are absorbed in the game but they eye the clock, waiting for it to reach 17 minutes and 14 seconds. For Catalans, 1714 is a defining date in their history. On 11 September, in that year, the Bourbon forces entered Barcelona and the war was lost. The defeat still rankles, and is commemorated as *La Diada Nacional de Catalunya,* the National Day of Catalonia. Now at 17 minutes and 14 seconds precisely, the fans spread wide their arms and shout, 'Independence!'

On 11 September 2012, over a million people took to the streets in a massive demonstration for independence. It surprised Catalans and jolted the rest of Spain. The Spanish prime minister dismissed the gathering as 'a rabble', a word once used to describe the Moors. That caused offence. The education minister, José Ignacio Wert, told Parliament he intended to 'Spanish-ise' Catalan schools and that provoked fury. For older Catalans it recalled the dictatorship of General Franco when the traits of regional identity were ruthlessly stamped on. School children were urged to report those speaking Catalan. Now, on the streets, it is easy to find those who say, 'We have our own language and culture and we want to be a nation.'

The main party that favours independence hands out the EU flag at its rallies. It is done to reassure. An independent Catalonia would apply to join the European Union. Brussels, instinctively, is against the break-up of states but, ironically, the union provides cover for peoples determined to root their identity in becoming a nation. In the midst of an economic depression, Spain is having to confront the question as to whether it will stay together as one country or break up. Madrid says it will use the full force of the law to prevent the Catalans holding a referendum about independence. The prime minister insists there is no right to self-determination under the Constitution. The European crisis is shaking the foundations of modern Spain and reviving memories of ancient divisions.

Economic recovery is long predicted but it recedes into the future: not before 2014, government ministers estimate nervously. There are some green shoots. Spanish wages are falling compared to Germany and the country is clawing back some competitiveness. Spanish exports are performing strongly but the national debt is still increasing. Many of the harsher austerity measures, passed hurriedly to keep the 'men in black' at bay, have yet to take effect. When they do, they will only depress the economy further. The promise is that one day, the re-engineered economy will bounce back and growth will return. What the government asks of the people is endurance, but they will not be patient for ever. Since the crisis began, 300,000 graduates have left Spain; a generation lost to the country.

European officials eye the streets anxiously. They fear the occupation of a central square that then is copied in country after country, in a continent-wide act of rebellion. The mood is sullen but it has not turned against the idea of Europe itself. 'Will there be social unrest? Will there be tensions?' asks President Van Rompuy. 'Of course,' he replies. He accepts time is running out. 'If there is no return to growth in two years' time, then nothing that has been said about the crisis can be guaranteed,' he says.

Chapter 17
Ciao! Dolce Vita

Nature made Cortina d'Ampezzo exclusive. It is a resort gated by its mountains, bound in by its valleys. It is known as 'the jewel of the Dolomites'. It is flashy and wears its money easily: a place to display wealth and not disguise it. Since World War One it has attracted the aristocratic crowd, pitching up and settling into the nineteenth-century villas and mansions. It has been the retreat for Hepburn and Hemingway and has had its brush with Bond: part of *For Your Eyes Only* was shot on its bobsleigh run.

In the late afternoon the Monti Paldi, 'the pale mountains', glow pink and red. It is the call to join the evening *passeggiata* in Piazza Venezia, a parade of furs and high-heeled boots, which precedes the slipping into Prada or Dolce & Gabbana before a visit to the wine bars. It is here over the New Year that money and all its restlessness briefly settles.

On the last day of 2011 the spell was broken. The town was raided. Tax collectors from the *Guardia di Finanza*, in their military uniforms, set up road blocks. The inspectors were looking for the owners of luxury cars: the Ferraris, the Maseratis and the Lamborghinis. In Cortina d'Ampezzo, the growl of high-performance engines is the soundtrack to the high mountain air. Slowly, with the veiled menace of a certain kind of politeness, the tax officials began logging the details of the owners and drivers. They would be checked to see whether their declared income supported the ownership of such a car. For a few hours the rich felt hunted. Wealthy Italians tried to ease their vehicles out of town unseen from the dreaded gaze of the *Fiamme Gialle*, the yellow flame of the *Guardia di Finanza*. The mayor of Cortina, Andrea Franceschi, was enraged, protesting it was a Hollywood spectacle intended to justify further tax increases by the government. One man, sliding and slithering for the exit, compared it to the McCarthy era in the States. 'You're guilty by suspicion,' he said.

The raids expanded. In January 2012, the financial police fanned out in Milan and pulled over the drivers of 350 Porsches and SUVs. Their names and vehicle registrations were passed to the national tax agency. Portofino and Florence were also in the net. Over time, the financial police assembled a picture of wealthy Italy, of Fellini's fabled *La Dolce Vita*. Of the 12 million Italians who claimed to earn 50,000 euros or less per year, over 200,000 of them drove high-powered luxury cars, while 26,000 of them owned a yacht. Some 600 of these lower-tax-payers commuted to work by private plane. There were people declaring annual incomes of less than 30,000 euros who were driving cars that cost 200,000 euros.

These round-ups, which unashamedly targeted the appearance of wealth, never failed to unearth tax evasion. There was the builder in Florence who was driving a Mercedes who had no tax records, while his wife was receiving social assistance. There was the Ferrari-driving plumber who had hidden away 2 million euros by operating two sets of accounts; the one that showed the much lower income was for the tax man. In Bergamo, they found the driver of a 200,000 euro Ferrari 131 who had avoided paying 3 million euros in taxes since 2007. The police discovered 19 luxury cars owned by businesses that had posted losses the previous year.

All of these raids and searches were ordered at the highest
level of government. It was a great shaking of the tree of the
rich to see what would come tumbling down. The Italian
prime minister, Mario Monti, had declared war on tax evaders. The sixty-nine-year-old former economist liked the word
'war' and used it often. 'Some measures adopted by the
government against tax evasion,' he said, 'may seem like war
measures and, in reality, they are.' He depicted the round-ups
as a battle for national survival. In 2010, Italy had discovered
from comparing satellite images with the official land register
that a million homes had been built illegally: if they had been
registered, it would have boosted tax revenues by nearly 500
million euros a year. Officials calculated that the Italian
government was losing between 120 and 240 billion euros a
year from undeclared income. It was not just a tidy sum; it
would transform Italy's economic crisis, wiping out the country's annual deficit of 45 billion euros. It would also slice into
Italy's debt mountain of 1.9 trillion euros.

Monti launched an advertising campaign depicting tax
evaders as parasites. He was not just out to catch tax cheats;
he wanted to change Italian culture. He no longer wanted it to
be socially acceptable to hide income. So the raids were high
profile: somehow the papers knew when the internal revenue
service had entered a well-known restaurant in Trastevere in
Rome and had scrutinised the books and the cash register
receipts. The papers splashed the confiscation of a fifteenth-
century castle, with its road lined with lemon trees and a
hundred statues, linked to a prominent fashion family.

The fashion élite was caught up in this new cycle of virtue.
Domenico Dolce and Stefano Gabbana, the stylists for
Monica Belluci and Angelina Jolie, were accused of evading

paying more than 400 million euros in taxes by setting up a holding company in Luxembourg. They denied the charges, and it led one of the designers to opine, 'Maybe it would be better to leave the country.'

Passione Rossa is the Ferrari owners' club where enthusiasts can share their passion for the Prancing Horse, the *Cavallino Rampante*. When some Ferrari drivers decided to go on a drive around Sicily, the police were waiting for them as they drove off the ferry in Palermo. After these police raids, the owners were wary of meeting, of arranging events or even seeing each other. Fabio Barone, who heads the club, says, 'Many Ferrari owners want to get rid of their supercars after the financial police came to one of our events near Rome and checked every driver.' The head of Ferrari, Luca Cordero di Montezemolo, warned of 'demagogic spectacularisation' – of targeting luxury to make theatre.

During this period, too, the former prime minister Silvio Berlusconi was convicted of massive tax evasion in a trial involving his television company.

The Monti government estimated they recovered 12 billion euros in 2011, more than in the previous year. Tax evasion and corruption were engrained in Italian society. The national tax agency calculated that 4.3 million households – roughly 20 per cent of the total – spent in a way that was inconsistent with their reported incomes. Ground down by austerity, some Italians began turning on suspected tax cheats. Thousands of people rang a police hotline to report stores and restaurants that had failed to issue a tax receipt.

It became smart to be understated and to shun the labels and the luxury brands. The growl of the Ferrari could still be heard in the land but heading north, out of Italy. In the first five months of 2011, the export of second-hand, high-performance cars exported from Italy tripled to 13,633 cars. The sales of the super luxury models fell by 47 per cent. The fastidious Mario Monti was unrelenting. He accepted that 'harshness' was an essential part of his policy. He said that 'practices that are deeply rooted in the Italian mentality, such as tax evasion and nepotism, are attitudes that are not worthy of a developed G8 member country.'

Some of the rich howled. Flavio Briatore, the motor racing impresario, said: 'Italy is now a country where, if you own a yacht and tie up in port, you are either a bandit or a thief.' Italy, in their view, had fallen into the hands of an ascetic leader, inflexible and unbending. Monti had been educated by Jesuits and remained committed to his Catholicism. Some found him sanctimonious. In Brussels they referred to him as the 'holy man'. The joke went around that when you handed Mario Monti a Bible, 'He signs it.'

The prime minister believed that changing the Italian mentality was necessary, not just to save the country but also the euro. Despite over twenty European summits, it still remained the case that if Italy got into difficulty it could bring down the single currency with it. The creation of a permanent rescue fund for the euro-zone – the ESM – which came into operation in late 2012 had not removed that risk.

Monti had political space to attempt the difficult if not the impossible. His room to manoeuvre stemmed from the simple fact that he was not Berlusconi. He was also outside the despised caste of politicians. After Berlusconi's show-girls pantomime, Monti reflected Italy's other side. He was sombre, academic and grey. At public events he could be awkward, wooden, even unsure of his own gestures. He was not constantly selling himself and his seriousness earned him respect, and respect gave him the chance to reform. He took on the closed professions like the pharmacists and the taxi associations, insisting that outsiders could compete for their jobs. He challenged the much-cherished Article 18, which ensured that workers could not be fired without good cause and which gave dismissed workers the right to sue their companies to reinstate them. He backed a new law allowing shops, bars and restaurants to stay open 24 hours a day. He embarked on pension reform. In his first six weeks in office he increased the retirement age, raised property taxes and trimmed the costs of government. He proposed an anti-corruption bill that would bar anyone convicted of a serious crime from standing in national or local elections. Many of these reforms were long overdue in a society that had become sclerotic and resistant to change.

In Italy, as elsewhere in Europe, the fear of the euro's collapse had acted as a great catalyst for reform, but Italy was not ready for a cultural revolution. The problem was that it was trying to remake itself with a shrinking economy. Its recession was the worst in sixty years. Since 2007, 1.5 million jobs had been lost. The unemployment rate was over 11 per cent; for those under the age of twenty-four, it reached 35 per cent.

Stefano Meletti had worked in a Sardinian mine for twenty-four years and it was the only work he had known. The Carbosulcis mine supplied coal to a nearby power plant run by the state-controlled energy company, Enel. In the downturn, the demand for coal had fallen and the mine was no longer economic: lay-offs were announced. Around 100 of the miners, armed with explosives, barricaded themselves underground. They invited in reporters and the television cameras. Stefano Meletti, wearing a miner's helmet, stepped forward and said, 'We cannot take it any more.' With his voice rising he repeated the words, 'We cannot! We cannot!' There was a fierce intensity to him as he spoke. 'If someone has decided to kill miners' families,' he continued, 'we'll cut ourselves, we'll cut ourselves.' With that threat he pulled a knife from his back pocket and cut his arm twice. In the midst of this underground press conference, two of his colleagues grabbed Meletti's arms. One of them shouted, 'Do not make us lose our reason to live!' As they rushed Meletti to hospital, he was still shouting, 'We are ready to do crazy things!' It was just one of a number of industrial disputes which reflected the desperation of ordinary workers as businesses folded. Valentina Zurry, one of the women who worked in the mine, said that without her job, 'I'd have nothing to do but work on a little patch of land that my family owns.'

Italy's political culture had deep roots and was resistant to change. Sicily braced itself against reform as it had against its numerous invaders. Its local government was riddled with extravagance; politicians had rewarded themselves richly. To become a councillor was to gain, at a stroke, lifetime security. The Palazzo dei Normanni, 'the Palace of the Normans', in Sicily, is home to the regional assembly. The local councillors have built up so many benefits that they are said to cost the Sicilian tax-payer 500,000 euros for each member. State jobs are traded for votes, so as each election passes, the state pay-roll expands as further posts are created. It was how the island ended up with 26,000 forestry workers, all on good salaries.

Sicily had also been an EU favourite, lavishing it with funds to narrow the gap with northern Italy. Much of the money was siphoned off by the mafia or misspent on viaducts to nowhere, on couscous festivals and golf courses. Brussels, at one point, demanded that some of its money be returned.

When the island revealed it had debts of 5 billion euros, Mario Monti said in May 2012 that he was 'gravely concerned' that the island might default. It was suggested that the government might have to seize control of Sicily's finances. It has not yet proved necessary but some of Italy's regions, like in Spain, are struggling with their debts.

Since the start of Europe's crisis, Italy's gross domestic product has fallen by 7 per cent. Industrial production is down more than 20 per cent. For the past ten years, the country has flat-lined, with low growth. In 2012 the economy slipped into recession. Consumer spending fell, the sharpest drop since World War Two. This was the background against which Mario Monti was introducing 20 billion euros of austerity measures. His promise of a better future rang hollow at a time when 6 million people were having to take on a second job just to survive. Half a million households were struggling to meet their mortgage payments. Italy, like Spain and Greece, saw a steep rise in suicides: the Rome builder who shot himself over his failed business, or the seventy-eight-year-old woman who jumped to her death because of her reduced pension.

Italy's political class often appeared isolated and insensitive. Its Parliament, with its perks and privileges, costs more than those of France, Germany and the UK combined. One politician threw a party for 2,000 guests in Rome. They came in togas and white robes with laurel wreaths. It reminded some of a scene from the film *Satyricon*. Women were nuzzled by men wearing pig masks. Guests lounged on ancient steps decadently dropping grapes in each other's mouths. It led to an investigation as to how the event was funded. The pictures, widely distributed, only served to deepen the hostility towards the political caste that ran Italy.

The alienation was reflected in the streets, where the protests became more violent. In the heart of Rome, demonstrators attacked banks and burnt vehicles. There were glimpses of more dangerous times ahead. At one protest, close to the Senate, a masked man came armed with a sharpened metal stave. The police became less tolerant of the protests and there were allegations against them of brutality. An officer was seen firing three tear-gas canisters from the second floor of a Justice Ministry building on Via Aurelia. Commentators warned the country could return to the so-called 'years of lead' when Italy, in the seventies and eighties, had been scarred by political violence.

Through all this, the studious Mario Monti remained outwardly unperturbed. He had restored international respect for Italy. He was included in Europe's most important meetings and was fêted as the man who had helped save the European project by restoring sound government to the third largest economy in the euro-zone. Some time had been bought, but he feared the crisis was sowing a dangerous instability. He warned of the 'psychological dissolution' of the continent, where people gave up and lost faith in the idea of Europe. On several occasions he spoke to the German Chancellor of the risks of a sullen southern Europe turning against the north. Opinion polls in Italy suggested that 55 per cent had doubts about the euro and a third of those polled wanted to return to the lira. Silvio Berlusconi flirted with embracing this new scepticism. 'It was not blasphemy,' he said, 'to be against the euro.'

Out of this disenchantment with the old politics emerged a comic, threatening to uproot the political establishment. The wild-haired and acerbic Beppe Grillo had long delivered his jokes and stories to the television fringes. Over time, his comedian's blog, inchoate and iconoclastic, spawned a political movement. His postings seethed with disgust at corruption. He railed against France and Germany for imposing austerity on Europe. He favoured a vote on the euro and threatened to stop paying off Italy's debts. He mocked Prime Minister Mario Monti as '*rigor monti*' for turning the country into a corpse. His was the rage of the anti-politician. He launched one of his election campaigns in a wet suit. His headquarters was his website. He eschewed the TV channels and the papers for the internet and 'spontaneous' grass-roots gatherings. His 'Five Star Movement', as he called it, had some success and at one point attracted 20 per cent support in the polls. Grillo reflected Europe's uncertain mood, a disillusionment with conventional politics. The crisis had left the political landscape more fractured. Unconventional parties were springing up. The Italian columnist, Massimo Franco, said that Grillo was 'a thermometer of Italy's political temperature, and the success of a demagogue like him would send a dangerous message to our allies in Europe that credibility and sacrifice are no longer on Italy's agenda'. Grillo was not in a position to take power, but he could act as a spoiler, denying a workable majority to other political parties. In the Italian election of 2013 Grillo travelled the land in a camper van. He avoided TV interviews and the press. He based his campaign on the internet and rallies in the piazzas. He drew vast crowds as he raged against the political class in Italy and the European elite. 'People are killing themselves,' he said, 'because they don't have work. Italians are having to eat in soup kitchens.' He described a country heading down a similar road to Greece. He was denounced as a populist, a demagogue, as 'dangerous for democracy' but he tapped into the mood of anger and resentment. A wild-haired comedian was sending a message that many Italians no longer trusted the politicians that had led Europe into its crisis.

Mario Monti sees himself in a race against time. 'I'm very keen,' he said, 'to make sure that the changes we have already introduced on labour markets and tax evasion remain and take root, and are not washed away with the first rains.' What he fears is a return of political instability, and has offered himself as the saviour in waiting. 'If there is no majority capable of governing,' he said, 'then I am ready to continue.'

Italy's mood is unpredictable. Berlusconi is still active, seeking the political influence that can thwart the magistrates who are working to convict him. He has lost none of his political acumen, detecting a growing hostility to Monti's austerity programme. He accused the prime minister of pursuing recessionary policies that amounted to the 'mediaeval blood-letting' of a sick patient. He has also sensed increasing resentment towards Germany and its power. A poll found that 83 per cent of Italians thought Germany's influence in the EU was 'too strong'. Berlusconi was quick to accuse the Monti government of 'following the German-centric policies which Europe has tried to impose on other states'. The former leader believed it was smart politics to play the German card. Italy, with its political volatility, was still the country that could fatally undermine the European project.

As 2012 ended, Europe's crisis lay unresolved, although the markets were less skittish. The European Central Bank, in offering to do what it took to defend the currency, had bought time. Some deficits were coming down but debt, in many countries, was still rising. Many places were mired in recession with unemployment levels not seen since the thirties, and several countries were just beginning to implement the austerity measures which had previously been announced. The German Chancellor Angela Merkel said the crisis could last another five years, and that would test Europe's commitment to its dream.

Chapter 18
The Lost Continent

In the harsh winter sunlight, West Flanders defies the morning's snow. The flat lands bristle with energy. The trucks kick up the slush on the congested routes between Belgium and France. On the tablecloth-flat farms they are pulling beets from the soil. New companies line the highways. Yet it is impossible to escape the past's long reach. For this is a landscape of monuments, of trenches, of concrete shelters, of cemeteries and mine craters. These were the killing fields of World War One.

Ypres is a Flemish town, which at Christmas has its market, its outdoor ice rink, its decorated square beside the Lakenhalle: the Cloth Hall which in mediaeval times was one of the great trading centres. The town itself is a testament to resilience, to human hope, which insists on reclaiming and rebuilding. For by the end of 1917, not a single house, not a single tree, was still standing in Ypres.

This ruinous past is preserved by people like Piet Chielens, the curator of the Flanders Fields Museum. For him, the lessons of the Great War remain universal; how leaders in 1914 'let loose the beast' and how war develops its own logic. The Germans had planned a short, sharp, violent campaign intended to take them to Paris in forty days. Instead, the war ended as a giant siege that lasted for four years. Nobody had envisaged trench warfare. It emerged from a stalemate as great armies locked horns on the plains of Flanders.

There was the stubbornness of leaders who believed, certainly at Passchendaele, in bleeding the enemy white. New machines of war: tanks, self-propelled guns, *minenwerfer* mortars, gas cylinders and flame throwers, caused casualties on an industrial scale. In just the third battle of Ypres, 4 million rounds were fired from British guns alone. Even now, nearly a hundred years later, 200 tonnes of ammunition are unearthed each year. Over a third of them are highly toxic gas shells.

For Chielens, these battlefields still underpin the European narrative today. He believes, along with essayist George Santayana, that 'those who cannot remember the past, are condemned to repeat it'. So, each day in Ypres, at 7.45 p.m., the traffic is stopped from driving through the Menin Gate and, fifteen minutes later, volunteer buglers play the Last Post. With the exception of the German occupation in World War Two, this brief ceremony has been held every evening since 1928. It is rare when scores, if not hundreds of people, do not gather at this memorial to the missing. Across Europe there are similar acts of remembering two world wars: the placing of flowers at war graves, the visits to vast cemeteries overlooking landing beaches, the silent disbelief at the camps of internment and death. This is what drove the post-war leaders to construct a Europe where war would never again be possible.

In Berlin, the current Finance Ministry used to be the Reich Ministry of Aviation. The offices that are at the centre of fighting the crisis in the euro-zone were once the headquarters of Hermann Göring, the commander-in-chief of the *Luftwaffe*. Beside this imposing piece of Fascist architecture on Wilhelmstrasse is the Topography of Terror. It is a modern, light, plain museum of the Nazi era, built alongside what had once been the main driveway to Gestapo headquarters. The exhibition spares no detail: history's darkest moments were often captured on camera. There are the photos of the trains taking Jews to the death camps. There are high-ranking SS leaders posing for a group photo. There are the orders for the murder of patients: 'Those who do not work shall not eat.' Older visitors to the museum tend to be more silent: the events are closer to memory. Some of the younger Germans chatter and gossip as if this was another school trip. Beside the picture of Hitler presenting Himmler with an inauguration certificate as Reich SS leader, a young German couple kiss and then turn back to the exhibits. Others take pictures of each other on their mobile phones.

Despite all the best efforts to preserve history, the past recedes. Few of the generation that witnessed the continent's barbarity remain. The threat of war has subsided. Peace is taken for granted. The Cold War has ended. For those countries emerging from authoritarian rule, the European Union served as a beacon for democracy. Those defining periods, however, lie in the past.

Today Europe is searching for a new narrative, a new cause to inspire an increasingly sceptical continent. The struggle to save the European project is delivering more power to Brussels, less by design and more by necessity. In the era of austerity, its European quarter is cluttered with cranes. It has expanded regardless, despite the hard times elsewhere. The EU believes in itself and its manifest destiny. The creed is 'ever-closer union'. Yet for all that, the buildings betray an insecurity. They are solid, functional and bureaucratic. They lack ambition and boldness. The Justus Lipsius building, with its labyrinthine corridors, squats. The light scarcely intrudes. It is inward looking. There is not a Chrysler Building here, bursting with automotive confidence. Nor is there an Empire State Building, reaching high and defining the skyline.

It is not Europe's way. It does not flaunt. It builds its dream unobtrusively. There are founding fathers but their names are largely unknown. Schumann gets a roundabout and a metro station. Monnet and De Gasperi get the odd plaque. Their mission was to save a continent from its destructive instincts. It was not to defend or promote individual freedom. It was to build institutions that made war impossible. The founders and their successors believe in the enlightenment of the few, the guiding lights; the civil servants that graduate from the gilded schools. It remains at heart a project of the élite, designed by the few for the many.

In its hour of need, the European project faces a crisis of legitimacy. In election after election, fewer and fewer people bother to vote for the European Parliament. Polls suggest that even while the European Union acquires more power, its people have either lost enthusiasm for the dream or have grown indifferent to it. According to a poll by Eurobarometer, conducted late in 2012, only 30 per cent of Europeans view the EU in a positive light. That is down from 52 per cent just five years ago. The public are no longer instinctive believers; they just want jobs and security. They judge Europe less by its grand designs and more by whether it delivers.

Europe's leaders have cast around and settled on a new narrative to justify closer union. It is globalisation. The lesson of globalisation is that the small get trampled on and ignored. Individual nations lose their influence and their seats at the highest tables. The fear is that the new economic thoroughbreds like China, India, Brazil and Russia will shape the planet, with Europe as a bystander. Only bound together can the continent defend its interests and its values.

When the German Chancellor Angela Merkel chided the British for their wariness towards Europe, she cited globalisation. 'If you have a world of seven billion,' she said, 'and you're alone in the world, I don't think that's good for the UK. I believe you can be very happy on an island, but being alone in the world doesn't make you any happier.' Tony Blair, the former British prime minister, spoke of what drove the creation of the Union nearly sixty years ago. 'Then,' he said, 'the rationale was peace. Today it is power. In this new world, to leverage power, you need the heft of the EU.' In his view, it is only the European embrace that gives countries the collective weight they otherwise would lack. It has nothing to do with idealism but 'brutal real politik'. Britain, he argued, needed the EU to pursue its national interest.

For Europe's élite, one of the lessons of the crisis has been the power of the financial markets. They are footloose and fast, bound by neither time nor place. They are global in reach and only powerful blocs can stand up to them. 'Financial markets have become a "global supra-government",' said Roger Altman, the former United States Deputy Secretary of the Treasury. 'They oust entrenched regimes where normal political processes could not do so,' he said. 'They force austerity, banking bail-outs and other policy changes . . . They have become the most powerful force on earth.'

So the narrative of globalisation has been co-opted to justify closer union. Other parts of the world are less persuaded by the argument that only the big countries or the big blocks can protect themselves. Canada, Australia, Singapore, Turkey and countless other countries do not believe that unless they are yoked together they are marginalised in the global world. Influence, as Germany has shown, stems from economic power. Turkey has demonstrated it has much greater influence outside the EU than it could possibly have inside. And that is one of the many questions that hangs over Europe in its hour of insecurity: have its high priests misread the zeitgeist? Does power and influence derive from large organisations or does it, at root, come from economic success? Does the desire to centralise, to harmonise, to regulate, suit the digital age that empowers the nimble, the creative and the innovator? Globalisation can be summoned to appear for the defence of a deeper union; its arguments can as easily be marshalled to support a more adaptable and looser union.

After some hesitation, Europe's leaders have fiercely defended their currency and their dream. It would be a mistake to underestimate their commitment. They believe that if the euro-zone were to break up, it would not just sow economic turmoil but it would destroy the European project. Former French President Nicolas Sarkozy said, 'The euro lies at the heart of Europe. If it collapses, Europe will not survive.' For the German Chancellor, preserving economic and monetary union dominates her time and energy; she considers it is what history will judge her by.

She believes that only 'more Europe' can save the currency. She thinks it is inescapable that a political union will follow, although she shies away from using the words. Her advisers insist she does not work in terms of visions, so her idea for the future of Europe lies undefined. She holds confidential dinners at a castle at Meseberg, Germany's Camp David, where she test-runs her thoughts on visiting leaders, yet none of them comes away knowing what she really believes. The French are unclear as to the goal the Germans are working towards. It is, however, the European way to build 'step by step'. Many officials believe that avoids voters being given a say on the steady transfer of power from national parliaments to the European level.

These days a United States of Europe, for so long the vision that could only be whispered in Brussels, is discussed openly, even though senior European officials still manage to squirm at the words. The German finance minister, Wolfgang Schäuble, says that 'if the United States of Europe is understood to be like the USA, it will never happen', but he thinks someday Europe will have a new order and not the old nation states. It will not follow a script, but European integration will be built by 'trial and error, time and again'. The former German Chancellor, Helmut Schmidt, believes there will be no United States of Europe this century, but a debate about Europe's future design is under way. The Germans are discussing a federal system for Europe much as they operate in Germany. There are position papers that envisage a directly elected president of the commission served by two chambers: the European Parliament and the Council of Ministers. For the moment, it remains blue-sky thinking. The problem for Europe is that if it cannot sketch out where it is heading and level with its people, then loyalty will be begrudging at best. The risk is that Europe becomes absorbed in itself, in its own grand projects and its own institutions, whiling away years discussing treaty changes.

The euro was one of the foundation stones of integration but proved to be flawed in design. Yoking together such different economies was an act of hubris. Those early illusions have now been stripped away. Economic and monetary union, so far, has not delivered stability but division. One interest rate for all led to boom time and debt. Economies that were intended to grow closer together moved further apart. The remedy, designed in Germany, has been austerity and reform. Countries have been consigned to recession as they struggled to become competitive with the powerhouse of Germany. The levels of unemployment have not been seen since the thirties and a modern-day depression, with its upheaval of people, has descended on parts of the continent. The charge against Germany is that its policies have led to a prolonged recession. The risk is of a permament division between the creditor and debtor nations. The promise is that painful reforms will deliver better times later. In the meantime, the social fabric weakens. Many believe that Europe faces a choice: a political union where debt is shared, or the eventual collapse of the currency.

As leaders have scrambled to shore up the euro, they have, at times, appeared careless of democracy. It is often hard to know who to hold to account for decisions taken. The European Central Bank has become so powerful that it can determine the survival of leaders. Time and again, elected politicians defer to unelected European commissioners. It is bewildering for the citizen to know who is responsible. President Van Rompuy insists that all major decisions are taken by elected ministers and that the 'process has been super-democratic'. It is, however, far from direct democracy, where the people can help drive the agenda. Democracy works best when the lines between the decision-makers and the governed are short and transparent. Most people would agree that democratic control over tax and spending is one of the hallmarks of a democratic society, but what happens if that budget is determined by European officials? Who does the voter hold responsible? Officials, like Van Rompuy, question whether national parliaments are 'in the best position' to take the 'common interest' of the European Union into account – but who should make those judgements and what role is there for the views of the people? A new model of government is emerging in Europe, but democratic accountability is lagging far behind.

The crisis has confirmed Germany as Europe's indispensable nation and therein lies a great irony. The currency that was intended to bind Germany into Europe has ended up with the coronation of Germany as the dominant power. It has not sought this role and is not yet entirely comfortable with it. It has however insisted, as the price of its support, that other countries embrace reforms inspired by its own experience and history. At times, it has seemed that Germany is trying to economically redesign Europe in its own image.

It is the German period in Europe, and has led some to talk of a German rather than a European Union. Berlin, the great advocate of financial sobriety, can scarcely contain its new-found confidence. It is there in the restoration and revival of Unter den Linden, the thoroughfare that was developed as a via triumphalis after Prussia's victory in the Napoleonic wars. Now a forest of cranes has taken root, and not just to construct a new subway stop. Eventually, they will rebuild the Berlin Stadtschloss, once the royal palace for the Prussian kings. It is Europe's largest cultural construction project. The reputation of the Prussian King Frederick the Great, whose imposing equestrian statue stands close by, has been rehabilitated. Germany has become more confident with its past.

Ultimately, it will fall to Germany to decide whether it wants to shoulder the burden of saving Europe's currency. Sooner or later, Germany's leaders will have to tell its people that not all the money loaned to Europe's weaker nations will be returned. Germany is on the hook for 300 billion euros. Some of that will be lost, and Germany's tax-payers will be asked to do more if the euro is to survive. It will not be possible by wage cuts alone to restore competitiveness in Europe's weaker countries. Germany will be asked to transfer more funds. Its political class may be willing to make that sacrifice for the European common good; it is far less certain whether the German people are.

The half-moon hung low in the Mediterranean sky. In the blackness there was only a green light, flickering intermittently. The engines strained against the swell. On the deck were 299 men, 14 women and 5 children, packed in, their knees drawn up. They had been at sea for thirty hours. There was no space to stretch out or lie down. Occasionally, they would lean against each other in exhaustion. Sometimes they edged backwards or forwards to allow a man to urinate or vomit over the side.

They had long fallen silent as the African coast receded behind them. At the start of their voyage, a few photos had been taken, but the initial excitement of departure had given way to quietness. The Africans guarded their energy, absorbed in their escape. They had handed their savings to smugglers and wagered everything on this open barge, which did not even have cover for the wheelhouse.

The migrants, *i clandestini*, peered ahead, seeing nothing, suppressing the dark thoughts, the stories that were told along the coast: the wrecks, the bodies, the fights, the men thrown overboard. And then, splitting the dark, a white light, probing, intense, interrogating. The Italian Coast Guard cutter circled them. There were men in lifejackets, men with guns, and a loudspeaker voice telling them to follow.

The barge sat in the wake of the Coast Guard until a necklace of lights emerged, steady and moving closer. This, they hoped, was Europe. As they tied up there were whispered conversations, uncertainty about where they were and the reception they would receive. Once the boat was lashed to the quayside there was a surge, a push towards the narrow walkway, until the voice on the hailer ordered them to stay still.

Slowly they were led out onto the Lampedusa dock. They were told to sit in long lines and were handed bottles of water. They sat there with immigrant eyes: watchful, wary, alive and daring to hope they could find work in this place called Europe. Some had crossed half a continent to reach this point. Others had been Gaddafi's *gastarbeiters*, but long since been discarded.

One man spread his hands for inspection and said quietly that they were good for work. Another man from Nigeria, using his Sunday-school English, said he had come for 'greener pastures'.

But what was the Europe they had been drawn to? They did not know. They were following the scent of work but not only that. It was the promise of the decency and respect that they were shown on that Italian dock. Within forty-eight hours they would be put on ferries and dispersed to reception centres in Catania, Cagliari or Livorno – one more step into an unknown world that would challenge the dream that had brought them this far.

Europe is still a beacon but its welcome has become strained. The continent is in ferment. Around 26 million people are without work. Wages, benefits – the safety nets that had defined the European way of life – are being cut. Angela Merkel noted that Europe has 7 per cent of the world's population, 25 per cent of the world's GDP but spends 50 per cent of the world's budget on social welfare. The future of Europe's welfare democracies is uncertain with countries no longer able to sustain their levels of social spending.

Europe, like the migrants, had had its dream. It was flawed and proved dangerous. Its leaders were fearful of their currency breaking up with the risk of economic collapse, and yet they lacked the confidence to push forward and redesign their continent. They have not explained Europe's place in the new global order. They have held back, unsure of the assent of their citizens, who remain stubbornly committed to the nation state.

Many citizens still trust European institutions more than their own governments. The fear is that Europe will be condemned to be a museum, a walk in a piazza: comfortable but lagging behind the fast-charging emerging economies. What leaders cannot know is the patience of their own people. In the absence of conflict they had struggled to make the case for Europe and to answer the hanging questions: can this ambitious project liberate? Can it inspire? Can it release energy and dynamism? Above all, can it deliver for the 500 million people who belong in the Union? Europe, for the moment, is preoccupied with itself, trapped by its dreams and its contradictions. A continent lost.

Timeline

November 1989   Fall of the Berlin Wall

February 1992   Signing of the Maastricht Treaty, agreeing to the setting up of the euro and economic and monetary union in the European Union

January 1999   The launch of the euro, the single currency and the European Central Bank (ECB)

January 2002   Euro notes and coins begin circulating

September 2008   Financial crash in America and the collapse of Lehman Brothers

October 2009   Election of a new government in Greece led by George Papandreou

October 2009   Discovery that the Greek deficit is much larger than previously disclosed, so setting off the euro zone debt crisis

2 May 2010   Greece receives its first bail-out from the EU and the IMF. Loans total 110 billion euros

9 May 2010   Launch of a huge 750 billion euros

rescue fund – the European Financial Stability Facility – for the euro zone

18 October 2010	Chancellor Merkel and President Sarkozy meet in Deauville and agree that private investors should share the cost of future bail-outs
21 November 2010	Bail-out agreed for Ireland. The country is loaned 85 billion euros
April 2011	Bail-out agreed for Portugal. The country is loaned 78 billion euros
Summer of 2011	Agreement in principal for a second Greek bail-out with loans of 130 billion euros. It includes investors accepting losses, which reduces the Greek debt by 100 billion euros. The details are negotiated at a summit in October 2011 and signed off in March 2012
August 2011	Prime Minister Silvio Berlusconi of Italy announces an austerity package for his country
31 October 2011	Greek prime minister, George Papandreou, announces referendum on the terms of his country's second bail-out package
2 November 2011	G20 summit in Cannes. George Papandreou is summoned to explain the referendum he announced
9 November 2011	George Papandreou resigns

12 November 2011   Silvio Berlusconi resigns. He is replaced by the unelected economist, Mario Monti

9 December 2011   Britain's prime minister, David Cameron, uses his veto to block European treaties being changed to allow for greater control of tax and spending in countries which use the euro-zone. David Cameron wanted specific safegaurds for the UK

21 December 2011   Mariano Rajoy elected prime minister of Spain

12 March 2012   The euro group finally backs the second Greek bail-out

6 May 2012   François Hollande is elected president of France

10 June 2012   Spain agrees to a bail-out for its banks of up to 100 billion euros

26 July 2012   Mario Draghi, the president of the European Central Bank announces he will do 'whatever it takes to defend the euro'

8 October 2012   The permanent rescue fund, the European Stability Mechanism (ESM), comes into operation

February 2013   Italian election results in deadlock between the centre left right of Silvio Berlusconi. The big winner is Beppe Grillo.

Acknowledgements

It took time for it to be understood how profound the crisis in Europe was. Eventually, Europe's leaders defined it as the most serious moment on the continent since World War Two – some of them even said Europe was living through a Great Depression. I am grateful to those who urged me to tell this story.

In particular, I want to thank my agent, Catherine Clarke, for believing there was the need for a book on contemporary history in Europe's crisis.

I have been very fortunate that so many senior politicians and officials gave so generously of their time. In the book and in the source notes, most of them are mentioned by name. Most of them were candid and helpful; some of those who were at the centre of events understandably insisted on confidentiality and spoke to me off the record. Even though these have been the most difficult times for European officials, when they feared for the survival of the European project, they have never refused to talk to me and I am grateful for that spirit of openness.

Much of what is written in this book was experienced with colleagues. Jon Whitney was a first-rate companion during the French elections and on visits to Spain and Greece. I am grateful, too, to Wietske Burema for her commitment to the story, to Bruno Boelpaep for his enthusiasm and sense of the streets, and to Sean Klein. They have all been very patient.

Similarly, telling this story on television has always been a challenge, but I was fortunate to work with two outstanding cameramen in Xavier Vanpevenaege and Maarten Lernout. Both of them were very encouraging and helpful in retracing and recalling moments we had shared together.

I have been enormously assisted by the BBC's correspondents in Europe: Mark Lowen in Greece, Tom Burridge in Spain, Christian Fraser in Paris and Stephen Evans in Berlin. They have lived this story and freely shared their knowledge and insight with me, and I thank them for being so welcoming. The BBC itself was exceptionally tolerant of my frequent trips to European capitals to research this book, and I am grateful for its understanding.

I am particularly indebted to those who helped me with research: Clea Caulcutt in France, Electra Arzimanoglou in Greece, and Carlo Catalogna in Italy. Without their help and enthusiasm, this book would not have been possible. Andrea Vogt was very insightful with the final manuscript.

I want to thank Rupert Lancaster, my editor at Hodder, for his encouragement and for holding me to deadlines. There are also others who know how important they have been.

Above all, I want to thank my family for their love and support: Sally, Becky, Dan, Jon, Ava and Maya. No thank you would ever be enough.

Sources

Prologue. Delirium

p2. Mercedes ownership – as revealed in *Pope's Children* by David McWilliams.

p4–5. 'The euro is far more than a medium of exchange . . .' Wim Duisenberg, first president of ECB.

p10. George Papandreou: 'We were shocked . . .' Interview with author.

p10. George Papandreou: 'This is without doubt the worst economic . . .' Statement made a week after taking office in October 2009.

P 11. George Papaconstantinou: 'We are not Iceland . . .' Comment made in December 2009.

p12. 'No one can live beyond their means . . .' The EU's economics commissioner Ollie Rehn. June 2010.

p13. Angela Merkel: 'Europe's toughest hour . . .' German Chancellor's speech to her party in Leipzig in November 2011.

p13. Sir Mervyn King. 'The most serious crisis we have had . . .' Remarks made in October 2011.

p13. Nicolas Sarkozy: 'Those who destroy the euro . . .' Made in a speech in October 2011.

p14. Robert Schuman: 'The gathering of the nations . . .' This was Schuman's proposal of 9 May 1950.

p14. Merkel being 'risk averse . . .' From a Wikileaks cable attributed to a US diplomat in Berlin dated 24 March 2009.

p14. Alain Minc: 'Sarkozy is a man . . .' Interview with the author.

p14. Chirac on Sarkozy: 'Nervous, impetuous . . .' Taken from second part of Jacques Chirac's memoirs.

p15. The exchange between Merkel and Sarkozy. 'We are made to get on . . .' recounted in biography of Sarkozy by Franz-Olivier Giesbert.

p15. Nicolas Sarkozy. 'I've been spending more time . . .' Joke made at press conference after summit in December 2011.

p16. Nicolas Sarkozy to David Cameron: '. . . opportunity to shut up.' Exchange at European summit October 2011.

p16. David Riley on Italy. Statement made at conference in London January 2012.

p16. Berlusconi and 'football and girls'. Remark made to Gerhard Schröder in December 2003.

p17. 'France was having to adjust . . .' Charles Grant, Centre for European Reform.

p17. Rainer Brüderle. '. . . motor for the entire European economy . . .' Presenting forecasts January 2011.

p17. 'The Germans are going through a crash course . . .' *Die Welt*.

p19. Ulrike Guérot. 'This will backfire on us . . .' writing in November 2011.

p21. Paul Krugman: 'No, the real story . . .' *New York Times* article, 'The Making of a Euro mess.' 14 February 2010.

Chapter 1. The Dream

p26. Nicholas Ridley and 'a German racket . . .' From an interview with the *Spectator* in July 1990.

p26. 'They might make even more ground than Hitler.' Thatcher's meeting at the Elysée Palace on 20 January 1990. Official papers released by the Foreign Office disclose memos by Sir Charles Powell, foreign affairs adviser to Mrs Thatcher.

p27. Thatcher to Gorbachev. In September 1989, according to Russian official papers, she told the Russian leader, 'We do not want a united Germany.'

p29. Delors's comments on the Bundesbank were made in 1992 while president of the European Commission.

p29. Assessment of the Central Council of the Bundesbank made in 1990.

p30. Helmut Kohl made his comment about a 'castle in the air' in 1991.

p30. Helmut Kohl and 'Recent history . . .' On 6 November 1991, he delivered the warning to the Bundestag. It was revealed in the minutes and disclosed by Otmar Issing in his speech, 'The euro: a currency without a state.'

p30. In February 1998, 155 university professors published a statement in the *Financial Times* and the *Frankfurter Allgemeine Zeitung*.

p30. Wolfgang Schäuble: 'If we had waited . . .' Interview with author. December 2012.

p30. Herman Van Rompuy: 'The euro was not created . . .' Interview with author December 2012.

p31. Kohl and 'the weight of history.' Comment made in 1998 on the introduction of the euro. Government papers obtained by *Der Spiegel* in 2012.

p31–2. Miranda Xafa. Interview with Allan Little and Jane Beresford of the BBC in 2012. *Europe's Choice* BBC Radio 4.

p32. Otmar Issing: 'Never before had sovereign states . . .' From *The Birth of the Euro*, Cambridge University Press.

p32. David Marsh: *The Euro: The politics of the new global currency* is an invaluable source for the launch of the euro.

p33. Gerhard Schröder: 'We are witnessing the dawn of an age . . .' A New Year message January 2002.

p33. Carlo Azeglio Ciampi statement: 'A decisive step towards . . .' January 1999.

p33. Yves-Thibault de Silguy: 'We can never be an American . . .' 1999. An interview with the *New York Times*.

Chapter 2. Boom Time

p38. Adam Posen. 'It was as if Germany . . .' BBC *Hardtalk*. August 2012.

p39. Luis Linde. 'There was a sort of euphoria . . .' July 2012, testifying to a Spanish Parliamentary committee on economic affairs.

p40. José Ortega y Gasset. Early 20th century Spanish philosopher.

p46–7. Some details of the Fitzpatrick court appearance drawn from the *Irish Independent* 25 July 2012.

p47. 'We have seen white-collar . . .' A comment by John Gormley, leader of the Irish Green Party.

p48. Sean Fitzpatrick: 'The real thing in life . . .' Interview given to Tom Lyons and Brian Carey in *The Fitzpatrick Tapes*, Penguin Ireland, p54.

p50. Patrick Honohan and 'excessive overseas borrowing'. Remarks made in a June 2010 report on the banking crisis.

p51. Morgan Kelly: 'No longer a question . . .' Remarks made in May 2010.

p51 Paul Mangan-Ebbs. Interview with author, plus extra detail from Marketplace World.

p52. David McKittrick. The *Independent*. 31 January 2011. 'The banker who became Ireland's most hated man.'

Chapter 3. 'We ate the money together.'

p55. George Papandreou: 'I had asked . . .' Interview with author 2012.

p56. George Papaconstantinou: 'I got handed letters . . .' Interview with author 2012.

p57. Giorgos Koutroumanis: 'We found one pension . . .' Press conference August 2010.

p58. Andreas Georgiou. Interview with author.

p59. Foreign Office minister: 'a fitting repayment . . .' Source: *A Concise History of Greece* by Richard Clogg.

p60. Jens Weidmann: 'Many years of wrong developments . . .' Speech in Berlin. November 2011.

p60. Figures about Porsche Cayennes based on an article in the *Daily Telegraph* 'Fast cars and loose fiscal morals'. 31 October 2011. The article refers to original research by Professor Herakles Pole-marchakis.

p60. Theodoros Pangalos: 'We ate the money together . . .' TV interview 2010.

p60. Theo Waigel: 'You are not part of this . . .' Account based on *Der Spiegel* article 5 October 2011.

p60. Theo Waigel: 'mortal sin'. Interview with Austrian magazine *Profil*.

p61. Peter Doukas: 'Don't worry about persecution . . .' Interview with the BBC.

p61. Herman Van Rompuy: 'The euro became a strong currency . . .' Interview with *Financial Times* June 2010.

p62. Alistair Darling: 'No one in the Treasury . . .' Interview with the author.

p62. George Papaconstantinou: 'I remember at the end . . .' Interview with author.

p63. George Papandreou: 'I was chased around . . .' Interview with author.

Chapter 4. The Night they Almost Lost the Euro

p65. Paul Krugman: 'Social progress and justice . . .' Article *New York Times* 10 January 2010.

p65. Steven Hill: 'Europe is a beacon . . .' Source: *Europe's Promise: Why the European Way is the Best Hope in an Insecure Age* by Steven Hill.

p65. José Manuel Barroso: 'The European Union has had . . .' Speech, 3 September 2009.

p65. José Manuel Barroso: 'protective shield . . .' 5 February 2010.

p65. Angela Merkel: 'Cooking the books . . .' 24 March 2010. Berlin.

p67. Wolfgang Schäuble: 'Greece has to realise . . .' Comment made in February 2010.

p67. Angela Merkel: 'There are rules . . .' Speech made in February 2010.

p67. François Baroin: 'not economic or strategic . . .' Interview with author.

p68. Wolfgang Schäuble: 'We need tighter rules . . .' Comment made in March 2010.

p69. George Papandreou: 'the weak victim . . .' Speech made to Greek Parliament, 26 February 2010.

p70. Jean-Claude Juncker: 'instruments of torture . . .' 1 March 2010. Interview with *Handelsblatt*.

p70. George Papandreou's account of conversation with Merkel. Interview with author.

p71. Alistair Darling: 'Sarkozy did not want Strauss-Kahn . . .' Interview with author.

p74. Angela Merkel: 'We're at a fork in the road . . .' Speech to Bundestag 5 May 2010.

p75. Joseph Stiglitz: 'The very survival . . .' 5 May 2010.

p76. Wolfgang Schäuble: 'We must defend the . . .' Speech to Bundestag May 2010.

p76. Jean-Claude Trichet: 'I was quite strong . . .' Interview with author.

p77. Authoritative account of the crisis weekend in *Der Spiegel*. 17 May 2010.

p79. Alistair Darling: 'For at least six hours . . .' Interview with author.

Chapter 5. Greek Rage and German Resentment
The attack on the Marfin bank. Many details are based on an interview with Christos Karapanagiotis done by Irene Chapple for CNN, June 2012.

p87. George Papandreou. 'Even though things . . .' Interview with author.

p89. Hans-Werner Sinn. 'This tragedy . . .' Speaking at European House-Ambrosetti. September 2010.

p89. George Papandreou. 'We know the road to Ithaca . . .' Remark made 23 April 2010.

p90. George Soros: 'They didn't understand the problem . . .' Festival of Economics, Trento. June 2012.

p90. Winston Churchill: 'Hence we will not say . . .' The remark was made in 1941.

p91. Theodoros Pangalos: 'They took away the Greek gold . . .' BBC interview, February 2010.

p92. Joséf Schlarmann: 'Those in insolvency . . .' Interview with *Bild*. March 2010.

p92. The Venus de Milo was on the front cover of the German magazine *Focus*. February 2010.

p93. Peter Altmaier. 'When the euro was introduced . . .' Breakfast meeting at the German Embassy in London 2011.

p93. Stefan Zweig: 'besmirched . . .' from *The World of Yesterday*. His memoirs.

p94. Gerhard Schröder: 'We shall reduce social benefits . . .' Bundestag 2001.

p96. Helmut Schmidt: 'If we let ourselves be seduced . . .' December 2011. Social Democrats conference in Berlin.

p96. Jürgen Habermas: 'Self-absorbed Colossus . . .' June 2010 in article for the *Guardian* and *The Nation*.

p96. Wolfgang Schäuble: 'We don't want to dominate . . .' Interview with author.

Chapter 6. Opposite Twins

p98. Angela Merkel. 'We've done no more . . .' Speaking to trade unionists in Berlin. 15 May 2010.

p99. Giscard d'Estaing. 'Europe cannot move ahead . . .' German Embassy, Paris, 2010.

p100. Angela Merkel. 'stubborn old bag . . .' Account based on *Wall Street Journal*, 2 July 2010.

p101. Ulrike Guérot. 'Germany was moving away . . .' 26 November 2010, from essay: 'How European is the new Germany?'

p101. Merkel and swimming lesson. Revealed in biography of Merkel by Margaret Heckel. The remark, 'I am not spontaneously . . .' made to biographer Evelyn Roll.

p102. Angela Merkel and 'never underestimated . . .' Interview with *Time* magazine, 2010.

p104. Nicolas Sarkozy: 'They call me Sarko . . .' from Wikileaks cable dated 5 August 2005. Sarkozy describes himself to Allan Hubbard, the US National Economic Council director.

p104. Nicolas Sarkozy and '. . . In that case go to America.' From a Wikileaks cable.

p105. The Sarkozy interview with Franz-Olivier Giesbert is based on the account in the *New Yorker* magazine, 12 December 2011.

p107. François Baroin: 'It was difficult at the beginning . . .' Interview with author.

p108. Xavier Musca: '. . . extremely powerful . . .' Interview with author.

p109. The comment 'Nothing is working any more . . .' is taken from an article in *Le Point*.

p110. Alain Minc: 'She doesn't want . . .' Interview with author.

p110. Xavier Musca: 'When Sarkozy understood this . . .' Interview with author.

p110. Jean-Claude Trichet: 'Europe is undoubtedly . . .' Interview with *Der Spiegel*.

p111. Simon Schama: 'remote masters.' Article for *Financial Times*, 21 May 2010.

'Those on the receiving end of punitive corrections – in public sector wages or retrenched social institutions – will lash out at their remote masters.'

Chapter 7. Ireland: Hell was at the Gates

p112. Patrick Honohan: 'I hadn't seen anything . . .' Interview with author.

p112. Dr Alan Ahearne: 'It was war . . .' Account based on interview with the author and comments made to the *Irish Independent*, 9 October 2011.

p114. Jean-Claude Trichet: 'I have admiration for Ireland . . .' Interview with author.

p116. Mary O'Rourke: 'once again . . .' Comment made in November 2010.

p116. 'It has been a very hard-won . . .' Remark made by Batt O'Keeffe, the enterprise minister.

p116. 'burly and brusque.' Comment made by US Ambassador Thomas Foley in a Wikileaks profile.

p117. Angela Merkel 'We cannot keep . . .' Comment made 12 November 2010.

p117. George Papandreou: 'They will factor . . .' Interview with author.

p117. Wolfgang Schäuble: 'If you look at the debt . . .' Interview with author.

p118. Patrick Honohan: 'There was a lot of confusion . . .' Interview with author.

p120. Dick Roche: 'It is not just a question . . .' Interview on RTÉ news, 15 November 2010.

p121. Herman Van Rompuy: 'We're in a survival crisis . . .' Remark made 16 November 2010 in a speech to a Brussels think tank.

p121. Angela Merkel: 'I'm telling you . . .' 15 November 2010. After being re-elected as head of her party.

p121. 'geo-political hardball . . .' Comment made by Brian Lucey, economist from Trinity College Dublin.

p122. Patrick Honohan: 'I talked to Brian Lenihan . . .' Interview with author.

p122. Dermot Ahern: 'There were people from outside . . .' Comments made on 30 November 2010.

p122. Dick Roche: ' . . . rot could be halted . . .' Article in *Wall Street Journal*, 23 November 2011.

p123. Brian Lenihan: ' . . . hell was at the gates . . .' Interview with the BBC.

p123. ' . . . a few shillings of sympathy . . .' *Irish Times*. 11 November 2010.

p129. Herman Van Rompuy: 'Euro-scepticism leads to war . . .' November 2010. State of Europe speech at the Pergamon Museum in Berlin.

Chapter 8. The Shadow of Silvio

p133. 'Forza Gnocca.' Remarks made to MPs on October 2011. According to the paper *La Stampa*, Berlusconi said, 'Some of the polls say the best choice would be Forza Gnocca.'

p133. Remarks about President Obama were made in November 2008.

p135. Patrizia D'Addario's account drawn from her recording of the event and interview with the author.

p135. Silvio Berlusconi: 'I'm not a saint . . .' Speech in Brescia, July 2009.

p138. Comments by Nadia Macri were made in November 2010 in an interview with Italy's Sky News.

p139. 'Sick and of unsound mind.' Comment in the Catholic paper *Famiglia Christiani*.

p141. Luca Cordero di Montezemolo: 'The one-man . . .' Comments made in November 2010 at a function of the Italia Futura Foundation.

p141. Dolce and Gabbana: '. . . whole religious gorgeousness . . .' *Vogue* magazine, 26 February 2012.

p142. Two journalists from *Corriere della Sera*, Gian Antonio Stella and Sergio Rizzo, wrote *The Caste: How Italian politicians have become untouchable*.

p143. Jürgen Stark: 'Each country . . .' Interview with *Süddeutsche Zeitung* December 2010.

p144. 'It is exactly this talking against other people and about other people . . .' Comment made by Steffen Seibert at a government briefing. Autumn 2010.

p144. Jean-Claude Juncker: 'losing sight of the European public good . . .' Remarks made in an interview with Germany's *Rheinischer Merkur* on 25 November 2010.

p145. Otmar Issing: 'highly indebted countries could be encouraged to blackmail . . .' based on an article written by Mr Issing for the *Financial Times*, 8 August 2011.

p146. François Fillon: '. . . at a historic turning point . . .' Interview with *The Times* in January 2011 before delivering a speech to the City of London.

p146. Angela Merkel: 'Member states face many years of work to atone for past sins . . .' Comments made at a summit in Brussels in March 2011.

Chapter 9. Disobedience

p150 George Papaconstantinou: 'I would go to meetings . . .' Interview with author.

p152. George Papandreou: 'You think that lawlessness is something revolutionary . . .' Comments made in an address to Parliament in February 2011.

p154. Paul Krugman: 'The austerity delusion.' Article in the *New York Times* on 24 March 2011.

p154. Wolfgang Schäuble: 'we are facing the risk of the first uncoordinated state insolvency . . .' Remarks quoted in *Die Welt* in June 2011.

p156. President Obama: 'It would be disastrous for us to see an uncontrolled spiral . . .' At a joint press conference with Angela Merkel on 6 June 2011.

p156. 'Let's put all options on the table.' Interview with George Papaconstantinou with author.

p157. Wolfgang Schäuble: 'No, we didn't have a plan.' Interview with author.

p160. Ollie Rehn: 'We're at a critical point in the most serious crisis since the Second World War . . .' Comment made in June 2011.

p161. George Soros: 'We're on the edge of an economic collapse . . .' Speaking in Vienna on 26 June 2011. The full quote was, 'Let's face it: we are on the verge of an economic collapse which starts, let's say in Greece, but could easily spread.'

p162. Evangelos Venizelos: 'It was very fragile, very dangerous . . .' Interview with the author.

p163. George Papandreou: 'We have rendered our debt problem manageable . . .' Comments made to the Greek Cabinet on 21 July 2011. The full quote was, 'Today we can be proud that we will not leave our children an insurmountable problem because we have rendered our debt problem manageable.'

Chapter 10. The Turning of Frau Nein
p166. Thomas de Maizière: interview with author in 2009.

p167. 'Scarcely a people is less suited . . .' Quote from *Die Welt*, as translated by *Der Spiegel*, 29 November 2011.

p168. George Soros: 'Germany would only do the minimum necessary, so every opportunity was missed.' *New York Review of Books*. September 2012.

p168. Radoslaw Sikorski: 'I will probably . . .' Speech in Berlin, November 2011.

p169. François Baroin: 'It was not an economic . . .' Interview with author.

p169. George Soros: 'Germany dictates policies which lead to a spiralling debt with deflationary consequences.' World Economic Forum in Davos 2012.

p169. Alain Juppé: 'reawakening of the old demons . . .' December 2011. Comment aimed at Socialist party in France.

p169. 'The rise of the Fourth Reich' was a phrase used by columnist Simon Heffer in the *Daily Mail*. 17 August 2011.

p169. 'A German protectorate . . .' A phrase used by Georgios Trangas, a Greek journalist.

p170. 'It was a massive irony that old Europe's . . .' Simon Jenkins in the *Guardian*.

p170. 'The Germanisation of Europe.' The Spanish paper *ABC*.

p170. Letter to Mariano Rajoy from Angela Merkel. Source was the Spanish paper *Público*.

p170. Angela Merkel: 'There are lazy Germans . . .' Interview with *Süddeutsche Zeitung*. 26 January 2012

p170. Xavier Musca: 'She is something . . .' Interview with author.

p171. Helmut Kohl: 'She is ruining . . .' July 2011. Comments reported by *Der Spiegel*. The magazine says Kohl made them to an unnamed political colleague.

p173. Ralph Brinkhaus: 'Either we get more . . .' Comments made at the CDU Annual Congress in November 2011.

p174. Herman Van Rompuy: 'Germany and Angela Merkel . . .' Interview with author in December 2012.

p174. Angela Merkel: 'It does not make sense . . .' Comments made in Davos in January 2012.

p174. Tony Blair: 'Her constant fear . . .' Comments made to *Newsweek*, 28 May 2011.

p175. Jean Monnet: 'Europe would be born . . .' A quote from *Memoirs*.

Chapter 11. The Downfall of *Il Cavaliere*

p177. *The Economist*: 'The man who screwed . . .' 9 June 2011.

p179. 'It is probably the most opaque . . .' Sean O'Grady, the *Independent*. 25 July 2011.

p179. President Barroso: 'undisciplined communication and the complexity and incompleteness of the 21st July package . . .' In a letter sent to the euro-zone heads of government on 3 August 2011.

p180. George Papandreou: 'It would have meant . . .' Interview with author.

p180. Nicolas Sarkozy: 'We have done something historic. There is no European IMF yet – but nearly.' Remarks made at a close of the 21 July press conference in 2011.

p181. Jean-Claude Trichet: 'I have to say sadly . . .' Interview with author.

p181. Jyrki Katainen: 'very alarming . . .' Comments to public broadcaster YLE. 3 August 2011.

p182. The summing-up of the letter to Berlusconi was made to the author by Jean-Claude Trichet.

p184. Franco Frattini: 'threatening to leave . . .' Interview with author.

p184. Silvio Berlusconi: 'Our hearts are bleeding. This government had bragged that it never put its hands in the pockets of Italians but the world situation changed.' Speech to Italian people, 13 August 2011.

p185. Giulio Tremonti: 'Just as on the Titanic . . .' Comments made 14 July 2011.

p186. Giulio Tremonti: 'If I fall . . .' Comments made in July 2011 and quoted by Italian papers.

p186. Silvio Berlusconi: 'He wants to drag me through the mud . . .' Comments reported in Italian papers and in *Der Spiegel*.

p186. Jacques Delors: 'on the edge . . .' Interview given to Swiss and Belgian reporters in Brussels in August 2011.

p186. President Barroso: 'We are confronted . . .' 14 September 2011. A speech to the European Parliament.

p186. Alain Juppé: 'The dissolution of the euro-zone . . .' Interview given to FAZ. August 2011.

p187. Silvio Berlusconi: 'They can say about me . . .' A wiretap made in July 2011 but leaked in September 2011.

p187. Marysthell Polanco. Interview with author.

p188. Carlo Rossella: 'pushing public opinion . . .' Interview with author.

p189. Silvio Berlusconi: 'Nobody in the EU can appoint . . .' Remarks made in statement issued October 2011.

p189. Comments by Carlo Rossella and Franco Frattini made in interviews with author.

p192. Giulio Tremonti: 'In the eyes of both . . .' Several versions of this argument appeared in the Italian press, including *Corriere della Sera* and *La Repubblica*.

p192. François Baroin: 'We knew that if he accepted . . .' Interview with author.

p194. Silvio Berlusconi and Mussolini: 'Don't you understand . . .' From an interview given to *La Stampa*.

p195. Paolo Flores d'Arcais: 'He legitimised and made normal . . .' Editor of a left-wing monthly, *MicroMega*.

p 196. Mario Monti: 'I have always been considered . . .' Comments made during a panel discussion in Rome in November 2011.

p197. Vladimir Putin: 'He was the last of the Mohicans of European leaders.' Comments made in a session with academics at a Moscow Country Club in mid-November 2011.

Chapter 12. The 'Madman' from Athens

p199. George Papandreou: 'It was beyond normal . . .' Comments made to author.

p201. Evangelos Venizelos: 'The image created . . .' Speech to the Greek Parliament, 14 October 2011.

p201. Alistair Darling: '. . . something that would have been worthy . . .' Interview with author.

p202. Xavier Musca: 'Sarkozy and Merkel . . .' Interview with author.

p203. George Papandreou's account of reaction to the referendum was given to the author.

p203. Evangelos Venizelos: 'without my knowledge . . .' Interview with author.

p 204. Nicolas Sarkozy: 'Giving people a voice . . .' A statement issued by the Elysée Palace, 1 November 2011.

p205. François Fillon: 'The Greeks must decide fast . . .' Comments to the French National Assembly, 2 November 2011. 'Europe cannot be kept waiting for weeks,' he said.

p206. Nicolas Sarkozy and 'madman'. This was a private conversation between Sarkozy and President Obama. A microphone was open and the conversation was overheard by some radio journalists.

p207. Evangelos Venizelos: 'My duty was to protect . . .' Interview with the author.

p209. Jean-Paul Fitoussi: 'In Greece and even in Italy . . .' Interview with the *New York Times*, 2011.

p209. Herman Van Rompuy: 'We have together to fight . . .' Comments made in a State of Europe speech at the Pergamon Museum in Berlin in November 2010.

p210. Nicolas Sarkozy: 'Those who destroy . . .' Comments made in October 2011.

p210. Herman Van Rompuy: 'Don't ask me too much . . .' Interview with author.

p210. Nick Clegg: 'populists . . .' November 2011. In a speech warning Europe 'not to disappear into a windowless room to discuss treaties'.

p212. Jean-Claude Trichet: 'It was more than heated . . .' From an interview with the author.

Chapter 13: The British Outsiders

p218. George Osborne and 'remorseless logic'. Comment made at the *Daily Telegraph*'s Festival of Business in Manchester on 16 September 2011.

p218. Herman Van Rompuy: 'felt very uneasy'. Interview with author.

p 218. François Baroin: 'Sarkozy was convinced . . .' Interview with author.

p219. President Barroso: 'The entire world is watching . . .' Comments made on 8 December 2011.

p220. Volker Kauder: 'Now, all of a sudden, Europe is speaking German. Not as a language, but in its acceptance of the instruments for which Angela Merkel has fought so hard . . .' Speech to CDU Congress, November 2011.

p226. 'He cares more about the spivs . . .' Anne Applebaum.

p226. 'there is nothing to be sorry for . . .' A quote from *Le Monde*.

p227. General Charles de Gaulle: 'England is an island . . .' Speech by de Gaulle, 4 January 1963.

p228. Russell Bretherton: 'The future treaty which you are discussing . . .' The date of Britain's withdrawal from the talks was 7

November 1955. The speech was drawn from the account by Roy Denman.

p228. Harold Macmillan: 'Shall we be caught . . .?' This was an entry in Macmillan's diaries written on 9 July 1960.

p229. Pierre Moscovici: 'In essence, it is rather . . .' In a panel discussion in Berlin in October 2012, at an event organised by the Berggruen Institute.

p229 Jacques Chirac: 'What more does this housewife . . .' This comment was reportedly made during the February 1988 Brussels summit and received wide attention in the UK.

p231. Radoslaw Sikorski: 'Please don't expect us to help you wreck . . .' Speaking at the Global Horizons conference at Blenheim Place near Oxford on 21 September 2012.

p232. Peter Mandelson: 'European mandate . . .' Major speech on Europe delivered 4 May 2012 in Oxford.

p233. Herman Van Rompuy: 'seek to undermine . . .' Comments made in an interview with the *Guardian*. December 2012.

p233. Jacques Delors: 'If the British . . .' Interview given to *Handelsblatt* in December 2012.

Chapter 14. A Great Depression
p236. The account of Dimitris Christoulas's suicide was based on an interview done by the author with his daughter, Emy Christoulas.

p238. Dimitris Manikas: 'I was nothing without a job . . .' He was speaking by phone from prison.

p241. Luis Garicano: 'The euro has converted . . .' Article in the *Observer* 1 April 2012. A similar comment was made by Paul De Grauwe, professor of economics at the University of Leuven.

p241. 'You had the Great Depression . . .' The comment was made to Bill Clinton by Antonis Samaras in July 2012.

p241. Wolfgang Schäuble: 'unless Greece implements the . . .' Interview with the *Wall Street Journal*. January 2012.

p242. Anna Diamantopoulou: 'the product of a sick imagination.' Comment made on 27 January 2012.

p242. 'The unconditional surrender . . .' Comment made in the Greek paper *Vima*.

p242. Evangelos Venizelos: 'This was a permanent . . .' Interview with author.

p242. Wolfgang Schäuble: 'The promises from Greece are not enough for us any more . . .' Interview February 2012 with *Welt am Sonntag*. The minister also used the phrase 'bottomless pit'.

p243. Lucas Papademos: 'We are a breath away . . .' In a televised address to the nation in February 2012.

p244. Comments from Lucas Papademos made in interview with author.

p248. George Soros: 'Germany is acting as the task-master . . .' Speaking at the World Economic Forum in Davos, January 2012.

p248. Paul De Grauwe: 'I am afraid . . .' The professor of economics at the University of Leuven made the comments in February 2012.

p248. Mario Monti: 'a protest against Europe will develop . . .' Interview with *Die Welt* newspaper. January 2012.

p249. Wolfgang Schäuble: 'The Chancellor can count on my loyalty . . .' Interview with Reuters. December 2011.

p249. Wolfgang Schäuble: 'The crisis can only be solved through reforms . . .' Interview with author.

p250. Some of the details for the Lagarde/Merkel meeting have been drawn from a *New York Times* article by Annie Lowrey on 9 March 2012.

p250. Paul Krugman: 'By introducing a single currency . . .' Article in *New York Times*. 26 February 2012.

p252. Charles Dallara: 'somewhere between catastrophic . . .' Speech made in May 2012 on a visit to Ireland.

p252. Lucas Papademos. Comments made to the author.

p253. 'Resist the Demagogue.' An editorial in the *Financial Times Deutschland*.

Chapter 15. The Rebellion of Mr Normal
p259. François Hollande: 'My true adversary does not . . .' Speech in Paris. January 2012.

p259. Question to Mr Hollande at St Pancras was asked by the author.

p260. Alain Minc: 'That's his character . . .' Interview with author.

p260 'un sal mec'. Hollande was having breakfast with reporters in March 2012. His comments were carried by *Le Parisien* although there is some dispute as to the exact context in which the words were used.

p260. Nicolas Sarkozy: 'Perhaps the mistake I made . . .' Interview with RTL radio in April 2012 as his electoral campaign drew to a close.

p263. Nicolas Sarkozy: 'All of those who make remarks . . .' Comments made during the campaign in March 2012 and after terrorist shootings in Toulouse.

p263. Nicolas Sarkozy. In early March 2012 he came up with a raft of policies. Speaking in the Paris suburb of Villepinte he said, 'France will ask Europe to adopt a "Buy European Act" on a model of the "Buy American Act".'

p265 Nicolas Sarkozy and 'You won't hear from me again . . .' January 2012. Remarks made in French Guyana to reporters travelling with him. 'In case of failure,' he said, 'I stop politics. Yes, that is a certainty.'

p266. Yasmina Reza: 'combat the slippage . . .' In 2006, Yasmina Reza was granted access to Sarkozy during his election campaign and wrote *Dawn Dusk or Night*.

p266. Xavier Musca: 'Sarkozy is a man . . .' Interview with the author.

p267. François Hollande: 'It's not for Germany to decide . . .' 26 April 2012 on France 2 television.

p268. 'Chancellor Merkel's ideas had been beaten by . . .' Remarks made by Arnaud Montebourg, a French minister and ally of François Hollande.

p269. François Hollande: 'The Franco-German relationship has been exclusive . . .' Remarks made on 7 May 2012 in an interview given to Slate website.

p270. François Hollande: 'It is France's task to tirelessly . . .' Comments made in October 2012 in an interview with five European newspapers.

p270. Angela Merkel: 'We should give Europe a real right of intervention in national budgets.' Speech to Bundestag on 18 October 2012.

p270. The meeting in Rome was on 22 June 2012.

p271. François Hollande: 'Those who speak most passionately about political union . . .' In an interview with the *Guardian* and four other papers on 16 October 2012.

p273. A useful source on the state of the French economy is the *Economist* edition of 17 November 2012. 'The time-bomb at the heart of Europe.'

p274. Frits Bolkestein: 'We shall all have to work longer and harder . . .' See statement made to the Maastricht Centre for European Law. The Institutional Functioning of the EU. 2010–2011 Volume 1.

p274. Christian Saint-Etienne: 'We are on the verge . . .' Christian Saint-Etienne is a chair professor of Industrial Economics and has written *Le Joker Européen: the Real Solution to Exit the Economic Crisis*.

p274. Dominique de Villepin told Europe Radio 1 in June 2012 that 'Germany has lost faith in France.'

p274. Volker Kauder: 'It would be good if the socialists there . . .' In an interview with *Der Spiegel*, 9 November 2012.

p275. 'France is deeply nostalgic . . .' An essay written by Mathieu von Rohr and published in *Der Spiegel* on 12 August 2012.

p275. Michel Sapin: 'There is a state . . .' France's labour minister gave the assessment in a radio interview on 28 January 2013.

p276. Helmut Schmidt: 'The present German government has not understood that Germany must be bound into a union . . .' From an interview given to John Vinocur and published in the *New York Times* on 3 May 2010.

Chapter 16. Spain: Resisting the Men in Black
p281. Rogelio Barahona: 'The crisis has hit citizens so hard . . .' Interview with Reuters, July 2012.

p281: 'If you said what you have in mind . . .' Comment made by Spanish Socialist leader Pérez Rubalcaba in a pre-election debate on 7 November 2011.

p282. Austrian finance minister, Maria Fekter: 'No. Spain has to make an effort . . .'

p282. Caja de Ahorros del Mediterráneo. The best reporting on this was an article by Giles Tremlett in the *Guardian* on 8 June 2012.

p284. Luis de Guindos: 'the battle for the euro is going to be waged . . .' The finance minister made the comment on 19 May 2012. The minister continued that, 'Greece was the canary in the coal mine.'

p284. 'The men in black will not be coming . . .' Comment made by Cristóbal Montoro, the Spanish finance minister in June 2012.

p284. 'There will be no rescue . . .' Rajoy made this comment at a press conference on 28 May 2012.

p284. 'False pride.' The accusation was made in an editorial in the *Financial Times Deutschland*: 'That is either false pride or economic stupidity.' Made in June 2012 and reported in *Der Spiegel*.

p285. 'Spain is not Uganda.' These text messages were disclosed by the Spanish paper, *El Mundo*.

p286. Paul Krugman: 'You get a picture of a European policy élite . . .' *New York Times*, 10 June 2012.

p286. Soraya Sáenz de Santamaría: 'It's not about who leaves the euro . . .' Comment made by the minister to Reuters in May 2012.

p287. Niall Ferguson: 'They are going to be handing over very large sums to Southern Europeans for the foreseeable future.' Niall Ferguson in *Newsweek* on 'How Europe could Cost Obama the Election'. 11 June 2012.

p287. 'Certain leaders, led by Mrs Merkel, are fixated . . .' Comments made by French minister Arnaud Montebourg in June 2012.

p287. Jakob Augstein: 'Abrasive pro-austerity policies threaten . . .' A commentary written by Jakob Augstein for *Der Spiegel* on 8 December 2011. Augstein described Merkel as a 'radical politician, not a conservative one'.

p288. 'Blank cheque for the indebted states' was the headline in the mass circulation *Bild* in September 2012.

p289. Wolfgang Schäuble: 'Public disputes . . .' Interview with the author.

p294. The Spanish education minister, José Ignacio Wert, told the Spanish Parliament in October 2012 that he intended to 'Spanish-ise' pupils in Catalonia.

p295. Herman Van Rompuy: 'Will there be social unrest?' Remarks made to the author.

Chapter 17. Ciao! Dolce Vita

p297. Further details on the scale of tax evasion are contained in an article written by Nick Squires for the *Telegraph* on 6 January 2012.

p298. Mario Monti: 'Some measures adopted . . .' Comments made in November 2012.

p300. Flavio Briatore: 'Italy is now a country . . .' Comments made in August 2012.

p 302. The best account of Sicily's civil service is to be found in a book called *La Zavorra: Waste and privileges in the Free State of Sicily* by Enrico Del Mercato and Emanuele Lauria.

p305. Massimo Franco: 'a thermometer of Italy's political temperature . . .' Political columnist in comments to the *Washington Post* in September 2012.

p305. Some comments and background based on an interview Beppe Grillo gave to the author in February 2013.

p305. Mario Monti: 'I'm very keen to make sure that the changes . . .' Interview given to Michael Day in Milan for the *Independent*. 15 October 2012.

Chapter 18. The Lost Continent

p307. Comments made by Piet Chielens were made to the author.

p311. Angela Merkel: 'If you have a world of seven billion . . .' Comments made to the European Parliament on 6 November 2012.

p311. Tony Blair: 'Then the rationale was peace. Today it is power.' A speech delivered at the Business for New Europe event at Chatham House on 28 November 2012.

p311. Roger Altman: 'Financial markets have become a "global supra-government" . . .' Comments made in December 2011 in an article in the *Financial Times*.

p313. Wolfgang Schäuble: 'If the United States of Europe . . .' Interview with author.

Index

Adenaeur, Konrad 271–2
Alamanou, Ada 148–9
Alcalá de Henares 279–80
Altmaier, Peter 93
America 39–40, 72–3, 79–80,
    171–2, 210
    see also Obama, President
    Barack
Anglo Irish Bank 47–8, 50
Araujo, Mayor Gemma 290–1
Athens 240
Attikis Platia 255–6
Attikon Cinema 245
austerity measures
    in Greece 62, 65–6, 89–90,
        107, 150, 161, 200–1
    in Ireland 114
    in Italy 301–2, 303
    packages across Europe 111
    in Portugal 125–8
    proposal by Germany 19, 248
    in Spain 281–2, 291–2, 295

bail-outs
    Greece see Greek bail-outs
    Ireland 2–4, 115, 116–20,
        122, 123
    Portugal 126–7

Spain 285, 285–6, 287, 290
Bankia group 283
Barcelona 293
Baroin, François 67, 192, 218
Barroso, José Manuel 13, 65,
    71, 75, 107, 169, 186, 206
Bello, Javier 280
Berlin Wall 24–5
Berlusconi, Silvio 'Il Cavaliere'
    Angela Merkel, snub to 139–40
    character 16, 132
    conspiracy fears 192, 196
    ECB demands, acceding to
    - 183–4
    European leaders' loss of faith
        in 188–90
    female friends 134–5
    Italian finances 182
    letter of reform 191
    Parliament, loss of support in
        191, 192, 193
    parties 137–8
    playing the German card
        305–6
    politician and showman
        132–3, 138–9
    prosecution charges against
        187–8

resignation as Prime Minister
193–4
sarcophagus, building erected
at home 140
summary of time in office
195–6
vote of no confidence in
131–2
Bild 92, 231, 246
Blair, Tony 311
BMW 95–6
borrowing costs
in Germany 94, 143
in Greece 66, 69, 72, 109
in Ireland 49, 50, 51, 117,
118
In Italy 142, 177, 181, 191,
193, 194, 288
in Portugal 126
in Spain 181, 284, 287, 288,
289
in weaker euro-zone countries
75, 76, 77, 168, 288
Brandenburg Gate 24
Bretherton, Russell 228
Britain
EU, future relationship with
227, 229–30, 232–3
EU indecision, irritation over
217
EU treaty change 220, 222,
223, 224–5, 225
euro, doubts over design of
217
euro-zone bail-out fund,
position on 81
European anger at 225–6

European integration,
support for 218
island mentality 227–8
relationship with France
215–16
see also Cameron, David
Bruni, Carla 212, 215, 216
Brussels 64, 177–8, 309–10
Bundesbank 28–9, 288–9

Caja de Ahorras del
Mediterráneo 282–3
Cameron, David 161, 215,
229–30, 233
improved poll ratings after
EU veto 227
Nicolas Sarkozy, relationship
with 216, 216–17
Castellón airport 35–7
Catalonia 293–4
Celtic Tiger 2, 3, 47–8, 49, 50,
114, 124
Cenicientos 278–9
Chancusig, Luciano 42–5, 45–6
Chielens, Piet 307, 308
Christoulas, Dimitris and Emy
236–7
Churchill, Winston 215,
227–8
City of London 221, 223
Ciudad Real airport 37
Common Market 228, 229
competitiveness
in the EU 230
in Germany 17, 94, 251
in Greece 150
in Ireland 114

in Portugal 125, 126
in southern European
  countries 248
Cortina d'Ampezzo 296
Cowen, Brian 113, 116, 119,
  122, 124
credit ratings agencies 55, 61

d'Addario, Patrizia 134
Dallara, Charles 252
Darling, Alistair 62, 71, 72, 73,
  78, 79
debt
  Greek 10–12, 31–2, 54–6,
    59–60, 61, 154–5, 246
  Irish 49, 50–2, 115
  Italian 16, 142, 177, 191
  Spanish 39, 278–81, 282–3,
    286–7, 290–1, 295
Delors, Jacques 28–9, 186, 233
democracy 209
Deutsche mark 26, 28, 68, 93
Diamontopoulou, Anna 242
Dolce, Domenico 298–9
Draghi, Mario 188, 287–8, 288,
  289
Dublin District Court 46–7

East Berlin 23
East Germany 23–5
Egana, Amaia 292
El-Mahroug, Karima 'Ruby
  Rubacuori' 136–7
euro-zone
  bail-out fund 77–81, 145,
    179, 211–12
  deficit limits 11

fear of breakup 12–13, 72–3,
  74–6, 219
single currency 4–5, 28, 30–4,
  76–7, 144–5, 163
systemic flaws in 219
see also European Central
  Bank; interest rates
Eurobonds 77, 143, 185
European Central Bank (ECB)
  33, 51, 80–1, 119–20, 182,
  287–8, 289
European Commission
  confidence of leaders 64–5
  Greek bail-out fund 71, 73
  politicians' lack of financial
    understanding 179–80
  saving the euro 77, 78, 79–82
  summits 178–80, 202–3,
    222–5
  see also Barroso, José Manuel;
    Brussels
European Financial Stability
  Facility fund 77–81, 80,
  145, 179, 211–12
European Stability Mechanism
  145
European Union
  accountability of 314–15
  confidence and success of 20
  crisis of legitimacy 310
  criticism of leaders 209
  critics of EU dismissed as
    populists 210–11
  divisions over Britain 230–1,
    233
  economic pact between
    governments 225

French/German domination
of 14, 99
integration of nations 311–13
North/South divide 143–4
treaty change 214, 219–25
see also European
Commission; monetary
union

Fabra, Carlos 35–6, 37
financial markets
confidence in ECB bond-
buying scheme 288–9
fear of euro-zone collapse 74–6
Greek bail-outs and 72,
178–9, 200, 246, 247–8
hostility towards 69–70
power of 311
regulation of 222
sharing cost of future bail-outs
116–17
Spanish debt and currency
fears 181, 283–4, 286–7
Fitoussi, Jean-Paul 209
Fitzpatrick, Sean 46–8, 50, 52
France
British criticism of banks,
irritation at 216
British terms for EU treaty
change, rejecting 223–4
commemoration of British
support 215
economic power and
stagnation 272, 273–4
elections 258–66
European Union, leading role
in 14

financial crisis, loss of
influence during 276
German influence,
resentment at 276
major international
companies in 273
partnership with Germany
14, 99, 101, 108–10, 175,
261–2, 267–9, 271
political and diplomatic
power 272
public sector expenditure
272–3
relationship with Britain
215–16
traditional lifestyle,
preservation of 275
see also Hollande, François;
Sarkozy, Nicolas

G20 summit 191–2
Gabbana, Stefano 298–9
Gaddafi, Colonel 133
Gaulle, Charles de 106, 215,
227–8, 271–2
GDP (gross domestic
product)
Greek 11, 12, 56, 60, 61, 65,
153, 243
Irish 49
Italian 131, 142
Spanish 39
Georgiou, Andreas 58–9
Germany
borrowing, people cautious
about 94
budget commissioner for

Greece, appointment of
241–2
economic power 17, 94–6,
167, 272, 315–16
European Union, leading role
17, 19, 167, 315–16
European unity, commitment
to 28–9
financial crisis, growth of
influence during 275–6
Greece, loss of patience with
242–3
Greek austerity measures,
seen as author of 248
Greek debt, options to deal
with 68
Greek workers, perception of
91–2
inflation during the Weimar
Republic 93
inward-looking French,
perception of 275
Italian bail-out 143–4
labour market 94
parliamentary democracy in
108
partnership with France 14,
99, 101, 108–10, 175, 261–
2, 267–9, 271
phobias and stereotyping of
169–70
resentment towards German
austerity policies 170
reunification 25, 26, 27, 28
Spanish bail-out 287
see also Bundesbank;
Deutsche mark; East

Germany; Merkel, Angela;
West Germany
Giulio, Tremonti 185, 185–6,
191–2
globalisation 88, 310–12
Golden Dawn 255–6
Gorbachev, Mikhail 27
Great Depression 128, 234,
241, 250, 251
Greece
anarchists 85, 88, 88–9
austerity measures 62, 65–6,
89–90, 107, 150, 161, 200–1
bankruptcy, facing up to
243–4
banks, threat of run on 253
budget commissioner,
opposition to 242–3
business closures 240
communists 244
credit rating loss 152–3
culture of resistance 153
debt 10–12, 31–2, 54–6,
59–60, 61, 154–5, 246
divisions in society 152
economic reform, lack of 241
elections 252–4
enforcers 255–6
euro, consequences of leaving
252
euro-zone, withdrawal and
expulsion threats 156–7,
160
European Union, resentment
towards 66–7
exodus from cities to the
country 241

financial accounts, improper 55–6, 58–9

general strike 83, 85, 86–7

Germany, anger towards 20, 88, 90–1, 92–3, 243

government, weakness of 87

handouts 238

healthcare shortages 239, 240

military high command, dismissal of 199

pawnshops and gold dealers 239

police forbidden from university grounds 87–8

political class, loss of credibility 152

private sector job losses 149

protests 151–2, 161–2, 244–5

public sector job growth 57–8

single currency, joining 31–2

social hardship 159

solidarity of people 149

soup kitchens 148, 236, 237

state benefit claims, fraudulent 57

suicide 236, 238

Syntagma Square, encampment and protests 83, 85, 158–9, 161–2, 201, 245

see also Papaconstantinou, George; Papademos, Lucas; Papandreou, George

Greek bail-outs

European Commission, agreement of 71, 73, 74

first bail-out 72, 151–4

second bail-out 160, 162–3, 178–9, 200, 242, 246, 246–7

terms of 74, 242, 246

workers, impact on 83–4

Greek Presidential Guard 85–6

Grillo, Beppe 304–5

gross domestic product (GDP) *see* GDP

Gutierrez, Antonio 33–4

Habermas, Jürgen 96

Hollande, François

Angela Merkel, relationship with 267–9, 269–71

canvassing votes in London 258–9

David Cameron, meeting with 233

economic beliefs 270

election campaign on economic growth 266–7

inauguration as president 267

Nicolas Sarkozy, assessment of 260

self-description 259

taxing the rich 260

world of finance, view on 259

Honohan, Patrick 49, 50, 121–2

House of the Gladiators 130, 130–1

IMF (International Monetary Fund) 2–3, 54, 71, 73, 74, 108–9

interest rates

euro-zone 5, 29, 57

in Greece 59–60

in Ireland 48–9
International Monetary Fund
  see IMF
Ireland
  austerity measures 114
  bail out 2–4, 115, 116–20,
    122, 123
  banking system 48–9, 50
  banks, run on 118
  brain drain 124–5
  campaign for national dignity
    112
  Celtic Tiger 2, 3, 47–8, 49,
    50, 114, 124
  debt 49, 50–2, 115
  emigration 5–6
  EU bail-out agreement,
    government denial 118–19
  euro currency 4–5
  European identity 4
  government guarantee of
    deposits and loans 50, 51,
    113, 115
  interest rates 5, 48–9
  property boom and crash 4,
    5, 49, 51–2
  'war room' 111, 119
  wealth, rapid expansion of 46
  see also Cowen, Brian
Issing, Otmar 32, 145
Italy
  austerity measures 301–2,
    303
  blurring of image and reality
    132–3
  change of mentality 300
  debt 16, 142, 177, 191

economic and social reforms
  184–5
economic stagnation 131,
  142, 301, 303
elite, privileges of 142
euro, growing opposition to 304
European Central Bank,
  threat from 182, 182–3
historic remains, crumbling
  of 130–1
international influence, loss of
  139
pension reform 188
political class, extravagance of
  303
political culture 302–3
political establishment, threat
  to 304–5
protests 304
scandals 136–7, 137–8
single currency, joining 31
style and fashion 141–2
tax recovery 299
undeclared income 297–9
unemployment 301–2
wealthy, raids on 296–9
see also Berlusconi, Silvio;
  Monti, Mario

Jenkins, Roy 231
Jerez de la Frontera 280
Johnson, Boris 227
Juan Carlos I, King of Spain
  291
Juncker, Jean-Claude 144, 170,
  222
Juppé, Alain 169, 186, 219

Justus Lipsius 177–8, 309–10

Karlas, Manolis 53–4
Katarachias, Costa 66
Kauder, Volker 220–1, 274
Kelly, Morgan 51
Kifissia 57
Kohl, Helmut 26, 27, 102
Konstandaras, Nikos 245, 254
Krugman, Paul 21, 64–5, 154,
   250–1, 286

La Línea 290
Lagarde, Christine 79, 80, 155,
   247, 249–50, 250
Lario, Veronica 136
Le Monde 226
Le Pen, Marine 263–4
Lehman Brothers 5, 40
Lenihan, Brian 113, 120, 121,
   123
Libya 217

Maastricht Treaty 28, 68, 93
Macmillan, Harold 228–9
Maizière, Thomas de 79, 166
Mandelson, Peter 231
Manikas, Dimitris 238
Marfin bank 84, 86–7, 88–9
markets, financial *see* financial
   markets
Meletti, Stefano 301–2
Merkel, Angela
   austerity measures for Greece
      107
   Britain, support for remaining
      in EU 231

character 14, 165–6, 166–7,
   170–1
civilian honour award from
   President Obama 171–2
competing obligations to euro
   and Germany 213
David Cameron, discussion
   of treaty change 221
economic and work ethic
   beliefs 169, 185
economic restructuring and
   reform 211
EU discipline over national
   budgets 219–20
EU treaty change 214, 219–20,
   221, 222, 224–5
euro-zone crisis 98
European Financial Stability
   Facility fund 80
European unity, belief and
   commitment to 172–3
financial crisis, preventing
   reoccurrence of 174
François Hollande,
   relationship with 267–9,
   269–71
'Frau Nein' nickname 168
German policies, facing
   criticism of 171
methodical and cautious
   approach 167–8
Nicolas Sarkozy, relationship
   with 15, 99–100, 106, 110,
   170–1, 175, 211, 261
power and influence 166–7
private investors' proposal
   116–17

recession, on cause of 166
second Greek bail-out,
defence of 246
Silvio Berlusconi, causing
affront to 189–90
upbringing 101–3, 172
Meyer-Landrut, Nikolaus 214
Minc, Alain 14, 107, 110, 260,
262, 266
Mitterrand, Françoise 26, 27,
28
monetary union 16, 21, 28–34,
77–81, 218, 254, 312–14
see also euro-zone; single
currency
Monti, Mario 196, 224–5, 248,
269, 304
reform programme 298–301,
303, 305
Monument to the Discoveries
127
Mozambique 128
Musca, Xavier 108, 110, 170–1,
202–3, 204, 205, 266

national budgets 107, 210, 214,
219, 261, 270, 282
Northern League '*Lega*' 184, 188

Obama, President Barack 79,
156, 169, 171, 178
Oktoberfest 17–19
Onassis, Aristotle 56
Osborne, George 78, 218

Papaconstantinou, George
55–6, 62–3, 150, 156, 160

Papademos, Lucas 237–8, 243,
244, 252–3
Papandreou, George
background 9–10
German reparations 67
negotiation with Angela
Merkel 70
presentation to EU leaders 62
referendum proposal 202–5
resignation 207–8
'scenario zero' presentation
156–7
second Greek bail-out 200
summoned to G20 summit
204–5
vote of confidence in 157,
162
Papathanasopoulou, Angeliki
84–5, 86–7
Papoulias, President Karolos
199
Patission Street 235
Pioz 279
Polanco, Marysthell 187
Pompeii 130
Portugal 125–8
Presidential Medal of Freedom
171

Quinn, Sean 50

Rajoy, Mariano 281, 281–2,
285
Rehn, Olli 118
Reims Cathedral 271, 272
Rompuy, Herman Van
defence of the EU 129

euro, analysis of 30–1, 61
fighting Euro-scepticism 209
Greek election results 254
influential figure in Europe
173–4
membership of the EU 233
Royal Hospital 215

Samaras, Antonis 254, 256–7
Samos 53–4
Santamaría, Soraya Sáenz de
286
Sarkozy, Nicolas
Angela Merkel, relationship
with 15, 99–100, 106, 110,
170–1, 175, 211, 261
appeal to silent patriotic
majority 262
attacks British challenge to
EU treaty change 225–6
birth of daughter 212–13
character 14
David Cameron, relationship
with 216, 216–17
defence of the euro 129
ECB, increased role for 211
election campaign 261–6
espousing French values 263
euro-zone, Greece leaving
206
Eurobonds 77
financial crisis 13
France, romantic view of 106
François Hollande, criticism
of 260, 265
George Papandreou, anger at
206

German economic model,
admiration for 262
German indecision, irritation
with 69
Greek referendum proposal
204
hosting the G20 summit
204–5
nationalistic appeal to people
264–5
people weary of 261
Silvio Berlusconi, causes
affront to 189–90
upbringing 104–5
Schäuble, Wolfgang 30, 67, 68,
78, 249
Schengen agreement 263
Schmidt, Helmut 96, 213, 276
Schröder, Gerhard 262
Schulz, Christian 247
Sicily 302–3
Sikorski, Radoslaw 168–9
single currency 4–5
criticism of 163
danger of collapse 76–7
division of north/south
countries 144–5
introduction 28, 30–4
in Spain 9
Sinn, Hans-Werner 89
Sócrates, José 125, 126
solidarity
of euro-zone countries 204
European ideal 156
French notion of 15, 107, 213
German response to calls for
100, 144, 147, 155

in Greece 149
tax 161, 200
Soros, George 82, 89–90, 161, 168, 248
Spain
  airports 35–7
  austerity measures 281–2, 291–2, 295
  bad loans held by banks 282
  bail outs 285, 285–6, 287, 290
  bank rescue 283
  bankrupt towns and cities 278–80
  Catalonian demands for independence 293–4
  concealment of downfall 277
  debt 39, 278–81, 282–3, 286, 286–7, 290–1, 295
  evictions from homes 292
  golden years 9, 40–1
  green shoots of recovery 295
  infrastructure development 35–7, 38
  local government funding 280
  nepotism 283
  property boom and crash 6–8, 38, 39–40, 42–5
  protests against austerity measures 284, 291–2
  rail network 293
  savings withdrawals 283–4
  single currency 9
  social deprivation 277–80
  unemployment 8–9, 40, 277
  unpaid workers 279
  vanity projects 38–9

St Pancras station 258, 259
Stability and Growth Pact 219
Stadiou Street 83
Stiglitz, Joseph 248
subprime mortgages 40
Syntagma Square 83, 85, 158–9, 161–2, 201, 245

Thatcher, Margaret 26–7, 229
Theodorakis, Mikis 90
Thorning-Schmidt, Helle 224
Topography of Terror 308–9
Trichet, Jean-Claude 76, 119, 181, 211–12
Tsipras, Alexis 243–4, 253–4

unemployment
  across Europe 128, 251, 306, 314
  in France 273
  in Greece 72, 153
  in Italy 301
  in Portugal 126, 127–8
  in Spain 8–9, 40, 277

Venizelos, Evangelos 162, 201, 203, 207, 242, 243
Versailles Treaty 201

Wall Street Journal 246
Washington, summit 72–3
Weidmann, Jens 60
welfare states 20–1, 111, 274
West Germany 25, 26
World Wars 307–8

Xafa, Miranda 31–2

Yeats, W.B. 3
Ypres 307, 308

Zakynthos 57